GRAHAM GREENE

HARVEY CURTIS WEBSTER

NATHAN A. SCOTT, JR.

FRANCIS L. KUNKEL

DOMINICK P. CONSOLO

DAVID H. HESLA

A. A. DEVITIS

HERBERT R. HABER

ROBERT O. EVANS

KAI LAITINEN

JOHN ATKINS

MIRIAM ALLOTT

JACOB H. ADLER

CAROLYN D. SCOTT

NEIL BRENNAN

Graham Greene

SOME CRITICAL CONSIDERATIONS

EDITED BY *Robert O. Evans*

UNIVERSITY OF KENTUCKY PRESS

CᴏᴘʏʀɪɢʜT © 1963 by the University of Kentucky Press. Printed in the United States of America. Library of Congress Catalog Card Number 63-22005.

The publication of this book has been made possible partly through a grant from the Margaret Voorhies Haggin Trust, established in memory of her husband, James Ben Ali Haggin.

INTRODUCTION

THE BOOK ONE SETS out to make, even when one is collecting the writings of others, does not necessarily end as it began, and this collection of essays has certainly come to a conclusion far different from that I once expected. The original intention was to collect a series of essays that would cast light on an author in progress, an important one, perhaps even a great one, highly representative of his era—but still a collection that would attempt only a partial evaluation, for there was indication that Greene was approaching the apex of his importance but had not reached it. During the three years and more, however, while the essays were discovered and selected, or written for this collection—two-thirds were written for inclusion here and the remainder chosen as representative of Greene criticism—Greene published a new novel, *A Burnt-out Case*, and later, in an interview, suggested that he may have reached the end of his career. "I have not written a new novel since *A Burnt-out Case*," he told Guy Martin in the fall of 1962 ("The Heart of the Graham Greene Matter," *Réalités*, December, 1962). "Nor am I working on a new one. My last book exhausted me completely. . . . It may be time for me to think about retiring." If so, these essays stand in a different relation to the author's work from that originally planned; that is, they cannot be accepted just as indications of direction. In a much more definite sense they exist as fixed judgments of an artistic career, even though most of them were actually written before the last novel appeared and only one, Carolyn Scott's "The Witch at the Corner: Notes on Graham Greene's Mythology," makes any real attempt to consider that book, and that attempt almost as an aside, for her main concern is with Greene's short stories.

I am attempting to explain how the essays in this book came into being and what they try to accomplish. This volume was intended to be more than a collection of previously published essays; those that are reprinted here, however, have been selected according to certain principles. A glance at Brennan's bibliography at the end of the volume, the most extensive ever compiled for Greene, will indicate some of the problems of selection. For example, I have chosen to omit Morton Zabel's fine essay, "Graham Greene: The Best and the Worst," because it is extremely well known, though Professor Zabel was kind enough to permit its inclusion. The essays reprinted have either been ones that seemed to have special merit but might otherwise be easily overlooked or those that added, in some fashion or other, to the general scheme of the book. Thus, to demonstrate the first principle, Nathan Scott's essay, "Graham Greene: Christian Tragedian," was selected for its intrinsic merits and because it originally appeared in an obscure periodical, now defunct, and might otherwise be missed. To illustrate the second criterion, John Atkins' essay, "The Curse of the Film," which appeared as a chapter in his book *Graham Greene*, has been reprinted to demonstrate an aspect of Greene's career that sheds unexpected light on his work as a novelist, particularly on his cinematic technique.

So much for principles of selection. The essays are all critical, some highly academic, others much lighter in vein.

None are reviews. The audience for which they were written varies from the general reader to the student in the university attempting to learn more about what makes Greene tick, though it is hoped all the essays will have something to offer the reader of criticism as well as the student or specialist. The essays themselves fall easily into two groups, those that deal with Greene's work as a whole, or at least with elements of his work larger than single books or separate techniques, and those that deal with smaller, particular considerations. In fact most of the essays, it will be seen, deal with one or more of the novels, keeping in mind Greene's own distinction between novels and entertainments. That distinction, however, is superficial, for the same themes appear in novels and entertainments and the same techniques, more or less, appear in both. Greene's labels, if there is any validity in them at all, serve simply as an indication of degree. The novels deal seriously with life; the entertainments deal with it less seriously, or rather their focus is slightly different, excepting only *Our Man in Havana*, Greene's attempt at satire. Even then it is difficult to maintain such a distinction, as the reader of these essays will discover. For instance, some of the authors find it impossible to discuss the serious aspects of the supposedly important works without referring to the lesser, and Greene himself seems to have had the same difficulty. At least he vacillated about the label that should be applied to *Brighton Rock*, calling it first an entertainment and then a novel.

Indeed the majority of Greene's works arise out of a single milieu, known familiarly to critics and Greene fans as Greeneland, a milieu whose distinguishing aspects are sometimes found more densely in the entertainments, say *Gun For Sale*, than in the novels themselves. The key word in Greene's milieu is *seediness*, with the sense of failure it suggests. Greene implies it, or says it outright, over and over again in his works, and he mentions it particularly as the essential characteristic of the 20th century in his travel book, *Journey Without Maps*: "Seediness has a very deep appeal: even the seediness of civilization, of the sky signs in Leicester Square, the 'tarts' in Bond Street, the smell of cooking greens off Tottenham Court Road, the motor salesmen in Great Portland Street." In the bulk of his important work that is the condition from which Greene begins, whether the book is set in London or in Africa. He is, of course, drawing a caricature of the real world, or at least the world as most of us think of it, but for Greene this reality, however distorted, is the essence of the human condition in the present time. He is concerned with the predicament in which man finds himself, and that concern necessitates an artistic starting place.

Greene's view of the world is highly individual, not only because of his fascination with seediness but also because he approaches the world from a point of view different from that of the average protestant, liberal Englishman (or, for that matter, American), a point of view different from that of the majority of English writers. It is not just a matter of Greene's being more intellectual, though that too is true. Coupled with the seediness he finds everywhere as characteristic of our society is his own, special Catholic vision, for Greene was, as a young man, converted to the Church of Rome. This conversion, he tells us in *Journey Without Maps*, was intellectual rather than emotional, thus reversing what must be the usual process—I should argue, however, that if the novels are any evidence the emotional conversion eventually followed. Until *Brighton Rock* the novels, not very successful it must be noted, were not especially concerned with religious themes or theological questions, though these were certainly never entirely absent. Until then Greene's vision, like Conrad's, was essentially ethical, though the milieu from which he projects this vision was very different from Conrad's. But after *Brighton Rock*, the first of a series known as "Catholic novels," Greene deals heavily in theological matter.

That label "Catholic novels" is itself ambiguous, for Greene is never a Catholic novelist in the sense that Mauriac defines when he distinguishes between the Catholic novelist, who writes for the propagation of the Faith, and the Catholic who writes novels, employing values learned in his Faith but seeking essentially, in his own way, for the truth. The matrix of ideas from which Greene draws after *Brighton Rock* is certainly Catholic, but the intention is to find and express truth rather than to write propaganda. *Brighton Rock* itself, perhaps originally planned to be a thriller, expresses Catholic themes which, though they have appeared in embryo in the earlier books, now appear intensified, with the purpose of illustrating certain truths about the human condition. *Brighton Rock* also introduces a distinct change in method and style (a fine development of what has been called the cinematic technique; see Consolo, "Graham Greene: Style and Stylistics in Five Novels," following) that arose perhaps from vital necessity. The earlier books had been financial failures, or near failures, and Greene was living on a three-year allowance from his publisher. As with Faulkner, when he wrote *Sanctuary*, it may have seemed necessary for him to alter his methods to produce a reasonably popular success.

Nevertheless, the Catholic ideas that permeate *Brighton Rock* are so strong as to overwhelm the readers of Greene's works with their intensity and originality of treatment. *Brighton Rock* marks a turning point in its treatment of the Catholic themes, though Atkins, in his book, refuses to distinguish it quite so sharply. Perhaps he is right, for the aspects of *Brighton Rock* that appear so striking to the reader are not really new in Greene; they have all been there undeveloped before. However, it seems to me that the focus of the intellectual background, from *Brighton Rock* through

The Power and the Glory to *The Heart of the Matter*, has altered. It is now Augustinian, perhaps in deference to Greene's intellectual training before his conversion, though Greene never follows dogma slavishly. It has been argued (in Hesla's essay, "Theological Ambiguity in the Catholic Novels") that what I may be calling Augustinian really constitutes a flirtation with heresy in the form of Gnosticism, and certainly in these books Greene's vision of the universe is not the usual triple-storied, heaven-earth-hell version, but one that is dangerously dualistic (though Hesla carefully distinguishes between Greene's sort of Gnosticism and that of the second century). While there is some validity to the argument, I should nevertheless contend that until *The Heart of the Matter* Greene is essentially orthodox, or at least within the folds of an orthodox position. His deviations to that point are mechanical and superficial. It is true he ends *Brighton Rock* ambiguously; a priest makes a highly favorable reference, in his discussion with Rose who is struggling for salvation, to Charles Péguy, who never came into the fold. But many Catholics have discovered a saintliness in Péguy and would probably not consider the reference out of key. Anyhow, the item is superficial when considered in relation to Greene's repeated concern with salvation in orthodox terms, a concern that occupied much of his attention throughout the book. Perhaps something of the same sort might be argued about *The Power and the Glory*, and indeed Atkins says as much and more in his essay, "Altogether Amen," following.

After *The Heart of the Matter*, where Greene seems much more openly attracted to heresy than in the earlier books—especially because of its denouement in which Scobie commits suicide—I descry not so much St. Augustine behind Greene's ideas, or in his intellectual background, as Kierkegaard. Greene himself acknowledges a debt to Kierkegaard (in the interview with Guy Martin). It is easy to assume, if one thinks of Sartre instead of Kierkegaard, that a drift towards existentialism is a move in the direction of atheism, but I have argued elsewhere that Greene's variety of existentialism is essentially Catholic (see "Existentialism in Greene's *The Quiet American*," *Modern Fiction Studies*, Autumn, 1957). When Greene wrote *The Quiet American*, he adopted directly much of the terminology of existentialist writing. His key word was *engagé*, much as Hemingway's was *nada* in the story "A Clean Well-Lighted Place." Miriam Allott does not agree; she finds Greene's main concern in *The Quiet American* to be orthodox Catholicism (see "The Moral Situation in *The Quiet American*," following), but many of the other writers in this volume (Kunkel, Consolo, Hesla, and especially Haber) refer to the matrix of Geene's ideas at this time in what are essentially existentialist terms. But the point to bear in mind is not just where Greene found his ideas but what they are, and what relation they have to the work of art itself; Greene's books are not, of course, a vehicle for the expression of one philosophy or another. They employ ideas as background, much as they use the milieu. Each in its way is an important aspect worthy of examination, as the essays in this book make eminently clear.

After *The Heart of the Matter*, Atkins suggests (in his book) that Greene felt the need to rehabilitate himself and wrote *The End of the Affair* along more orthodox lines. But perhaps, despite the series of miracles that seems to revolt Atkins, and doubtless many protestant readers, there is in that view an oversimplification. Greene's ethical teaching has been essentially that in the milieu in which modern man finds himself the only possible solution is *imitatio Christi*. But in making his point he has at times strayed from the path of dogma, just as, in a sense, in creating his intellectual background he adopted only an aspect of the Christian world vision. The idea of creation as a joyful work of God is conspicuously absent in Greene. As Hesla points out, the imitation of Christ in *The End of the Affair* (and in *The Heart of the Matter*, too) tends really to become an imitation of God. From an orthodox point of view such dualism is dangerous; for example, Scobie's suicide, obviously impossible for an orthodox Catholic to accept without assuming it implies damnation, may, if one so interprets the book, seem to be a usurpation of God's own prerogative. A somewhat similar argument could be made about Bendrix in *The End of the Affair*, despite the ambiguous implication in the book that God will eventually catch up with him, for in the very power of his hatred Bendrix usurps functions not intended for human beings. Such questions present a series of knotty difficulties for orthodox interpretation, but from the existentialist point of view, while heretical situations are not avoided they no longer seem very important. The matrix of ideas encourages a shift in focus. Sarah has been able to make a great leap from a life of sin to one of sanctity. Bendrix, ironically, informs God he will not follow her; he will not *leap*. The word is his; it is of course the French word *saute*, used by existentialists to describe the means of rising from one plane of existence to another, higher one. The existentialist background may not be essential to an interpretation of the novel, but it affords a means of evading apparently heretical ideas that Greene has fostered. In *The Quiet American* the case is even plainer.

But what about the last book, *A Burnt-out Case*? Much of the background of ideas there arises quite naturally out of the earlier works; yet there is an essential difference. It lies, to some extent at least, I think, in Greene's approach there to the idea of a teleological universe. Prior to *A Burnt-out Case* there has been no salvation possible in this world; that is why the important characters are so often driven towards suicide, as Hesla points out. But in the last novel, though the ending is quite as amibguous as in the others, there is a new, different tone. The novel ends with a conversation between the Superior and Dr. Colin over the grave of Querry, who has been slain by Rycker. "Naturally. *Le crime passionnel,*" the Superior says in answer to the speculation that Rycker will be acquitted. "Everybody will have got what they wanted—it's really quite a happy ending, isn't it? Rycker feels he has become important both to God and man . . . Mme. Rycker will soon be free to go home. . . ." Dr. Colin interjects, "You can hardly say it was a happy ending for Querry." "Wasn't it?" the Superior asks. Now this is a very different tone from the flat resignation of this world and a hint of glory in the next that prevails in the other books. Where does it come from in Greene's intellectual background? It would likely have arisen from some conviction recently shaped in the writer's mind, and the only work of sufficient power and importance that Greene might have come upon about the right time, assuming as one may that Greene is not likely to be found rediscovering ideas already well known, would be Teilhard de Chardin's *The Phenomenon of Man.* And Greene has subsequently admitted (in the interview with Guy Martin) that Teilhard de Chardin made an "enormous impression" upon him: "I think it is one of the key works of our century. It influenced me when I wrote *A Burnt-out Case.* Read it and you'll see."

So much then for the intellectual background of Greene's work and the way in which it becomes a major concern of these essays. Those not directly involved in discussing this matter are devoted to more particular considerations. Some are focused on style (Consolo); others on different aspects of Greene's work, such as the drama (Adler) and the short story (Carolyn Scott), or on a particular novel (Atkins, "Altogether Amen"), but all are in some way or another concerned with the ideas that underlie Greene's writing. Why? Though Greene's view of man's predicament is deliberately distorted, nevertheless it is a recognizable one.

The situation from which men like Greene rebel in the 20th century is that liberal, optimistic view of the world nurtured by the Enlightenment and brought to fruition in the 19th century vision of man's predicament as one due either to economic causes (Marx) or to psychological ones (Freud). It is a view of a world in which man is naturally good but forced to evil by circumstances that might be brought within his control. We all know the clichés, for they are still at the root of popular philosophy. Change the economic conditions, do away with want, and crime will disappear. Or, understand one's neuroses and psychoses and one will adjust. There is no original sin; man is by nature a good creature. For a long time now this has been the rationalist point of view. But Greene, like Professor Joad, a one-time rationalist, has rejected it, Greene for religious reasons, Joad for intellectual. Both have turned to Christianity for a solution, Greene after investigating the seediness of our world, Joad after the lesson of the brutality of two wars. This direction, I think, is dominant in the British novel of Greene's generation. The same path, after another fashion, is followed by Evelyn Waugh. Something akin to this might even be said of the French novel of the same era, particularly of Mauriac (the question is investigated by DeVitis in his essay, "The Catholic as Novelist: Graham Greene and François Mauriac," following). It is too much, of course, to claim that this return to Christianity will become the central direction in English literature in the second half of the 20th century. Already a new school of novelists has sprung up—writers like Amis, Shillitoe, and Wain—with very different concerns, and we cannot yet dismiss as secondary such writers as Angus Wilson, C. P. Snow, or Lawrence Durrell, each of whom, in his own way, seems much closer to Greene and Waugh than the new generation. The Catholicism of Greene and Waugh may place them somewhat outside of English tradition, but their concern with the world that envelops us, a concern which has caused them to make a decision like

Newman's, may force them back into the main stream. We shall simply have to wait and see what the literary historians of the future decide.

In any case Greene's position is now secure. If not *the* major writer, he is certainly *a* major writer—the bibliography at the end of this volume is all the evidence needed to support the claim. He is also a masterful technician; whatever history decides about his position will not affect that. And, except when he departs from the genres he has learned to control, he is a master storyteller, a spell-weaver of the first order. It is to be hoped this collection will assist in examining these last contentions, for it is in the light that criticism casts on literature, in the extension of meaning that it assists and encourages, that the worth of criticism depends.

I wish to acknowledge my debt to the authors who have shown so much patience with the editor of this collection and to the others in whose debt we all rest. Mr. Maurice Beebe, the editor of *Modern Fiction Studies,* encouraged the initial attempt and allowed us free use of the material in his bibliographical checklist. Mr. Atkins not only contributed a chapter but kindly permitted use of material from his book, *Graham Greene.* In a sense Mr. Kunkel extended the same permission, though his chapter was contributed before the appearance in print of his book. Dr. Robert Jacobs carefully read and criticized the introduction. The tedious, initial proofreading was done by a contributor, Mrs. Carolyn D. Scott, without whose assistance the book might never have been finished. To Mrs. Mary Gracey, who typed the bulk of the manuscript, and to Mrs. Pauline Brooks, who typed the bibliography, I am also much indebted. The University of Kentucky Research Fund kindly assisted in the expenses incurred in preparation. And I am especially indebted to Professor Ants Oras, who translated from the original Finnish Mr. Laitinen's essay.

R. O. E.

CONTENTS

Harvey Curtis Webster

THE WORLD OF GRAHAM GREENE

IN HIS PERCEPTIVE essay about Dickens in *The Lost Childhood* (1951), Graham Greene remarks that he is "inclined to believe" that "the creative writer perceives his world once and for all in childhood and adolescence, and his whole career is an effort to illustrate his private world in terms of the great public world we all share." Whether this is generally true or not, Greene has made out a convincing case for its truth about himself. When, at the age of ten, he read H. Rider Haggard's *King Solomon's Mines*, he was most impressed by the figure of Gagool, the old witch, for someone very like her waited for him in dreams "every night in the passage by the linen cupboard, near the nursery door," and she still continues to appear, "when the mind is sick or tired . . . now . . . dressed in the theological garments of despair." The more heroic Quartermain and Sir Henry Curtis seemed too heroic to him at the same age: "These men were like Platonic ideas: they were not life as one had already begun to know it." Even in his most recent books— *A Burnt-out Case* (1961) and *A Sense of Reality* (1963) —the image of Gagool continues to linger in the passageway, taking the form of a leper or a cave under the garden, and in these, as in earlier volumes, no heroic characters appear.

The years between ten and fourteen, when "the future for better or worse really struck" with the reading of Marjorie Bowen's *The Viper of Milan,* accentuated the feeling of despair that frequently masked itself as boredom.' In *Journey Without Maps* (1936) he recalls seeing a dead dog in the bottom of his pram, where it was placed by his nurse to get it out of the way after it had been killed in an accident. This, the first thing he remembers, "was just a fact," and was later joined by a recollection of a man who rushed out of a cottage with a knife in his hand to kill himself and the memory of wishing to experience "the pleasure of cruelty" with a girl who lived close by when he was fourteen. It was also during these years probably (Greene is not very exact in his chronology) that he tried three different ways of suicide, ran away from Birkhamsted school (where his father was headmaster) because of boredom that had reached "an intolerable depth" and started the six month psychoanalysis that taught him correct orientation and wrung him dry, "fixed in boredom," though it left him also with the habit of analyzing and using his dreams as he tells in *In Search of a Character* (1961). The consequences of this fixation in boredom-despair appear to have never left him for long. At the age of seventeen he began his several times repeated experiments with Russian roulette, pulling the trigger of a revolver with one of its six chambers loaded, not knowing whether he would shoot himself with the loaded chamber or not. It seems likely that his later dangerous ventures into Africa, Mexico, and Indochina served much the same purpose as the Russian roulette he abandoned, that these journeys were night journeys like Marlow's in *The Heart of Darkness,* Celine's in *Journey to the End of Night,* and Orwell's among the down and out in Paris and London. We have Greene's word for the fact that, after almost dying on his dangerous trek through Liberia, he "discovered in himself a passionate interest in living," though he had always "assumed before, as a matter of course, that death was desirable." This experience, like the experiences with attempted suicide and Russian roulette, "was like a conversion" which at least left "a little sediment at the bottom of the brain" that enabled him to strengthen himself "with the intellecual idea that once in Zigi's town" he had "been completely convinced of the beauty and desirability of the mere act of living." Why despair and boredom were and continue to be so prominent a part of Greene's character, he nowhere reveals unless it is by the implication in all his work that they are the inevitable consequence of some terrible calamity in which "the human race is implicated." But his revelations about himself do make it easier to understand why he early preferred *The Viper of Milan* to the books of Anthony Hope, Haggard, and Westerman. For Greene, *The Viper of Milan* colored and explained:

the terrible living world of the stone stairs and the never quiet dormitory. . . . It was no good in that real world to dream that one would ever be a Sir Henry Curtis, but Della Scala who at last turned from an honesty that never paid and betrayed his friends and died dishonoured and a failure even at treachery—it was easier for a child to escape behind his mask. As for Visconti, with his beauty, his patience and his genius for evil, I had watched him pass by many a time in his black Sunday suit smelling of mothballs. . . . Goodness has only once found a perfect incarnation in a human body and never will again, but evil can always find a home there. Human nature is not black and white but black and grey. I read all that in *The Viper of Milan* and I looked around and I saw that it was so.

Marjorie Bowen gave him the pattern he believes he has exemplified: "perfect evil walking the world where perfect good can never walk again, and only the pendulum ensures that after all in the end justice is done."

With the not small qualification that he rarely approximates perfect evil in the characters he creates, this is the pattern of Graham Greene's world. Hell lies about his children in their infancy, and one begins to believe in heaven only because one believes in hell. All societies, the creation of grey and black characters, are "in a true sense discarded from" God's presence, and as Cardinal Newman says, "implicated in some terrible aboriginal calamity," comparable to the one in "A Discovery in the Woods." England is a place where men "live in an ugly indifference"; America is where the disparity between the comfortable and the improverished shows up most shockingly against the background of "the drugstore and the Coca-cola, the hamburger, the graceless sinless empty chromium world." Mexico and Russia, *all* welfare states, are the worst because they offer inadequate palliatives: "even if . . . there were no God, surely life was happier with the enormous supernatural promise than with the petty social fulfillment, the tiny pension and the machine made furniture." Even primitive societies are better, for in Liberia and Querry's Congo one can have "moments of extraordinary happiness, the sense that one was nearer than one had ever been to the racial source, to satisfying the desire for an instinctive way of life, the sense of release, as when in the course of psychoanalysis one uncovers by one's own effort a root, a primal memory," and there one finds too, among the natives in the interior "gentleness, kindness . . . honesty which one would not have found, or at least dared to assume was there, in Europe." On his return from each of his journeys among the less "civilized" to the "seedy level," he knows, as he did after his trip to Liberia, that "this journey, if it had done nothing else, had reinforced a sense of disappointment with what man had made out of the primitive, what he had made out of childhood."

An exceedingly pessimistic reading of life and the world

in which it is lived, more Jansenist than Catholic, as Sean O'Faolain has pointed out. A Roman Catholic since 1926 and, one assumes, as good a one as he can be, Greene, when he writes, is at least as much the product of his lost childhood as a Catholic "with an intellectual if not an emotional belief in Catholic dogma." In the November 1948 issue of *Partisan Review*, Graham Greene wrote, "Literature has nothing to do with edification." And he continued, "I am not arguing that literature is amoral, but that it presents a personal moral, and the personal morality of an individual is seldom identical with the morality of the group to which he belongs." Never a liberal who "thought men could govern themselves if they were left alone to it, that wealth did not corrupt and that statesmen loved their country"; once briefly a communist; never a capitalist with "the power of elimination" that enables one to forget "the people behind the shares"; always inclined to prefer the ruled to the rulers; frequently and surprisingly, considering his view of life, a popular success; never quite consistent in his representation of the views I have outlined above—Graham Greene above everything else is an artist committed to the faithful representation of his personal vision, a vision he realizes with nearly progressive fidelity in his novels.

II

BEFORE HIS first published novel, *The Man Within* (1929), Graham Greene published a volume of poems, *Babbling April* (1925) and wrote two novels and part of a third that have never been printed. The poems confirm what he has said about himself in "The Lost Childhood" and elsewhere. Sensations do not delight him: he is "ignorant of the way to speak to God, whether Father, Majesty, or simply You There"; his ideal of happiness is to be like "the insentient stone"; he thinks of love as "a brief ecstasy and a lengthy

pain." Most significantly, in "The Gamble," about the playing of Russian roulette, he wonders:

> Will it be mist and death
> At the bend of this sunset road,
> Or life reinforced
> By the propinquity of death?

The first three novels Greene published show, as Kenneth
Allott and Miriam Farris say in their study, *The Art of
Graham Greene,* "the divided mind." Andrews in *The Man
Within* is "embarrassingly made up of two persons, the
sentimental, bullying, desiring child and another more stern
critic," the "man within . . . that's angry with me." Oliver
Chant, the protagonist of *The Name of Action* (1930), is
unable to decide whether he is for or against dictator
Damassener, who is trying to coerce the people of Trier
into puritanical moral conduct, but he is glad, as one
presumes Greene is, that life is uncertain "in place of the
regular succession of meals, theatres, parties. . . ." The two
protagonists in *Rumour at Nightfall* (1931), appear to be
two sides of one personality rather than separate individuals.
Crane, a coward who fears and hopes to believe in God,
is opposed to the rather indifferent Chase throughout most
of the action, but in the end he becomes a whole person
because of the guilt he suffers. "I suffer, therefore I am," he
thinks. Querry, in *A Burnt-out Case,* thinks very much the
same, though he feels differently.

Except in *The Man Within,* which is still a readable and
significant novel, Greene succeeds poorly in dramatizing the
divided self. There are good things in both *The Name of
Action* and *Rumour at Nightfall,* of course. The characterization of Demassener who sometimes thinks he is "the only
man existing who can see . . . things as they must appear to
a God who is not smirched by living in the world," is
admirable caricature, but those who conspire against him

and the protagonist Chant are types. Despite the awkward-
ness of the device of presenting two aspects of a character
as separate persons and the implausible melodrama of the
action, *Rumour at Nightfall* is the better, particularly in the
minor characterizations, such as that of Riego, who worries
more about the souls of his men than the success of their
actions, and in the incidental descriptions that suggest
Greene's mature manner, such as the following about a
brothel:

A manageress in velvet with a mass of hair and a smile. A
drawing room with cheap mirrors and a red plush sofa. And
finally a rather squalid bedroom with lace curtains, not quite
clean sheets, a dressing table littered with hair combings . . .
and a naked, ill-shaped prudish woman, who is determined to
give as little as possible for your money.

But neither of them have either the technical or the
substantial interest of *Stamboul Train* (American title,
Orient Express) which followed in 1932 or of *The Man
Within* that preceded.

The Man Within has the intensity of a nightmare
occasionally interrupted by pleasant dreams. From the first
page, when Andrews is discovered in full flight from his
friend Carlyon whom he has betrayed, to the conclusion
when he feels he has conquered the lower self that led him
to betray his smuggling comrades and behave with scarcely
intermitted cowardice, the reader identifies with the intense
struggle that goes on within him, is carried ahead by nightmare plausibility. If Greene had not, by the intensity of his
own identification with Andrews, made the reader live
within Andrews, a good deal might not seem probable: the
extent of Andrews' hatred for his father, a good leader of
the smugglers with whom the son is compared invidiously;
the rapt love he feels for Elizabeth because, like a mother,
she shelters him from Carlyon's pursuit (his still warm cup
of tea from which she drinks to make Carlyon believe he has

left becomes a chalice symbolic of the sacred love he does not believe he deserves); the very profane love of Lucy that he wins by testifying in court against the smugglers (typically, after they have slept together, Lucy says, "Have you enjoyed yourself?" and Andrews replies, "I've wallowed"). But Greene's art, here as in many of the novels and entertainments that followed, is equal to his intent of making you see, feel, and live within the bad dream of life *The Man Within* presents. Even after you have put down the book, you wonder which is dream, which reality, and you are left, as in Greene's other books and in Webster's plays, with a residual enlightenment about the horror of existence for those who live with minds alternately haunted by Heaven or Hell.

Stamboul Train, which followed the lesser successors to *The Man Within,* is the first of what Greene calls his entertainments. In these novels, as Allott and Farris point out, there is a "comparative lack of development in the characters . . . wilfull use of interesting background for its own sake," and a linking up of "the various section of his narrative by coincidences and improbabilities." These entertainments, as a rule, move so rapidly in short, sharp cinematographic flashes that the reader has no more wish to weigh probabilities than he does when he watches a good Hitchcock film. So, in *Stamboul Train,* he does not consider the unlikelihood of the many unusual characters who are thrown together on one train and experience so many sensational events. One does not question the probability of the relationship among Dr. Czinner, the socialist leader, Myatt, the insecure Jewish businessman, Carol Musker, the homely dancer traveling to a foreign engagement, Miss Warren, the aggressive lesbian reporter, and the popular "cheerful" novelist Savory. Nor is one upset by the sudden melodramatic events that bring death to Czinner and turns Carol into Miss Warren's next convert to lesbianism. It is an entertainment, perhaps, only because the unlikely characters and happenings seem so removed from our everyday realities that one reads for the surface effect only. But the aftertaste suggests a world similar to that of *The Man Within* and the other novels: a world in which betrayal, lust without love, and violence without motive are more likely to occur than fidelity and true love and kindly, gentle action.

III

As we approach the novels that preceded *The Power and the Glory* (1940: American title, *The Labyrinthine Ways*), it is necessary to remind ourselves that the real world in which Greene lived was full of lust, betrayal, violence, and exploitation, that during the years in which he wrote *It's a Battlefield* (1934), *England Made Me* (1935), *A Gun for Sale* (1936: American title, *This Gun for Hire*), *Brighton Rock* (1938), and *Confidential Agent* (1939) everybody's world was a fallen world. The years that saw the Great Depression, Manchuria, Ethiopia, the Spanish Civil War —these years formed what can easily be seen as a "low, inglorious decade," a little worse even than the decades that have followed. Graham Greene cannot be accused of misrepresenting the Thirties in his savagely pessimistic novels. Indeed, because his novels are as critical of communists as of capitalists, of the men who hold up the law as of those who are lawless, it is possible that the novels from *It's a Battlefield* to *Confidential Agent* give a more accurate picture of the thirties than do the novels of Steinbeck and Dos Passos for America, than do those of James Hanley and George Orwell for England.

It's a Battlefield (1934) is a more fully realized novel than any Greene published earlier. Like *Stamboul Train* it is cinematographic in technique, giving a broad social picture, relying on suggestion for emotional depth. It is,

however, more carefully centered than *Stamboul Train.*
All of the action circles about the attempt to reverse the
sentence of death passed on Jim Drover, a Communist, who
killed a policeman for striking his wife while the police were
putting down a Communist demonstration. Involved in the
effort are Jim's brother, Conrad, who is not a Communist
but believes injustice has been done, Milly, Jim's wife who
sleeps with Conrad out of loneliness and pity, Surrogate, a
Fabian turned Communist who would just as soon have Jim
die as a Communist martyr, the Assistant Commissioner
who knows all justice is imperfect and rarely dares to think
of anything but doing his job, and a number of others who
represent differing and representative attitudes towards
Communism and social justice. The point the action as a
whole emphasizes is that each of those involved in the
battlefield centering about Jim Drover tends towards the
condition of "the private soldier fighting in a fog, like the
men at Inkerman, in a fury of self-preservation," that in
such a mixture of ignorant motivations justice happens only
accidentally. Greene's point is brought out most effectively
when, after the muddle is nearly over, the prison chaplain
resigns because he "can't stand human justice any longer."
When the Assistant Commissioner replies that divine justice
is "much the same," the chaplain replies, "Perhaps. But one
can't hand in a resignation to God. . . . And I have no
complaint against His mercy."

Judged by conventional standards of realism, the novel
is not an entire success. Though all of the characters have
an exterior plausibility and depth is suggested, the fury of
self-preservation the characters are made to exemplify is
overdone. Nevertheless, if one views the novel as a pro-
jection of Greene's peculiar—and powerful—nightmare vision
of the worst that usually happens, the novel is good.
Greene's skill is so great that one believes thoroughly while
he reads and continues to wonder afterwards if Greene's

exaggeration may not be closer to the truth than the cosier realisms we prefer to accept.

England Made Me (1935) is at once more plausible and less important. The portrait of Krogh, based upon the figure of the Swedish match king, Kreuger, is impressively probable, and so is the portrait of Minty, the ticket of leave man who clings pathetically to the respectability of a Harrow tie while he buys and sells scandal and rumors of misfortune. What keeps the novel from impressiveness is the supine conduct of the two chief characters, Anthony and Kate Farrant. One believes in and remembers their almost unnatural attachment to each other, but it is difficult to feel any identification with two characters so dedicated to letting what must be, be. Their only gesture against the domination of Krogh seems half-hearted and theatrical, and one scarcely cares when Anthony is killed by Krogh's chief henchman and Kate decides to leave Krogh. Though, like most of what Greene writes, it is eminently readable, it does not leave you wondering or worrying about either man's or God's injustice.

In *The Confidential Agent* (1939), D, the economic materialist with whom Green identifies, speaks of the fear "of other people's pain, their lives, their individual despairs. He was damned like a creative writer to sympathy." It is Greene's damnation to sympathy that makes his nightmare picture of the world bearable and believeable. Though one does not always find plausible what his characters do or the background against which they act, his identification with extreme characters in extreme situations is so adequate that we live the books until their nightmare becomes our own. He does not portray "perfect evil walking the world," unless the perfect evil is the background of modern society rather than the men who make it. Neither the communists nor the Assistant Commissioner in *It's A Battlefield,* neither Krogh nor the Farrants in *England Made Me* are portrayed without

sympathy. Except for Sir Marcus in *A Gun for Sale*, Hall in
England Made Me, and Ida in *Brighton Rock*, he identifies
sympathetically with all his characters, Catholic or op-
ponents of Catholicism, murderers, or those set to catch
murderers. This identification and his nearly unorthodox
conception of the mercy of God that may save Pinkie, Scobie,
the whiskey priest, and all the rest of his sinners, may make
him a poor apologist for Catholic orthodoxy as it is conventionally viewed, but it does make him a good artist,
angry with circumstances that corrupt but (usually) gentle
with the corrupted—as perhaps God is, too.

Though it is flawed by a happy ending that can only
satisfy the most wilfully sentimental reader, *A Gun for Sale*
(1936), which would have been a good novel with the last
chapter omitted, and *The Confidential Agent* (1939), which
would have been a good novel with the omission of the last
page, illustrate this quite as vividly as the books he labels
novels instead of entertainments. Raven, the paid killer who
nearly starts a war with the innocence of a man who is just
doing what his managers say he should do, has everything
against him. Hare-lipped and too poor to do anything about
it, fatherless from the age of six when his father was hanged,
motherless when his mother cuts her throat on the kitchen
table, he seems predestined for efficient killing that does not
touch the heart. He is thoroughly plausible as one who is
comforted by the kind feeling of Anne who does not notice
his hare-lip and listens to his confessions like a psychiatrist
or priest. When she betrays him, our sympathy is with
Raven, who has by then killed Sir Marcus, the evil capitalist,
and his henchman. Indeed we have something of the same
feeling for him one has for Macbeth though it is tinged
with the feeling one has for pathetic Falder in Galsworthy's
Justice. If Greene's theology were different, he might have
concluded with "The President of the Immortals had finished
his sport with Raven."

In *The Confidential Agent,* D obviously is suggested by the idea of a sympathetic creative artist who has accepted economic materialism with such dedication that he is obsessed by the need to get coal for the Loyalist government of Spain during the time of Civil War and non-intervention. Though the novel is full of the improbabilities Greene allows in an entertainment, the characterization of D is quite as moving as that of Raven. His side, Loyalist though not called so, is shown to be as flawed as Jordan's in *For Whom the Bell Tolls,* but one sympathizes, as I believe Greene did, with his feeling that the poor right or wrong is quite as justifiable as my country right or wrong. Unobtrusively, Greene does make his religious point, as he does with Raven when Ravel feels he might not have had to kill if he had had a priest-like listener, when D thinks, "If you believed in God," you could leave punishment to Him. But also you agree with D who "hadn't that particular faith," and believed "unless people received their deserts, the world . . . was chaos." One is happy with him when he learns that the coal that did not go to the Loyalists at least did not go to the rebels who almost thwart him. Indeed it is with the rebels and the business men who will sell to anyone for a profit, as it is with the ordinary people who have never had a war within and do not expect one without in *A Gun for Sale,* that one is really angry. If they do not make the circumstances that make D and Raven, they are at least responsible for the continued existence of injustice.

Brighton Rock (1938) was at first labelled an entertainment by Greene, later called a novel. Though there are incidents that require an unusual willingness to suspend disbelief, it deserves the name of novel because of its overall probability and seriousness. I do not mean to imply that it is a realistic novel, though it is based upon an actual series of murders that occurred in Brighton. None of Greene's novels are that. It is a thoroughly realistic night-

mare that suggests by exaggeration truths about men and
the moral and social universe God may have made.

The center is Pinkie, a lapsed Catholic who retains a
knowledge of good and evil as distinguished from the more
secular conception of right and wrong, who believes in Hell
and lives in it, dimly perceives the possibility of a Heaven
that is not his destination. Like Raven, he has never known
love, unless it was his parent's weekly exercise in bed that
he witnessed and which made him think of sexual desire as
a sickness. His desire for recognition, the closest he can
come to something like love, has made him a killer, an inept,
merciless leader of a gang. He is not sentimentalized, hate
runs stronger than blood in his veins, but he is presented as
salvageable human material in his awkward and diffident
approach to love for Rose, who resembles an animal in whose
hole for hiding "were murder, copulations, extreme poverty,
fidelity, and the love and fear of God." Both Pinkie and Rose
seem more worthy of salvation than their pursuer who
believes in the secular punishment of wrong by right, the
big-breasted Ida, with her merciless compassion for Rose
and her sense of "fair play" as an eye for an eye that means
death for Pinkie. One does not like to believe that such
people exist, but they do in the terrifyingly convincing nightmare world of the book that does, after all, resemble life
more than our day dreams. One hopes strenuously, while
and after he reads, that the priest Rose visits after Pinkie's
death is right when he tells her, "You can't conceive, my
child, nor can I or anyone—the . . . appalling . . . strangeness
of the mercy of God."

IV

GREENE'S MORE recent novels—from *The Power and the
Glory* (1940) to *A Burnt-out Case* (1961)[1]—are, with the
exception of *The Third Man* (1949), *Loser Takes All* (1955)

and *Our Man in Havana* (1959), his best. One continues to find the familiar obsessions with the awfulness of life on earth, with the strangeness of the mercy of God, so odd "it sometimes seems like punishment." Now, however, it is with the mercy of God and the need to believe in it and with the way awfulness is made by idealists who fancy themselves God that Greene is mainly preoccupied. Because of this modification of his view of God and the world, the novels are less realistic nightmares, more realistic novels in which nightmares appear. Because he has matured both as thinker and artist, his control of his material is better, too. Though he continues to use, when it is necessary, the vivid cinematographic technique he used first in *Stamboul Train*, the quick flashes that suggest a multiverse are nearly always subordinated to the steady progression of a conflict in which only a few characters are involved.

To see how much he has progressed as an artist one has only to compare *The Lawless Roads* (1939) with *The Power and the Glory* (1940). In *The Lawless Roads* righteous indignation at the treatment of Catholics in Mexico often obscures his vision; in *The Power and the Glory* he dramatizes fully and fairly the insights that are nearly buried in *The Lawless Roads:* that the peasants are perhaps "the population of heaven," that "these aged, painful, and ignorant faces . . . are human goodness"; that even the communists are compelled to their view of the world, for "no one can live without a philosophy"; that what is typical of Mexico is perhaps typical of the entire human race; "violence in favor of an ideal and then the ideal lost and the violence just going on."

Where the whiskey priest goes, pursued by God and the police, he finds human goodness. He finds it most among the peasants who risk danger by coming to him and by sheltering him, in the mestizo Judas who shamedly betrays him, in Coral Fellows who lost her faith at the age of ten.

He finds it even in the Lieutenant, his and God's opponent, who despite his mystical "certainty in the existence of a dying, cooling world" where people should have the "right to be happy in any way they chose," befriends him as long as he does not know he is a priest. Certainly Greene does not sentimentalize the goodness of any of these: the peasants haggle over the price of a baptism, the mestizo betrays him, the Lieutenant orders his execution. But without Greene's picture of limited human goodness, both the priest's fearful efforts to serve people and God's effort to save the priest would seem utterly futile.

But it is mostly what happens within the priest that holds us. He is so thoroughly oppressed by the awfulness of the world, "the way things happen," and the evil he sees in himself—his early mistaking of ambition for a sense of vocation, his dreams of luxury, his sleeping with Maria and his love of his child above other children when he should "love every soul as if it were one's own child," his cowardice and his drunkeness—that his persistence in his priestly function seems a form of saintliness. Indeed, as we watch him learn in his corruption what he had not known in his innocence, we agree that "when you visualized a man or woman carefully, you could always begin to feel pity," that hate, even of his opponent, the Lieutenant, "was just a failure of imagination." As he argues Catholicism with the Lieutenant while he is nearly overcome with fear of death, he seems specially favored by God, certainly not despised. Assuredly all but the blindly prejudiced must agree with Greene's judgment of the man upon whom he based his characterization (in *The Lawless Roads*): "who can judge what terror and hardship and isolation may have excused him in the eyes of God?"

In the entertainment that followed—*The Ministry of Fear* (1943)—Greene develops further the preoccupation, appearing in *The Power and the Glory*, with the excesses of a secular power that is not checked by men who believe in a supernatural power greater than themselves. Like all of Greene's entertainments it relies a great deal on coincidences and does not attempt depth of characterization, but it does probe the problem of idealism run amok in idealists (like Dr. Forrester and Poole) who "don't see blood like you and I do. . . . It's all statistics to them." The central character, Arthur Rowe, unwittingly becomes the possessor of some films the Nazis and their idealist allies need. As a consequence he becomes involved in melodrama that includes two bombings, confinement in a sanatorium with amnesia, and being pursued by and pursuing the secret agents who form a Ministry of Fear in England. The action, of scenario swiftness, is handled admirably, but what remains after the pleasure, is a brooding worry over a world in which man does not seem worthy to prevail. "Let not man prevail," Rowe reads in a Roman missal, "and the truth of the appeal chimed like music. . . . It wasn't only evil men who did these things. Courage smashes a Cathedral, endurance lets a city starve, pity kills. . . . We are trapped and betrayed by our virtues." This irony is dramatized vividly by the entire novel, for almost everyone means well and expects to accomplish too much—even Rowe, who had killed his suffering wife out of pity. Although it is clear that the Nazis and the idealists who "can bear . . . other people's pain endlessly" if it seems justified by their ends are worse than those who cannot outlive pain "like sex," it is clear that we are all involved in a Ministry of Fear greater than any the Nazis ever made, "a Ministry as large as life to which all who loved belonged. If one loved one feared." And there is the further implication that it is only God's mercy that permits escape. The three later entertainments—*The Third Man* (1949), *Loser Takes All* (1955), and *Our Man in Havana* (1959)—are entertainments only. Fast pace and plot ingenuity are their virtues. *The Third Man* is the more typical of the three because it does suggest one of Greene's preoccupations: "In these days . . . nobody thinks in terms of human beings." Greene himself properly characterizes *Loser Takes All* as a "frivolity," and though *Our Man in Havana* is unique in the gaiety of the fun it pokes at secret agents and their superiors, it is not profound.

The Heart of the Matter (1948) is, in its different way, quite as good as *The Power and the Glory*. Appropriately its epigraph is from Péguy: "No one knows as much about Christianity as the sinner unless it is the saint." Even more than in *The Power and the Glory*, where evil is externalized in the Lieutenant, the conflict is within the protagonist. Scobie, the sinner, is also an upright man, so unimpugnably honest that the civil servants under him dislike him and the Commissioner above him looks upon him as his logical successor. Like Greene himself when he made his journey without maps and when he served in West Africa during World War II, Scobie is kind to the African natives, to his subordinates, to everyone, even the smuggler Yusef. Like Greene again, Scobie is a Catholic convert married to a woman who was born Catholic. I do not mean to imply that Scobie is a self-portrait; I only suggest that there is an autobiographical reason why Greene identifies with him so perfectly. Perhaps he is what Greene felt he might become, as are all of his heroes except Pinkie.

Scobie's gentleness is interpreted as the consequence of pity which resembles the damnation of the creative artist, sympathy. He does not, in any ordinary way, love his wife Louise, who wants him to get ahead, to move some place where cultivated company is possible, who cannot comprehend his love of Africa. Scobie loves Louise most in her times of ugliness, "when pity and responsibility" reach the "intensity of a passion in him." Because of the "pity that smouldered like decay at his heart," Scobie becomes involved in an impossible series of situations. He borrows from Yusef so that Louise can get away to something like happiness in South Africa; he falls in love, during her absence, with Helen Rolt, for with her he feels to excess "the loyalty we all feel to unhappiness, the sense that that is where we really belong." Deeply involved in the complications to which pity leads him, he can only wonder, "If one knew . . . the facts, would one have to feel pity even for the planets? if one reached what they called the heart of the matter." He wonders, he cannot accept. He cannot accept the Church's dogma that "one should look after one's own soul at whatever cost to another," since he feels one cannot truly love God "at the expense of one of his creatures." Consequently he succumbs to despair, "the price one pays for setting oneself an impossible aim," kindness to everybody that hurts no one. It is, he thinks, "the unforgivable sin, but it is a sin the corrupt or evil man never practises. . . . Only the man of good will carries in his heart this capacity for damnation." His despair leads him to suicide which he tries to make appear a natural death so that his wife and Helen Rolt will not suffer. This is not because he does not recognize the probability of his own eternal damnation whether he says an act of contrition before dying or not. His wife, a more devout and/or orthodox Catholic, is appalled, but the priest to whom she talks says, "don't imagine you—or I—know a thing about God's mercy. . . . The Church knows all the rules. But it doesn't know what goes on in a single human heart."

In my account of the novel, brief as it must be, I have stressed the structure at the expense of the texture, which is everywhere realized admirably. One gets to know the people, the weather, the insides of houses and the suggestive outsides of the minor characters, the total atmosphere of the place where Scobie's tragedy occurs. Without the texture, one would not care about or believe the meaning Greene unobtrusively conveys. But it is the meaning, artistically translated into an ambiguity as obscure as the will of God, that remains with us forcibly. One is left wondering about the close alliance of sin and virtue, perplexed, whether one is Catholic or agnostic, about the working and judgment of whatever transcends the world we see and die in.

Most of the critics consider either *The Heart of the Matter* or *The Power and the Glory* Greene's best novels, *The End of the Affair* (1951) and *The Quiet American* (1955) inferior. Though there are things in both of them that hurt effectiveness—the planting of Sarah's baptism as a Catholic in *The End of the Affair* to make plausible her wish to be buried a Catholic, the inept moment in *The Quiet American* when Pyle thinks of the shine of his shoes rather than of the bloodshed his ignorant idealism has caused—I consider *The End of the Affair* Greene's best novel and *The Quiet American* very little below his best level. Perhaps this is because I believe flawed intensity is to be preferred to perfection without intensity. Without detracting from the excellence of any of the early novels, I would maintain that these two novels are the most intense he has ever written, both because they are more deeply felt and because this deep feeling is represented by a greater concentration on fewer characters and because the cinematographic flashes are reduced to a minimum.

In *The End of the Affair* the reader identifies closely with the good-and-bad man and writer, Maurice Bendrix. He is, he says, at the beginning, writing a record of hate "far more than of love." He hates particularly Sarah Miles, who became his mistress while he was trying to get material from her about her husband, Henry Miles, a prominent civil servant, whom Bendrix despises as a representative of unimaginative beauracracy. Whatever he says in favor of either, he writes on the first page, can be trusted. "I am writing against the bias because it is my professional pride to prefer the near-truth, even to the expression of my near-hate." As his record continues to struggle towards the near-truth, it becomes clear that his hate of both Henry and Sarah is caused by jealousy, for Sarah, after being his mistress for five years, suddenly and unaccountably breaks with him after an intense meeting that is followed by his close escape from death by a buzz bomb. As he thinks, she either returns to her husband or goes on to another lover. His hatred of her is the consequence of great love intensely shared. The description of this love affair is the first in Greene to be presented as true passion that brings real happiness while it lasts. Out of the desire to hurt both Sarah and her husband, Bendrix hires a private detective who uncovers evidence of her apparent double infidelity and brings to him, finally, Sarah's journal that covers the time of the affair and afterwards.

Reading it, "over and over again," he has to skip "when a passage hurts him too much." So does the reader, for the journal shows that Sarah gave up Bendrix because she made a promise to God that she would leave him if He restored Bendrix to life after his actual death from the buzz bomb he thought only stunned him,[2] and it is mainly about the conflict between her "ordinary corrupt human love" and her desire to love God who has saved Bendrix and deprived her of him with that "odd sort of mercy" that "sometimes looks like punishment." The intensity of her struggle to give up a human love that has enabled her to understand how God can be intensely loved and hated is as excellent a piece of writing as one finds anywhere in modern literature. Sarah finds it as difficult to believe God can love her immortal soul as she does the giving up of Bendrix. No excerpts can do the journal justice, but he who reads it is convinced that Sarah means the words that come repeatedly to Bendrix's mind after reading it; "But You are good to me. When I ask you for pain, You give me peace. Give it him too. Give him my peace—he needs it more."

Her ultimate forgetfulness of herself in her love of God who can work miracles for others turns her into a saint. The ill son of the detective who followed her is made well by one of her books; the rationalist to whom she goes to cure herself of her growing love of God has a disfiguring birthmark removed by her touch. In the end, Bendrix is still unconverted, but the reader feels sure he cannot escape, though the last words of the book are, "O God, You've done enough, You've robbed me of enough, I'm too tired and old to learn to love, leave me alone for ever."

What has caused most modern readers to refuse to acknowledge the book's excellence, as it has, I suppose, kept most viewers from accepting Greene's miracle play, *The Potting Shed* (1958), is the occurrence of the miracles and the conversion of the adultress Sarah into a saint. As Greene comments in *The Lawless Roads*, "We are too apt to minimize the magic elements in Christianity—the man raised from the dead, the devils cast out. . . ." Evidently most modern readers cannot agree with Hardy, the agnostic, who would go to the manger on Christmas Eve, hoping the miraculous were so, or with that devout agnostic, Gilbert Murray, who felt the same. Greene has not converted me (though I believed as I read), but he has made me grateful for the experience of, for a time, believing as he does. I must agree with William Faulkner, certainly no orthodox or unorthodox Catholic, who called *The End of the Affair* "one of the best, most true and moving novels of my time."

The way Greene shocks one into taking a position that it is disreputable to take in a sophisticated gathering is again illustrated in *The Quiet American*. Greene's tale of Pyle, the innocent American, "impregnably armoured by his good intentions and his ignorance," a man who must blame even the violence he causes on the Communists, has not been very sympathetically received. It is too clear that the narrator, Fowler, though he shares only some of Greene's views, as Greene has pointed out in a letter printed in the New York *Times*, does believe American foreign policy in Indochina and elsewhere is dominated by an innocence that is "like a dumb leper who has lost his bell, wandering the world, meaning no harm," dominated too by diplomatic correspondents "who get hold of an idea" and then alter "every situation to fit the idea." Greene's dramatic pillorying of such innocence is not, of course, confined to what he observed of Americans when he spent some months in Indochina. The Englishmen who belonged to the Ministry of Fear and the Mexicans who pursued the whiskey priest are found guilty (in so far as a novel can hand down decisions) of similarly well-intentioned idealism.

Esthetically, the book is very good indeed. The I, Fowler, is a convincing portrait of a man who refuses engagement only to become involved in it when he sees the harm Pyle's naivete is doing. Another plausible part of his motivation is the fact that he is jealous of Pyle who has taken from him his native mistress, Phuong, and envies him his faith in God though he distrusts the faith. The characterization of the others—the soldiers reluctantly managed by politicians who will ultimately settle for a state of affairs similar to what prevailed before the fighting started, the Vietnamese, the other Americans, the Communists, everyone but Phuong who becomes a sterotype once one finishes reading—is intentionally shadowy. The action of Pyle in trying to form a Third force that is neither Communist nor imperialist is thoroughly plausible, the jungle warfare managed with a skill comparable to John Hersey's in *Into the Valley*. It is, furthermore, like all of Greene's later novels, religious as well as political in theme. The never obscured significance of the whole action is the awfulness of what occurs when man alone tries to prevail and the last sentence implicitly decries even Fowler's intervention in Indochinese affairs that helped cause Pyle's death: "Everything had gone right with me since he had died, but how I wished there existed someone to whom I could say that I was sorry."

This sentence, the latter part of it, states again the fundamental preoccupation of Greene in all the better novels from *The Man Within* to *A Burnt-out Case*. With an art and an insight that approaches the consummate, Greene is always mainly concerned with man's hope of God and the danger of his too frequent hubristic self-reliance. His novels are never cosy. They all emphasize the loneliness of human beings that has caused even the pretentiously rational to invent God or something very like him—"a being capable of understanding," as we almost never do, ourselves and others. Perhaps, he overdoes his case against contemporary man and what, without God, he has made and may make of this world, but who can disagree with Fowler's casual comment after seeing an American film: "It was what they call a film for boys, but the sight of Oedipus emerging with his bleeding eyeballs from the palace at Thebes would surely give a better training for life today."

Nathan A. Scott, Jr.

GRAHAM GREENE: CHRISTIAN TRAGEDIAN

Graham Greene's first novel—*The Man Within*—
appeared in 1929, and, as we stand at a remove from it of
more than twenty-five years, it begins now to seem that the
stature which he has won requires that we judge him in the
terms that we use for judging the major novelists of this
century.[1] Yet Greene has not been often fortunate in the
quality of the discriminations which his critics have brought
to bear upon his work. He has been accused, and generally
with irrelevance, of excessive morbidity and, on occasion,
by reason of his preoccupation with evil, has been called a
Manichean. He has also been charged with too strong a
predilection for melodrama, and, perhaps even more frequently, for horror and violence. But these are objections
which may well be only acknowledgments, however wrong-
headed and lacking in cogency, of the deeply penetrating
moral and religious concern which is central to his entire
work and which gains its special form of statement by
reason of the spiritual circumstances of his time.

Greene, it must be remembered, has a profound and
radical affiliation with Catholic Christianity, and wanting,

as a Christian artist, like Dante in the fourteenth century, to disclose the point of juncture between nature and grace, he has used violence and melodrama as instruments for awakening his age out of its lethargies, for destroying its specious securities and revealing its underlying nightmare and tragedy. He has wanted to "prohibit sharply the rehearsed response,"[2] to resurrect the heart through terror and to exhibit the world itself, in all of its degradation, as the country wherein man's spiritual nature is to be rediscovered. But since Greene has known at what a discount a Christian reading of the human situation has been in the modern world, he has resorted to those devices of indirection which the Christian artist has so frequently employed in our period, himself concealing the true motives of his work beneath the conventions of the "thriller."[3] And there is little doubt but that the furtive lust and the shabby little slum rooms, the vitriol and the razorblades, the chases and the explosions have effectively hidden his larger purposes from many of his readers. Too frequently the verdict has been that his main contribution to the furniture of the contemporary imagination is simply a "shabby Inferno" of "soured virginity, soured spirituality, soured kindliness . . . the world of the Slump, as well as of the Fall."[4]

Greene belongs, of course, to that English generation of W. H. Auden and Stephen Spender, Rex Warner, and Christopher Isherwood, which grew to maturity in the years between the two great wars and which was profoundly affected, at an impressionable age, by the general European *malaise* that was brought overwhelmingly into focus by the call to arms in Spain in the summer of 1936. It was a world unforgettably described by Auden in his *New Year Letter* of 1940, where he speaks of how,

> taut with apprehensive dreads,
> The sleepless guests of Europe lay
> Wishing the centuries away,

> And the low mutter of their vows
> Went echoing through her haunted house,
> As on the verge of happening
> There crouched the presence of The Thing.

But Greene's response to the developing crisis differed from that of his contemporaries who were bent on invoking all the militant formulas of leftist politics and who were seeking a way out of their own disquiet through Freudian psychology. It was not that he turned away from the contemporary world, but, rather, that the ruined cities and the putsches and mobilizations of western Europe in the Thirties—which he looked at as steadily as did the early Auden and Spender and Orwell, or Continental writers like Malraux and Silone —pointed, for him, not simply to a breakdown in the machinery of modern society but to something in the nature of man which could not be grasped by the mathematically precise assignations of guilt and innocence characteristic of leftist liberal thought. As Auden, again, was to say in the *New Year Letter,* himself now having passed through his youthful Marxism and expressing here, one feels, a sensibility very close to Greene's: "The situation of our time / Surrounds us like a baffling crime." And all of our equipment for the detection and containment of the malevolent forces only

> Extends the area of the crime
> Until the guilt is everywhere,
> And more and more we are aware,
> However miserable may be
> Our parish of immediacy,
> How small it is, how far beyond,
> Ubiquitous within the bond
> Of one impoverishing sky,
> Vast spiritual disorders lie.

It is as Arthur Rowe, the hero of *The Ministry of Fear,* says: "The world has been remade by William Le Queux." Released from imprisonment for the mercy-killing of his

wife, we meet him against the background of war-torn
London, stumbling into a charity bazaar in a Bloomsbury
square where he wins a cake which contains the micro-
films of a naval secret that is being sought by Nazi spies.
Before he is fully sensible of his plight, he has become
involved in an intricate web of espionage and murder and
is himself an outlaw, having been framed by the ruthless
amoralist, Willi Hilfe, for a nonexistent murder. And in the
midst of this macabre entertainment[5] he cries out to his
dead mother in a dream: "I've killed my wife and the police
want me."

His mother smiled at him in a scared way but let him talk:
he was the master of the dream now. He said, "I'm wanted for a
murder I didn't do. People want to kill me because I know too
much. . . . It sounds like a thriller, doesn't it?—but the thrillers
are like life . . . it's what we've made of the world since you died.
I'm your little Arthur who wouldn't hurt a beetle, and I'm a
murderer too. The world has been remade by William Le
Queux."

So Greene has chosen in many of his novels to render
the contemporary world through the medium of the "thriller"
—not at all, though, as some of his critics have hinted,
because he wishes to cater to the plain reader's desire for
circuses, but, rather, because he has felt that it makes
possible a more effective imaginative seizure of the infernal
realities of our time. And it is this searching moral purpose
behind the frequently Gothic exterior of his books that
gives him the kind of importance as a novelist to which only
a very few of his contemporaries can lay any claim.

II

IN HIS EARLIER novels—*Stamboul Train* (1932), *It's a Battlefield* (1934), *England Made Me* (1935), and *A Gun for Sale*
(1936)—Greene created (as did T. S. Eliot in his early

poems) a kind of abstract of our modern Inferno, and it is the adjective "seedy," recurring again and again, which is the focally descriptive term. We are brought up against a whole series of displaced persons, lonely and uprooted, whose seedy world, in all of its moral neutrality, is—as it is said of the Swedish industrialist Krogh in *England Made Me* —a wilderness of their own contriving. In *Stamboul Train* there is, for example, the hypochondriacal Mrs. Peters, who whines ceaselessly about her digestion: " 'Get me a sandwich. . . . I'm so empty I can hear my stomach. . . . No, I won't have any more of this foreign beer. My stomach won't stand it. Ask them haven't they got a Guinness. I'd just fancy a Guinness.' " Or there is the joyless lesbian relationship between Mabel Warren, the foreign correspondent, and the beautiful and vacuous Janet Pardoe, who is "lovely." And we also have the vain and smug little writer of popular fiction, Savory, whose bit of success has very greatly enlarged his sense of the role he must play in the world. In *It's a Battlefield* there is Kay Rimmer, the sister-in-law of the doomed Communist murderer, Jim Drover, who comes alive only in the moment of copulation, who "never felt more at home than in a bed or a man's arms." She is in love with the young Frenchman, Jules Briton, but she cannot resist the exquisite flat and the luxurious rose-colored, semicircular bed of Surrogate, whom she meets at a Communist meeting. And there is the pathetic figure of Conder, who, in the loneliness of his squalid little bed-sitting room, seeks to redeem his sense of failure in fantasies of being a successful journalist and business magnate, and, particularly, of being a family man.

It is perhaps in *England Made Me*—which Greene properly regards as being, after *The Heart of the Matter* and *The Power and the Glory*, his most successful book—that he gives us his finest evocation of our "fallen" world. Kate Farrant, the mistress and secretary of the Swedish financier, Krogh,

brings her weak, shifty, but charming scapegrace brother
Anthony to Stockholm (and there are hints of incest in their
relation), where she hopes to place him in Krogh's organiza-
tion. The great man takes him on as his personal bodyguard
and is soon captivated by Anthony's debonair amiability.
But Anthony meets the English tourists, Mr. and Mrs.
Davidge, and falls in love with their daughter, Lucia, whose
teenage frankness about sex and whose prattling simplicity
make her a little pathetic and yet, perhaps because of the
very freshness in her unformed youth, somehow desirable.
Her background of Coventry, Woolworth's, and Wotton-
under-Edge represent "home" to Anthony, and for this he
proposes to break with Krogh and Kate, promising Lucia,
on the morning he sees her off at the railway station, to
meet her on a certain day not far hence at the Moroccan
Cafe in the High Street at "home." But he never arrives
there, for before he can leave Stockholm he is murdered by
Hall, Krogh's devoted henchman, who fears that Farrant,
having made so many discoveries about the precariousness
of their financial enterprises, may betray them all. After
Anthony's death, Kate decides to leave Stockholm. But she
does not intend to return to England: "I'm simply moving
on," she says to Minty, the newspaperman. "Like Anthony."

Now this is the basic situation of the novel into which
Greene draws a host of memorable figures whose wretched
loneliness very largely defines the tone of the book. There
is Krogh, the self-made business magnate, whose vast wealth
cannot purchase for him any felicity of soul, whose exterior
presents to the world the formidable solidity of success, but
who is really, as Kate realizes in a moment of sympathy,
". . . one of us, fighting for his own security like one of us,
he's not the future, he's not self-sufficient, just one of us, out
of his proper place." He lives, without love, in a "wilderness
of his own contriving," his deepest pleasure consisting in
gazing at the initials of his own name flashing at him in

the electric lights that adorn every doorway in his great office building. Or there is the little newspaperman Minty, an expatriate, who lives on Krogh, since everything that happens to Krogh is "news"—a man utterly without connections, without roots, who hopes, that morning when Anthony takes Lucia to his room simply because there is nowhere else for them to go, that they have come to see him as a friend, and who is bitterly disappointed when he realizes that it is only his bed that they want. " 'Poor devil,' " they say, as he leaves. " 'It's a dreary world.' " And finally there is the "depraved innocence" of Anthony, who has emerged from a long series of seedy, disreputable confidence games with his slick, shiny exterior unscathed but without either wisdom of the mind or peace of heart. Ironically, he dies by drowning—ironically, because his baptism comes too late. Kate Farrant says of them all (including, one imagines, Hall, who makes her think of "some great pain hopelessly demanding sympathy"): "we're all thieves. . . . Stealing a livelihood here and there and everywhere, giving nothing back. . . . No brotherhood in our boat. Only who can cut the biggest dash and who can swim."

So it is not surprising that betrayal, as Walter Allen has observed, is a frequently recurring theme in Greene's earlier books.[6] There is Conrad Drover, for example, in *It's a Battlefield*, who sleeps with his doomed brother's wife, as there is also in the same book the habitual infidelity of the effete Communist intellectual, Surrogate, to the memory of his wife who had known the inner falseness of his life for what it was. Or there is the hare-lipped killer of *A Gun for Sale* who is betrayed by Anne, the first person he ever dares to trust. It is a world of violated trusts and broken loyalties —such a world as Gauguin was thinking of when he remarked (and Greene has quoted this sentence): "Life, being what it is, one dreams of revenge." Which is perhaps the explanation of another characteristic theme in these books:

namely, criminality, the violent lawlessness of those like Josef Grünlich in *Stamboul Train* or Conrad Drover in *It's a Battlefield* or Raven in *A Gun for Sale* who strive toward further self-definition through an act of revenge.[7] And they have, of course, significant affinities with many of the major heroes of modern literature—with Lafcadio of Gide's *Les Caves du Vatican*, with Joe Christmas of Faulkner's *Light in August*, with Jeremiah Beaumont of Penn Warren's *World Enough and Time*, and with Meursault of Camus' *L'Étranger*, to name only a few.

The shabby little shyster lawyer of *Brighton Rock*, Mr. Prewitt, reminds us at one point that, when Faust asked Mephistopheles where Hell was, Mephistopheles replied: "Why, this is Hell, nor are we out of it." And so too does it seem that many of Greene's early novels are, at bottom, saying: "Why, this is Hell, nor are we out of it." For he is always juxtaposing the special personal failures recorded in these books against the background of the collective tragedy of the modern world—the furious schismatism of the Communist Party in *It's a Battlefield*, the unconscionable incitation of international war by armament manufacturers in *A Gun for Sale*, the internecine struggles generated by Franco-feudalism in *The Confidential Agent*, the Mexican church suppression in *The Power and the Glory*, and the Nazi fifth column in *The Ministry of Fear*. "Each of these novels," says Allen, "is the microcosm of the violence of a continent," and each is "reminiscent in a very real way of the world of the old Icelandic sagas and eddas. 'Though he believe it, no man is strong.' "[8]

III

IT IS THAT hauntingly memorable book of 1938, *Brighton Rock*, which marks a kind of transition in Greene's work from the early novels to the major books of his maturity—

The Power and the Glory (1940), *The Heart of the Matter* (1948), *The End of the Affair* (1951), and also the interesting entertainment, *The Ministry of Fear*, which appeared in 1943. In the book of 1938 it became clear that the forlorn world of dereliction that Greene had been portraying in his earlier novels was not simply the squalid arena of futility and meaninglessness that has been so thoroughly explored in modern fiction but was, rather, a world of dimensions, not truly to be understood except *sub specie aeternitatis*. Indeed this book brings to a kind of terrifying conclusion the first phase of his work, and Greene here gives us an even more sombre description of dereliction than anything that had gone before.

Fred Hale serves his newspaper as its mysteryman, "Mr. Kolly Kibber": in this role he patrols the Brighton seaside, leaving cards along his route, to be picked up by visitors, and he is prepared to give a reward to the person who identifies him. Hale is the betrayer of Kite, the former leader of some seedy racecourse gangsters, whose present leader is the brutal and sinister seventeen-year-old criminal, Pinkie. And for this act of treachery Hale is murdered by Pinkie's henchmen who take his life by cramming down his throat a long piece of the hard candy known as "Brighton Rock."

Shortly before Hale is killed, he is "picked up" by the plump and sensual Ida Arnold, a coarsely amiable tart who, after his death, sets out to track down the murderers. "'I'm going to make those people sorry they was ever born. . . . Right and wrong. . . . I believe in right and wrong.'" When Pinkie discovers the interest she is taking in the affair, he mistakenly dismisses her, saying: "'She don't matter . . . she's just a buer.'" And he is, of course, mistaken, for Ida's persistent investigations are to be his undoing. But his miscalculation is inevitable, for Pinkie is incapable of understanding that Ida loves life so deeply that she is "prepared to cause any amount of unhappiness to anyone in order to defend the only thing she believes in." And thus she is a more dangerous adversary than Pinkie realizes, for Fred Hale's murder figures in her imagination as an assault upon that than which there is nothing more sacred—namely, life itself. "'I like fair play,'" she says. And she feels the necessity for no stronger equipment than this in the realm of fundamental belief: she simply loves the world with a cheery gusto and abandon. The word "stranger" means nothing to her: "there was no place in the world where she felt a stranger. . . . There was nothing with which she didn't feel kinship": for her the "world's all dandy." But for Pinkie the world is like a ". . . jail, it's not knowing where to get some money. Worms and cataract, cancer. You hear 'em shrieking from the upper windows—children being born. It's dying slowly." He says on one occasion to Rose, the little waitress who loves him and who is also a Catholic: "'These atheists, they don't know nothing. Of course, there's Hell. Flames and damnation, torments.'" And when Rose anxiously adds: "'And Heaven too,'" Pinkie replies: "'Oh, maybe, maybe.'"

Now it is in the struggle between Ida and Pinkie that Greene offers us his chief dramatic image of what he believes to be the radical antithesis between the secular and the religious view of the human situation. Ida, it will be remembered, believes that God doesn't mind "a bit of human nature." But Pinkie, despite the desecration of his piety, never forgets that, when he commits murder and takes Rose as his wife in a civil marriage, he has chosen to be damned: it is significant that the words of the petition for peace from the *Agnus Dei* are often on his lips. And though his desperate efforts to evade the machinery of Ida's justice finally culminate in his suicide and hers is the final triumph, she never really gets to Pinkie, nor even to Rose, who says to Pinkie: "'I'd rather burn with you than be like her.

She's ignorant.'" As, of course, Ida is, for she knows only Right and Wrong, and nothing of Good and Evil: she is the type of the "natural man," and this is why, within the logic of the novel, her complacent vulgarity and her jolly, good-humored sensuality strike us as being, however robust, something less than human. For, as T. S. Eliot has said in his essay on Baudelaire,

So far as we are human, what we do must be either evil or good; so far as we do evil or good we are human; and it is better, in a paradoxical way, to do evil than to do nothing: at least, we exist. It is true to say that the glory of man is his capacity for salvation; it is also true to say that his glory is his capacity for damnation. The worst that can be said of most of our male-factors, from statesmen to thieves, is that they are not men enough to be damned.[9]

And it is with these—that is, those who "are not men enough to be damned"—that Greene so richly populates the world of *Brighton Rock*, setting their velleity against Pinkie's energy of will, their abstractedness against the burning reality of him the very purity of whose malevolence discloses, in a paradoxical way, the grace for which he hungers.

IV

BUT CAN ANYTHING good and gracious come out of the rubble of such extreme secularity? This is, one feels, the great question that Greene is implicitly raising and answering in the books that appeared during the Forties—*The Ministry of Fear, The Power and the Glory*, and *The Heart of the Matter*—and in the latter two he has created something closely approaching tragedy.

How, though, it will be asked, is it possible for a Christian novelist to manage a rendering of the human story that is at once genuinely tragic and genuinely Christian? Is it not the case that "if God is in fact the Lord of life and

history, the deep wound of tragedy is no longer deep?"[10]
This is a question that both theologians and literary critics
have often posed, by way of denying the possibility in
literature of such a thing as "Christian tragedy," it being
assumed, on the one hand, that tragic art must be purely
tragic, and, on the other, that the Christian drama takes
us beyond the dimension of tragedy. But Professor Preston
Roberts has reminded us of the error in both assumptions.
For Christian theology, on the one hand, says Roberts,

does not simply deny or cancel out tragedy. It shifts the locus
of tragedy from God, nature, others, or our own essence to an
aspect of ourselves and others—an aspect which is rendered
sufferable, meaningful, and transformable by virtue of a conjunction between God's freely given grace and our freely received
faith. Chance, necessity, and judgment remain. . . . The consequences of sin are not erasable or completely reversible. . . .
There is always the generic contract between what might have
happened and did not happen and what may or can still happen.
. . . No man falls so far as to be cut off from all possibility of
salvation, and no man rises so high as to be beyond all possibility of reversion, stasis or further ascent.[11]

And, on the other hand,

. . . dramatic tragedy is not simply and purely tragic. The
meaning . . . is not all despair and doom. . . . Some of the
greatest of dramatic tragedies . . . turn upon the theme of man's
idolatory and pretension rather than upon the themes of man's
suffering nobility or piteous abnormality. They move from defeat
to victory, from doom to grace, and from tragedy to peace.[12]

So it appears that a "Christian tragedy" is possible, since
"the events and meanings of which Christian theology
consists . . . are not simply and purely 'beyond tragedy,'
and literary tragedy 'is not simply and purely tragic.'"[13]
And it is in the direction of a narrative art which incor-
porates this kind of complex insight that Greene seems to
be moving in his more recent novels.

The world into which we are taken by his books of the Forties at once resembles and differs from that of classical tragedy, on the one hand, and that of Christian tragedians like Hawthorne and Melville and Dostoievski, on the other. Greene's hero, characteristically, is not the great individual of Greek tragedy: he is, rather, the little man, who is, however, very much in the manner of Greek tragedy, immediately placed in a situation that makes him guilty. This situation is simply his membership in the "fallen" world that forms the stage upon which the drama of redemption is to be played out. But the fact that the protagonist is in a situation that makes him guilty at the ouset does not predetermine the issue of the action, as in Greek tragedy where whatever the hero does must be wrong (Oedipus must either persist in searching out the cause of the Theban plague or allow the city to be destroyed). For, although not unaffected by the consequences of his own and others' sins, there yet remain vents of freedom through which it is possible for him to transcend the moral ambiguousness of human existence, to the extent of being able to hear and accept the summons to reenact our Lord's Passion. And his heroism is defined by his acceptance of this task.

Greene's hero seems to be endowed with the *hamartia* or tragic flaw laid down by Aristotle as an essential requirement of the tragic man; but this flaw is neither a constituent element of his nature as a finite creature, as in classical tragedy, nor does it issue from an abuse of freedom motivated by pride, as is the case with the Christian tragic hero. He is a man whose dominant emotion is pity, "the terrible promiscuous passion which so few experience" and which is nurtured, says Greene, by "the conditions of life." It is, indeed, the quality of his compassion, his inability to resist the impulse to bear the griefs and carry the sorrows of his fellow creatures—it is this which makes him a hero: he would have the chastisement of their peace upon himself

and, with his own stripes, would have them healed. He is
the man whose life is governed by "the horrible and horrifying emotion of pity": for him the great uncanonical
sacrament is the sacrament of the brother. But the very
imperiousness of his compassion frequently commits him to
a position where the felt claim upon him of another's need
conflicts with and cannot easily be adjusted to other situations, less immediate and pressing, in which he knows
himself to have contrary obligations. Yet so urgent is the
immediate and present claim upon the moral imagination
that it cannot be resisted, its opposition to other obligations
notwithstanding. And thus "the imitation of Christ" becomes
a tragic spectacle, in so far as it becomes, ironically, the
occasion for the hero's betrayal into sin: yet it is not (as
with, say, Brigitte Pian in Mauriac's *La Pharisienne*) the sin
of self-righteousness, nor is it (as with Sophocles' Oedipus)
the sin of *hybris*: his *hamartia* consists simply in the frailty
of the human creature who is unable to be a priest to
others without himself being succoured by divine grace.
But this is not a fact which leaves us feeling angry or
desperate, since the pathos of the hero's situation is tran-
scended in the great denouement of the action which consists
in the disclosure of a conjunction between human charity
and divine charity.

The plot that involves Greene in the exhibition of this
pattern manifests several consistencies as between *The Ministry of Fear, The Power and the Glory,* and *The Heart of
the Matter;* and, though each of them deserves the most
careful scrutiny, I must here, for the sake of brevity, concentrate upon *The Heart of the Matter,* which presents its
most searching and profound version. Like Arthur Rowe in
The Ministry of Fear (who kills his disease-ridden wife out
of pity) and the fallen whiskey priest in *The Power and the
Glory* (who, as he contemplates the uncertain future of his
little illegitimate daughter, prays: " 'O God, give me any

kind of death—without contrition, in a state of sin—only save this child' "), the hero, Major Scobie, who is a commissioner of police in Sierra Leone, wonders whether, if one knew all the facts, one would not " 'have to feel pity even for the planets? If one reached what they called the heart of the matter.' " And, though his vulnerability to suffering is his virtue, it is also his flaw, for by it he is to be brought to the brink of damnation. His story reminds us, in fact, of the priest's description of Péguy in the final pages of *Brighton Rock*, as he tries to comfort Rose after Pinkie's death: " 'He was a good man, a holy man, and he lived in sin all through his life, because he couldn't bear the idea that any soul could suffer damnation . . . He never took the sacraments, he never married his wife in church. I don't know, my child, but some people think he was—well, a saint.' "

Scobie is a man of middle age, a convert to the Roman Church, whose life with his nagging, restless wife Louise has long since ceased to be an affair of ecstasy and passion. But, though he no longer loves her, he remains bound to her "by the pathos of her unattractiveness." And, in order to secure the money for her South African holiday, away from the heat and the damp, the ants and the cockroaches of their drab, northwest African coastal settlement, he enters into a financial arrangement with the Syrian usurer, Yusef —an arrangement which he knows his position as a responsible British colonial official ought to forbid.

During Louise's absence the survivors of a torpedoed ship are landed on the Sierra Leone coast, and among them is a nineteen-year-old girl, Helen Rolt, who has been widowed in the shipwreck. Toward this bewildered child-woman (who reminds us of Anthony's Lucia in *England Made Me*) Scobie extends himself in sympathy and compassion, and their friendship soon becomes a secret liaison. Then, Louise returns, and Scobie is faced with the necessity of deciding between his wife's claim upon him and that of

Helen, but, since any decision must result in suffering for either, there seems to be no line of action really open. He brings his problem before his priest in the confessional box, but, being unprepared to break off the affair with Helen, he cannot be given absolution. Yet, determined to avert his wife's suspicions, he has to pretend that things between them are as usual—which involves his accompanying her to the Communion rail, this being something that Louise, as a strict Catholic, insists upon. He knows, of course, that for him to make his Communion while in a state of mortal sin is for him to risk eternal damnation. But he cannot bring himself to make either Louise unhappy by revealing to her his affair with Helen—or Helen unhappy by breaking things off with her for the sake of Louise. So he goes to the rail with his wife, "watching the priest pour the wine and water into the chalice, his own damnation being prepared like a meal." As he takes God into himself, he prays: "'O God, I offer up my damnation to you. Take it. Use it for them.'" And he is "aware of the pale papery taste of his eternal sentence on the tongue."

But the intolerableness of his situation begins even more strongly to be felt as he realizes that the deception which he is practicing on Louise will require his committing again and again this act of eucharistic blasphemy. One night, as she calls to him to come to bed, a desperate prayer forms itself on his lips: "'O God . . . I can't give her pain, or the other pain, and I can't go on giving you pain. O God, if you love me as I know you do, help me to leave you.'"

His decision has, then, been made: he will destroy himself, for no longer can he shower blows upon the bruised face of Christ by falsely participating in the *missa fidelium*. So he studies the symptoms of angina pectoris and poisons himself with the tablets which his physician prescribes for the illness that he pretends to have.

Here, then, is Greene's *exemplum* of the Christian hero

in a tragic situation: here is the branch that grows out of the "stony rubbish" of our world—the man who, being caught up and possessed by the example of Christ's charity, discovers, as Christ discovered in Gethsemane, that goodness involves suffering, but who does not refuse that suffering, so profound is his compassion for his fellow creatures, his compassion being nurtured by "the conditions of life." And the fact that his attempt to reenact our Lord's Passion proves unsuccessful leaves us not with the pity and terror of Greek tragedy but rather with something like the sense of judgment and forgiveness of the Gospels. For, though Scobie betrays God, the last words on his lips, as he falls to the floor after taking the poison, are: " 'Dear God, I love . . . .' " And the resonances of meaning and implication that have been stirred up within us by the total action persuade us that he is himself loved and shall be forgiven in some "brave new world."

V

"MAN HAS PLACES in his heart which do not yet exist, and into them enters suffering, in order that they may have existence." So we are now reminded not only by the consistencies that have animated Greene's fiction in the past, but also by the epigraph (from Léon Bloy) that introduces his novel, *The End of the Affair.* In this book Greene foregoes the highly charged violence and melodramatic intensity that have been so much a part of his previous work: its scene is neither the agitated underworld of urban gangsters nor some torpid backwater of the tropics but a placid island of London suburbia, Clapham Common, against the background of which is told a tale of middle-class adultery and of a modern woman's submission to an *askésis* highly reminiscent of that *via negativa* of St. John of the Cross.

Between Henry Miles, a middle-aged civil servant, and

Sarah, his attractive wife, there grew up during the first
months of their marriage one of those curious misunder-
standings of the flesh which, when it arises between a husband and wife, if they remain with each other afterwards,
often results in their being "kind" to one another for a lifetime. This has for several years been the character of the
life that Henry and Sarah have shared; but she, in her
robust sensuality, has good-naturedly taken her pleasure
wherever it was to be had. And so, when the writer Maurice
Bendrix, in gathering material for a story, seeks to study at
first hand a senior civil servant, he has little difficulty in
getting "copy" from Sarah Miles, who is the wife of such a
man: as their relation develops, he falls deeply in love with
her and she with him, and this is the beginning of the affair.

But the novel does not begin at the beginning, but
somewhere near the end, on a dark, wet January night in
1946, as Bendrix, out for a stroll in spite of the weather, sees
Henry "slanting across the wide river of rain" on the Common. Bendrix overtakes his neighbor who invites him into
his study for a drink, and there the worried husband, never
suspecting that Bendrix was at one time his wife's lover,
confesses his fear that his wife's affections have strayed
elsewhere. Many months have now passed since Bendrix
and Sarah last met, prior to which they had been lovers for
five years, and Bendrix had, throughout this time, been
given to periodic outbursts of unjustified suspicion and
jealousy: it was simply his nature not to be without fear in
love. So now he is curious to discover the identity of the
rival who displaced him, and, when he learns that Henry
has thought of engaging a detective, he urges this course
upon him: indeed, he arranges to engage the operative.
But no evidence is found except Sarah's journal, to which
the whole of Book III, the central section of the novel, is
given over.

Now we are taken back—eighteen months before—to that

last night on which Bendrix and Sarah made love, during an air raid. We learn that during the raid Bendrix left Sarah and went downstairs, but on the way down a flying bomb exploded. For a few minutes afterwards he lay unconscious beneath a door. When Sarah found him, she thought him dead and refrained from touching his prone figure, lest if she took his hand "it would come away, all by itself, from under the door." Bendrix was, perhaps, only stunned, but Sarah, believing him to be dead, returned to his rooms, knelt down and prayed for the first time in many years to a God in whom she no longer believed: " 'Dear God. . . . I'll give him up forever, only let him be alive with a chance. . . .' " Then Bendrix walked in, and was alive, and Sarah thought: "now the agony of being without him starts," and wished that he was safely back dead again under the door.

" 'Now, of course, I know,' " Sarah states in her journal, " 'that this was hysteria.' " But, whether it was or not, it becomes the occasion for a human being—very modern, very sophisticated, very worldly in her sensibility—to begin to grope her way toward recovery of belief in God. For Sarah, whatever her weakness, is honest, and the vow must be kept, and her problem becomes that of discovering the identity of Him to whom the pledge has been made—together, indeed, with the identity of the one who made the vow.

At first Sarah feels nothing but a terrible loneliness and emptiness—in the apparently irreparable ruin of her soul's joy and happiness, nothing but a "cowardly need . . . of not being alone." Her descent is to sorrow and suffering and solitude. It is an *agonia*, an awful deprivation, a "dark night," and we are reminded of that "frontier" of which Eliot speaks in *The Family Reunion*, "beyond which safety and danger have a different meaning." The word which Sarah uses in her journal is "desert," for this is what she finds round herself, now that her relation with Bendrix has come to an end. And she wonders what one can build in the desert, how one can go on living, and whether God, if one could believe in Him, would fill the desert. " 'I have always wanted to be liked or admired,' " she says.

'I feel a terrible insecurity if a man turns on me, if I lose a friend. I don't even want to lose a husband. I want everything, all the time, everywhere. I'm afraid of the desert. God loves you, they say in the churches; God is everything. People who believe that don't need admiration, they don't need to sleep with a man, they feel safe. But I can't invent a belief.'

And she confides to her journal that

'That's asking me to believe too much, that there's anything lovely in me. I want men to admire me, but that's a trick you learn at school—a movement of the eyes, a tone of voice, a touch of the hand on the shoulder or the head. If they think you admire them, they will admire you because of your good taste, and when they admire you, you have an illusion for a moment that there's something to admire. All my life I've tried to live in that illusion—a soothing drug that allows me to forget that I'm a bitch and a fake.'

No, she decides, this God who supposedly is able to find something lovable in the bitch and the fake must Himself be the sheerest fiction.

But, finally, Sarah is driven, by utter loneliness, to the threshold of faith. For, as she says in her journal, " 'I want somebody who'll accept the truth about me and doesn't need protection.' " This is an inclination to which she offers very great resistance, and she even begins to take instructions from an old-fashioned rationalist who preaches against Trinitarianism and Immortality on London street corners. But he only succeeded in strengthening her growing belief. He argued against the arguments for God, when she had not known there were any—" 'except this cowardly need . . . of not being alone.' " And so there slowly grows in her, try as she does to smother it out, that delight which Augustine knew, the delight, that is, which is to be had in finding God by failing to find Him.

Sarah begins now to sense the possibility of her affair with Bendrix having itself been a figure in the tapestry of the divine Purpose. As she looks back and recalls the abandon with which they scattered themselves upon each other, in all the untidiness and disorder of their undeveloped hearts, it occurs to her that perhaps all the time He was there, encouraging each to give the other so much love that, when they had finished, there would be nothing left but Himself. And so the fallen soul embraces fatigue (as Porphyry advised), chooses the despair that has, as Kierkegaard says, "something of the eternal in its dialectic," chooses solitude, in order that it may go to the "desert,"

> to the empty land
> Which is no land, only emptiness, absence,
>   the Void,
> Where those who were men can no longer turn
>   the mind
> To distraction, delusion, escape into dream,
>   pretence,
> Where the soul is no longer deceived, for
>   there are no objects, no tones,
> No colours, no forms to distract, to divert
>   the soul
> From seeing itself, foully united forever,
>   nothing with nothing. . . .[14]

Sarah chooses, in other words, "the secret way," the way of "the dark night," of which St. John says in *The Ascent of Mt. Carmel*: "The journey of the soul to the Divine Union is called night for three reasons: the point of departure is privation of all desire, and complete detachment from the world: the road is by faith, which is like night to the intellect; the goal, which is God, is incomprehensible while we are in this life." And this is the journey that Greene's heroine undertakes: she dares "another intensity / For a

further union, a deeper communion. . . ."[15] So the end of
one affair becomes for her the beginning of another.

Bendrix had, of course, expected to discover that he had
been sexually wronged, but, when he completes his reading
of Sarah's journal, the old bitterness is dispelled. Certain
that they can resume their relation, he telephones her to
say that he is coming to her immediately; but Sarah, though
suffering from acute influenza, goes out into the pouring
rain to avoid him and seeks refuge in a nearby church.
Bendrix overtakes her and persuades her to seek a dissolution of her marriage in divorce. It turns out, though, that
Sarah was not strong enough to withstand exposure, and
she dies a few days later of pneumonia, but not before the
priest to whom she had been going for instruction has
assured her that her Registry Office marriage is valid and
cannot be dissolved: Bendrix learns this from a letter which,
having been misaddressed, reaches him only after her death.

Again, the affair would seem to be over. But after Sarah's
death Smythe, the rationalist preacher, is cured of a birthmark that had disfigured his face; a book which she had
owned as a child cures Parkis' little son (Parkis is the
detective whom Bendrix had engaged) of appendicitis. And
is a miracle wrought upon Bendrix also? There is, but it is
not so visible as these more spectacular occurrences. What
has happened is that suffering has brought new places
into existence in his heart, though at the end of the book
the transformation is by no means complete. He, of course
—the sensual, agnostic sophisticate—professes to be uncon-
vinced by these "miracles." He talks to Henry about "coincidences," such as having seen over and over again "two
cars with the same figures side by side in a traffic block,"
despite "ten thousand possible numbers and God knows
how many combinations." But his very contentiousness
makes manifest his deep suspicion that in the life of this
woman whom he loved supernature had invaded nature,

transcendence immanence, God man. Indeed, the thought that seems most to disturb him is that " 'if this God exists,' " and if Sarah, with her lusts and her adulteries and her timid little lies, " 'can change like this, we could all be saints by leaping,' " as she leapt, " 'by shutting the eyes and leaping once and for all. . . . It's something He can demand of any of us.' " But he resists it: he sits listlessly in his rooms and says to the problematic Person:

'You've taken her but You haven't got me yet. I know Your cunning. It's You who take us up to a high place and offer us the whole universe. You're a devil. . . . But I don't want Your peace and I don't want Your love. I wanted something very simple and very easy: I wanted Sarah for a lifetime, and You took her away. With Your great schemes You ruin our happiness as a harvester ruins a mouse's nest. I hate You, God, I hate You as though You existed.'

And we imagine that such a one as Augustine might have said to such a man as Bendrix: "Thou couldst not hate the Lord thy God, if thou hadst not already found Him; so rejoice, then, that thou hatest Him, for, in hating Him, thou hast found Him; and, having found Him, thou mayst, in time, by His grace, discover that thou shouldst love Him, even as He loveth thee."

VI

HERE, THEN, is a rising curve that is discernible in one of the most remarkable bodies of writing in the imaginative literature of our period, a curve which runs from the early studies of modern dereliction to the later studies of purgation and sanctity which (excepting the comparable work of Bernanos and Mauriac) are without parallel in the fiction of our time. He has found, as Morton Zabel has remarked, "an instrument for probing the temper and tragedy of his age, the perversions and the fears that have betrayed it, and the stricken

weathers of its soul."[16] And though, in his proven capacity
to negotiate the hazards of an art that accepts a kerygmatic
responsibility, he may not yet have satisfied all our questions
(particularly those which concern the rendering of religious
reality that is most adequate to the demands of a mimetic
art) he is today one of the most interesting and one of the
most promising novelists using the English language: as
F. R. Leavis says of Henry James, he has "*added* something
as only genius can."[17]

Francis L. Kunkel

THE THEME OF SIN AND GRACE
IN GRAHAM GREENE

IN A SHORT STORY about a Roman Catholic novelist, Graham Greene has one of the characters say that true literary criticism leaves the author's views out of account.[1] " 'A novel is made up of words and characters. Are the words well chosen and do the characters live? All the rest belongs to literary gossip.' "[2] But a critic cannot act on this advice; it leaves out of consideration the fact that the words an author chooses and the characters he creates depend upon his views. A critic must pay attention to problems of theme.

Greene never states his themes. He simply illustrates them in terms of the characters and action. Since he lives passionately in his ideas, his literary works never suffer from being abstract. It would embarrass him, he confesses, to discuss the ideas underlying his novels, because, in the act of writing, he is carried along by the unpredictable energies of his characters, rather than by the desire to express his thoughts about the problems besetting mankind,[3] though in Greene these problems derive from his central preoccupations, grace, sin, and the flesh.

Every novelist tries to treat significant human experience,

but the Catholic novelist tries to treat it at its roots—where God confronts man and grace encounters free will. Grace can act like a thunderbolt or grace can act like a leaven. Like Paul's, Sarah's conversion, in *The End of the Affair*, is quick and dramatic. The rehabilitation of the priest in *The Power and the Glory*, like that of Augustine, is slow and secret.

Among modern Catholic novelists only Mauriac conveys the triumph of grace with artistic skill comparable to Greene's. All Mauriac's action, like Greene's, is wound around the spool of sin and despair, salvaged only by a wretched, but indomitable, faith in the liberating grace of God. The comparison has been made most effectively by a critic: "More violently and perhaps more mysteriously than Mauriac, he (Greene) has joined his work with Catholicism. The debate he carries on is the oldest in the world—that between nature and grace. It is the debate of man placed between two worlds: an inaccessible heaven and an earth heavy and rich with the life it bears."[4] The agonies of sin —usually sins of the flesh—may shatter the sinner's complacency and reveal to him for the first time his lack of self-sufficiency and his need for God. In this way, carnal passion may be transformed finally into religious passion. So it is with Greene's Sarah Miles and Mauriac's Gisele de Plailly: these two erring women, responding to grace, turn from debauchery to the Infinite.

In implying that some characters are offered grace by God while others are not, Greene, however, parts company with Mauriac who makes no such neo-Calvinist division. Greene is generous in supplying grace in abundance to all the Catholic characters, even demoniacal Pinkie, but he is stingy where certain non-Catholic characters are concerned. Though it is denied them for different reasons, Ida and the police lieutenant are the two outstanding examples of char-

acters to whom grace is denied. The Lieutenant is cut off
from grace, because, warring with God, he hates Christianity; Ida is cut off, because, indifferent to God, she ignores
Christianity. Conflict in Greene's two-world view is generated by the antagonism which always exists between
characters who are given no access to God's grace and those
who are. But this central contrast, more pronounced in
Brighton Rock than in *The Power and the Glory,* has heretical implications: for the orthodox Catholic all virtues spring
from grace. Ida's justice and the Lieutenant's compassion
are no exception. To believe, as Greene obviously does,
that some characters are forever outside the pale of grace
and so incapable of religious belief and experience is to cast
a gratuitous slur on God's mercy and to flirt with Jansenism.
Greene's position here is inconsistent because ordinarily he
follows Pascal in setting no limits to God's mercy.[5]

The Tertullian contrast in Greene's fiction, "between the
supernatural man who lives on the plane of good and evil
and the natural man who lives on the plane of right and
wrong," has been put concisely by Francis X. Connolly. He
justifiably complains that

right and wrong are not really opposed to good and evil; the
same God who created the supernatural order created the
natural order. Grace perfects nature. Natural goodness invites
the free gift of grace. Greene's whole emphasis however would
tend to suggest that it is bad to be right, bad to be cheerful,
healthy, companionable. There is a trace of savage Manicheism
in his resentment of well-being.[6]

Now the unorthodoxy in Greene's novels would not be
important from a literary point of view—provided his world
seemed entirely authentic. But that is not the case in
Brighton Rock and to a lesser extent in *The Power and the
Glory.* The imaginative cohesion of these two books is
disrupted by the assumption that not everyone receives

grace. Helen Gardner rightly contends that Pinkie, Rose, and the priest are falsely romanticized and Ida and the Lieutenant falsely turned into semicaricatures on account of it.[7]

Greene does not swallow Jansenism whole, however. If he did, Ida and the Lieutenant would be his greatest sinners; for, according to Jansen, those who are not offered grace cannot help sinning.[8] Yet the only commandments Ida breaks, the first and the sixth, are the only commandments Pinkie keeps. And the Lieutenant, starved for grace, is a Lilliputian sinner by comparison with the priest. It is the pessimism of Jansenism that is most endemic in Greene.

Not only are the Catholic characters greater sinners, but they are frequently less happy in the state of grace than they are in the state of sin. Sarah Miles, for instance, is a carefree relaxed sinner before her conversion and life of virtue plunge her into woe. The nearer she approaches to God, the less joy she takes from the created world and human love. Pascal describes the wretchedness of man without God;[9] Greene describes the wretchedness of man with God.

It is interesting to compare Greene in this respect with Evelyn Waugh. In *Brideshead Revisited* the virtuous Catholics, with the exception of Cordelia, are a miserable lot. To be in love with God made Chaucer's Parson happy; it only makes Cordelia's brother, Brideshead, and her mother, Lady Marchmain, melancholy. Waugh, like Greene, does not find goodness keeping company with joy. Indeed the reverse is true; for Cara, the mistress of Lord Marchmain, takes the most joy out of life. And the most contented of all Greene's characters is jolly Ida, a woman of easy virtue.

Happiness, Greene implies, is incompatible with grace. "Happiness," he advises, "should always be qualified by a knowledge of misery."[10] Success too is suspect; a sense of doom hovers over it.

One looked around and saw the doomed everywhere—the champion runner who one day would sag over the tape; the head of the school who would atone, poor devil, during forty dreary undistinguished years; the scholar . . . and when success began to touch oneself too, however mildly, one could only pray that failure would not be held off for too long.[11]

Close to the heart of Greene's upside-down matter is Sean O'Faolain's witty observation concerning him: "Joyfully he reverses Browning. God's in his heaven, all's wrong with the world."[12]

"Goodness has only once found a perfect incarnation in a human body and never will again, but evil can always find a home there," Greene writes in *The Lost Childhood*.[13] The ease with which "evil can always find a home" in the human body is due to original sin. In the epigraph to *Another Mexico* Greene reflects his commitment to the doctrine of original sin by quoting a passage of Cardinal Newman which concludes: ". . . this living society of men is in a true sense discarded from His presence . . . *if* there be a God, *since* there is a God, the human race is implicated in some terrible aboriginal calamity."

For all this, Greene does not exaggerate the results of original sin. He never portrays man as so mired in sin as to be beyond the power of redemption. Those of his characters who are most strongly committed to sin always retain their freedom to renounce it, to respond to the tug of divine grace. Grace tries to get at the dying Scobie in the passage, "all the time outside the house . . . someone wandered, seeking to get in. . . ."[14] Even Pinkie, who has on his face the flush of the flames, recognizes before the end a counterpull, an enormous emotion beating on him. "It was like something trying to get in, the presence of gigantic wings against the glass."[15] The reader hears the fluttering of the wings of grace, the feathered glory striving, as the Boy disappears.

All of Greene's Catholic characters regard sin as an outrage perpetrated against the person of Christ. Contemplating his sins, Scobie "had a sudden picture before his eyes of a bleeding face, of eyes closed by the continuous shower of blows: the punch-drunk head of God reeling sideways."[16] This frighteningly anthropomorphic description finds a restrained counterpart in a passage from Waugh's *Brideshead Revisited.* In a self-flagellating speech, Julia Flyte, a bad Catholic, shows her agnostic lover what their sin means:

Christ dying with it, nailed hand and foot; hanging over the bed in the night nursery; hanging year after year in the dark little study at Farm Street with the shining oilcloth; hanging in the dark church where only the old charwoman raises the dust and one candle burns; hanging at noon among the crowds and the soldiers; no comfort but a sponge of vinegar and the kind words of a thief; hanging forever; never the cool sepulcher and the grave clothes spread on the stone slab, never the oil and spices in the dark cave; always the midday sun and the dice clicking for the seamless coat.[17]

For Greene's characters sin is intoxicatingly omnipresent. Even in infancy they exhale the scent of sin and corruption. Pinkie, for one, finds no innocence in childhood. "You had to go back a long way further before you got innocence; innocence was a slobbering mouth, a toothless gum pulling at the teats, perhaps not even that; innocence was the ugly cry of birth."[18] For Pinkie "hell lay about him in his infancy."[19]

Clouded by sin and corruption, Greene's own childhood was just as smoky as Pinkie's, if less pathetic, and was marred by some of the same kind of irrational violence. The shocking story, drawn from his own experience, that Greene tells in *Another Mexico* of the suicide of a fifteen-year-old girl, pregnant out-of-wedlock, anticipates a similar version recited by Pinkie.[20] Adumbrating the "faint secret sensual pleasure"[21] which Pinkie feels, fingering a bottle of vitriol, as Rose approaches, is the sadistic impulse experienced by Greene at the age of fourteen, as reflected in a passage from *Journey without Maps*: "There was a girl lodging close by I wanted to do things to; I loitered outside the door hoping to see her. I didn't do anything about it, I wasn't old enough, but I was happy; I could think about pain as something desirable and not as something dreaded. It was as if I had discovered that the way to enjoy life was to appreciate pain."[22]

In their degrees, all Greene's Catholic heroes and heroines are sinners; even those of them who eventually reach blessedness have en route been perilously close to damning themselves. The character Greene had so cherished as a boy in *The Viper of Milan*—"perfect evil walking the world where perfect good can never walk again"[23]—provides us with a clue as to why he has never created a figure of absolute goodness. Greene's practice at this point—concentrating exclusively on the love of God as it shines forth among the sinful—is in marked contrast to the practice of Georges Bernanos, who has no such compunction about portraying both extremes of the human spectrum. He populates his world with demons—M. Guérou in *L'Imposture,* the Abbé Cénabre in *La Joie,* and M. Ouine—and with saints—the diarist of *Journal d'un curé de campagne,* the Abbé Donissen in *Sous le soleil de Satan,* Chantal de la Clergerie in *La Joie,* and the Abbe Chevance in *L'Imposture.* Thus Bernanos remembers what Greene forgets: that the sinless also love God.

In limiting his universe to sinners, François Mauriac, who resembles in this respect Greene rather than his countryman Bernanos, defends the practice on the grounds that sinless Catholics, virgins and saints—such as the Little Flower and the Curé d'Ars—are not fit material for the art of the novel.

But how is one to describe the secret drama of a man who struggles to subdue his earthly heritage, that drama which finds expression neither in words nor gestures? Where is the artist who may dare to imagine the processes and shifts of that great protagonist—Grace? It is the mark of our slavery and of our wretchedness that we can, without lying, paint a faithful portrait only of the passions.[24]

Certainly Greene acts on this assumption. Never attempting a portrait of unsullied goodness, he works solely with imperfect human material. Like Mauriac, he is the novelist of the weak, the suffering, the misunderstood. His pity for all the exiled of the world and his rooted interest in the seedy make him temperamentally ill-adapted to be the portrayer of the sinless person.

Greene's very interest in the exiled and the seedy has led to a crucial misunderstanding of his position on sin and sinners. Most commentators persist in attributing to Greene a view on the relationship of sin to virtue for which I find little basis. And nearly all of them, in my judgment, err in their interpretation of Greene's attitude towards various kinds of sinners.

In the short story "A Visit to Morin," Morin, a Roman Catholic novelist whom Greene obviously intends to be identified with himself, is plagued by critics who applied the word 'pardox' to his work "with an air of disapproval" and "seemed to scent heresy like a rat dead somewhere under the boards. . . ."[25] In an effort to locate the exact spot, critics have pulled up nearly all of Greene's floor boards. On occasion I, too, have wielded a crowbar, but when George Orwell finds in Greene's novels the suggestion "that there is something rather *distingué* in being damned"[26] and Kenneth Tynan imputes to Greene the paradoxical idea "that sin holds within it the seeds of virtue,"[27] I think it is time to put a halt to housewrecking.

This glorification of sin and the accompanying notion

that damnation is somehow an immediate form of salvation have been termed "sin mysticism."[28] Herbert Haber documents Greene's purported "sin mysticism" at length. Analyzing the character of the whiskey priest, Haber concludes that he: "found the path 'to the good death,' to martyrdom and sainthood, through an immersion into the pentecostal flame of earthly sin. . . . Through adultery, the Priest finds in himself the capacity for love: he does indeed love the twisted fruit of that transgression—his child, Brigida. Through drunkenness, he becomes humble to the point of ungratuitous self-effacement."[29]

This point of view assumes that the priest's humility and selfless love have been caused by alcoholism and fornication. But it is faulty to perceive a cause and effect relationship where a mere priority in time exists. The priest and, for that matter, Sarah, also, grow spiritually not because they have sinned—sin is not the condition for their virtue—but because they have been engulfed by disaster, purified by pain. The priest's complacency is corroded by persecution, Sarah's lust by the self-enforced loss of Maurice. In other words, Greene is exalting the whiskey priest, not his whiskey-guzzling. Nor is it the sensuality and the unfaithfulness of Sarah that Greene extols; it is her self-control in the face of enormous temptation. It was after all the penitence of Magdalen, not her promiscuity, which won her salvation.

The sinner, never the sin, enlists Greene's sympathies. And even then it is only a special kind of sinner that Greene takes an interest in: the sinner, in Charles Péguy's paradox, who, together with the saint, is at the heart of Christendom.[30] Guilt-riven and tormented, this sinner is a recurrent figure in the art of many modern Catholic writers—Bloy, Mauriac, for example—who invariably endow him with two characteristics. He never abandons himself to sin without a soul-tearing struggle, and he continually fights his bondage. Far better than the externally pious Christian, who is smug about his success in keeping the commandments, the sinner knows that Christ alone can save him. Neither Greene nor the others are celebrating "sin as an incitement to salvation"[31] but rather the weakness of man and the power of God. Greene does not glorify sin; he glorifies humility. The priest's love for Christ, like that of Peter the prototype of all priests, is not augmented by his betrayal but by the sorrow that ensues from the betrayal.

Like St. Thomas Aquinas and countless theologians, Greene considers sins of pride worse than sins of the flesh.[32] If he seems too lenient towards fornication and adultery, it is solely as a reaction to complacency.

Alexander Boyle's judgment of Greene's art illustrates the general misunderstanding on this point. "There is a sort of inverted Phariseeism . . . which not only welcomes to its bosom the thief, the prostitute, and the murderer, but assigns as their portion indifference and contempt to those whose feet have rarely wandered from the path traced out before them at their First Communion."[33] Granted that Greene welcomes thieves, prostitutes, and murderers—in keeping with the Christian attitude of hating the sin but loving the sinner—and vouchsafes them a future; he does not assign contempt to the sinless for the obvious reason that his universe is limited to sinners. Although Boyle cites no examples to bolster his contention, Elizabeth Sewell, in a similar indictment, uses as evidence the pious woman in the Mexican prison *(The Power and the Glory)* and Aunt Helen *(The Living Room)*.[34] Admittedly Greene has no sympathy whatever for either of them, but he does not flail them for the reasons Miss Sewell supposes—bourgeois virtue, spiritual mediocrity. On the contrary, he denies them virtue, even mediocrity: he denigrates them for their self-righteous, outward piety, which hypocritically masks an unholy meanness of spirit.

To assume, as Dietrich von Hildebrand seems to do,

that Greene's Catholic novels imply that humility presupposes sin and that alcoholism or adultery are indispensable protections against Pharisaism[35] is to misread them. This assumption overlooks the fact that the privations of persecution, quite apart from his sensational sins, are enough to humble the priest. Furthermore, on the morning of his execution the priest begs God's pardon for *all* his sins and realizes "now . . . at the end there was only one thing that counted—to be a saint."[36] Where Scobie is concerned this assumption ignores the fact that he is more humble, in the sense of experiencing less moral superiority, *before* his adulterous liaison. Greene does not sprinkle holy water on sin, or endow it with the character of a *felix culpa,* or invite someone to sin with the hope of bringing about good results. Instead he instills a reverence for the individual person despite his sin and cultivates a more profound respect for the mysterious transforming powers of grace which can enable a penitent thief on the cross to 'steal' paradise.

The Catholic character who does not perfect himself in charity associates the flesh with revulsion. Ida's big breasts pointing through a thin summer dress stir Pinkie's disgust. Louise sitting up in bed under a mosquito net reminds Scobie "of a joint under a meat cover."[37] And Helen in a comparable position reminds him of a "bundle of cannon fodder."[38] On the other hand, the character who perfects himself in charity, far from detesting the flesh, sees the body as sanctified. The implications of the Incarnation—finding Christ in his fellow-men and, particularly and painfully, in those in whom His image was grotesquely distorted by sin and shame—exhilarate the priest.

At the centre of his own faith there always stood the convincing mystery—that we were made in God's image—God was the parent, but He was also the policeman, the criminal, the priest, the maniac and the judge. Something resembling God dangled from the gibbet or went into odd attitudes before the bullets in a prison yard or contorted itself like a camel in the attitude of sex.[39]

Sarah too pushes beyond the truth that the essence of man's likeness to God is intellectual and spiritual and wonders: "Could anybody love Him or hate Him if He hadn't got a body?"[40] Revering the body, despite its capacity for sin, she poses the question: "We can love with our minds, but can we love only with our minds? Love extends itself all the time, so that we can even love with our senseless nails; we love even with our clothes, so that a sleeve can feel a sleeve."[41]

Although many critics have singled out Greene's puritanism for comment,[42] how little puritanical he really is is evident as soon as he is contrasted with Mauriac. The latter is committed to the myth that the flesh is wholly evil, and all carnal love, even in marriage, is guilty. He quotes with approval Pascal's definition of marriage as "the lowest of the conditions of Christianity, vile and prejudicial in the eyes of God,"[43] and he speaks, in his life of Racine, of "that certitude fatal to human happiness, that carnal love is evil, evil which we cannot help committing."[44] It would be fatuous, of course, to contend that we are dealing with polar extremes—say Calvin and D. H. Lawrence; in truth the difference between Mauriac and Greene is a difference in degree. Yet, and this is the important point, Greene's characters do expect relatively more from sexual love than Mauriac's characters ever do. This is most clearly seen by juxtaposing the view of Mauriac's Brigitte—"All the miseries of our human state come from our inability to remain chaste"[45]—with the view of Greene's D.—"It was something to be in love with a living woman, even if you get nothing from it but fear, jealousy, pain. It was not an ignoble emotion."[46]

Dominick P. Consolo

GRAHAM GREENE: STYLE AND STYLISTICS IN FIVE NOVELS

THIS ESSAY IS A study of Graham Greene's technique in his five novels: *Brighton Rock, The Power and the Glory, The Heart of the Matter, The End of the Affair,* and *The Quiet American.*[1] Technique, taken in its larger sense to mean "any selection, structure, or distortion, any form or rhythm imposed upon the world of action,"[2] will be used interchangeably with style: the result of "an individual way of feeling and seeing" which compels "an individual way of using language."[3] Specifically, however, the focus is on point of view, on character, on structure, and some aspects of language, insofar as they inform a particular approach by Greene to his fictional world. Only slight consideration will be given to themes.

As Mark Schorer has said, "Technique is not a secondary thing . . . some external machination, a mechanical affair, but a deep and primary operation; not only that [it] *contains* intellectual and moral implications, but that it *discovers* them."[4] Despite the contention of a sensitive, perceptive, and satirical novelist that Greene does not have a literary style and that "the words are functional . . . simply mathe-

matical signs for his thought,"[5] in these five novels the style
is subservient to the meaning and the action and incorpo-
rates them.

Many of Greene's critics make at least passing reference
to his style, giving it a short glancing blow and careening
off into considerations of theology or metaphysics. Walter
Allen calls it a "swift nervous style," whatever that means,
"and a technique of montage which he owes to the film."[6]
His use of the camera eye is often mentioned, and Neville
Braybrooke holds that Greene's "technique is simple; it is
the adaption of the dramatic soliloquy to the confines of the
novel," only not in a Shakespearean way, however, for one
"has the impression not of somebody declaiming his thoughts
to the world at large, but of somebody whispering his
inmost doubts and conflicts to one by telephone."[7] What
there is here of critical flatulence has at least wit to recom-
mend it; whereas Arthur Calder-Marshall is merely misleading in saying that the "pace" in *The Power and the Glory*
is that of a "thriller" while "the total effect is dissipated in
the confusion of detail. . . ."[8]

It will not do, I think, to give the style a label, trail
behind it a series of qualifying phrases, and trust the con-
tainer to hold only or even as much as was meant to be
contained. Since Greene's style is cumulative, the best one
can with justice do is to concentrate on those central elements that reveal the method whereby he achieves his
effects. Of necessity, then, I must forego an examination
of minor elements of his technique—such as, the studied
detail, the rhythmic device, the rich mesh of image and
symbol—giving them but a cursory glance in passing.

First in importance among the essential elements to any
novelist is point of view, that is, the theoretical position the
novelist takes in respect to his own creation and to the
reader. In *Brighton Rock*, *The Power and the Glory*, and
The Heart of the Matter, the point of view is omniscient,

while in the last two novels, *The End of the Affair* and *The Quiet American,* the narrative unfolds through the eyes of one of its protagonists. The omniscient point of view allows a greater freedom in the handling of scene, characters, time and space simply because the invisible narrator is not committed to a static perspective. He can shift the focus insofar as his skill in handling the perspective is convincing within a particular temporal and spatial context. But the narrator who is himself a part of the action is limited, if he is not to violate probability, by his own intelligence. What the author gains in credibility through the use of an "eye-witness," therefore, must be worth the restriction this point of view imposes. One would expect, then, that the narrative method in Greene's first person novels would differ sharply from the earlier omniscient ones. And so, apparently, they do. But closer examination reveals this difference to be more *apparent* than *real.*

In speaking of Greene's fiction before *The Heart of the Matter,* Calder-Marshall points out that "In the old-fashioned sense, there is no 'comment'; no appeals to the 'dear reader.' The novel appears straight, fast, factual narrative with a concentration on objective details."[9] The verb *appears* is meant to prepare for what he later refers to as Greene's "comment metaphors," although he states emphatically that "the prose [is] carefully free from direct comment. . . ." Examination of the novels will show that this position is hardly tenable. Let it suffice at this point merely to quote Greene on his own view of the matter in his essay on Mauriac.

[Mauriac] is a writer for whom the visible world has not ceased to exist, whose characters have the solidity and importance of men with souls to save or lose, and a writer who claims the traditional and essential right of a novelist, *to comment* to express his views. For how tired we have become of the dogmatically "pure" novel [Flaubert, James]. . . . The exclusion of the author can go too far. Even the author, poor devil, has a right to exist. . . .[10]

Greene can be taken at his word, for his own novels are constructed with this insistence on the author's prerogative to express his views—a practice which is not much in favor, for it tends to rupture the illusion and destroy dramatic effect. Greene however believes otherwise, that the effect is heightened by an awareness of the author, for he continues:

In such passages one is aware, as in Shakespeare's plays, of a sudden tensing, a hush seems to fall on the spirit—this is something more important than the king, Lear, or the general, Othello, something which is unconfined and unconditioned by the plot. "I" has ceased to speak, I is speaking.[11]

This accounts in part for a certain basic similarity among Greene's novels and explains why the change in point of view—from omniscient in the earlier novels to inside narrator in the later ones—is more apparent than real. The author controls the work; he is always in charge and wants you to know it.

This singularity of Greene's technique is attributable also to his recurring images and to the use of a diction alternately plain and rhetorical. Many of his effects are achieved by juxtaposing these two levels of diction. His use of imagery is more complex, for it contributes not only to the atmosphere, but informs character and theme as well; it is a means of communicating the emotion in an attempt to get at the truth. In Greene's words:

By truth I mean accuracy—it is largely a matter of style. It is my duty to society not to write: "I stood above a bottomless gulf" or "going downstairs, I got into a taxi," because these statements are untrue. My characters must not go white in the face or tremble like leaves, not because these phrases are clichés but because they are untrue. This is not only a matter of the artistic conscience but of the social conscience too.[12]

Indeed, few clichés slip into his novels. His images are fresh and arresting, often taking the form of colliding opposites, like the notorious one from *Brighton Rock*: "Virginity straightened in him like sex." This is an example of the baroque quality of Greene's sensibility; one is startled but not quite drawn up short, for in their context, the small units seldom detach themselves from the character or the scene. Appealing strongly to the senses, Greene's images are drawn from various departments of life and nature; he is most fond of those having to do with animals, geography, travel, war, childhood, and the human body. They set the tone of the novels and, more importantly, objectify the emotional responses of the characters.

If Greene's characters tend to run to type, they are not spectral figures, mere shadow-shapes for the author as ventriloquist. They are typed by their intensity, their almost hypersensitive awareness of a reality beyond this one of the senses. These are the doomed, not necessarily the damned, weighted with consciousness of a morality surmounting human ethics, curiously static because they partake of that quality of ancient heroes whose fatality was shaped by their past. But they are not *predestined* to fall; "between the stirrup and the ground" time remains for the right choice to be made, the supreme choice of man for God. This is the battle Greene usually dramatizes in his novels—a soul at war with its past commitments, struggling by its free will to accept or reject its future.

Or characters are typed by their self-satisfaction and lack of commitment to the higher religious truths that Greene espouses. They are the foils: sensual and pleasure-loving like Ida Arnold, corrupt and insensitive like the racketeer Colleoni and the Mexican Jefe, sniveling and cowardly like Wilson, the secret agent; detached like Fowler, or misdirected like the atheistic Lieutenant and the Quiet American Pyle. Each has his role to play in Greene's fictional world; each is tailored to fit that world, and within this microcosm they seem credible.

What captivates the reader and draws him into the illusion whereby the credibility of character is achieved is Greene's story. Morton Dauwen Zabel has pointed out that the ideas come from contemporary newspapers:[13] The Brighton Race Gang murders, Garrido's persecution of the priests in Tabasco, wartime in the Gold Coast, war-torn London, and finally, the muddle of Indochina. With violence as their common denominator and betrayal their theme, a spell is woven about us from the opening pages as we are plunged in *medias res,* the precipitating factors of the conflict having already taken place. The method is classical. Only one causative agent remains to do its work—time. The inevitable is laid, yet anticipation predominates. The chase in its myriad forms gets under way and, disbelief suspended, we journey through a familiar land with all of the horror and fascination that attends a nightmare. Superficially, the basic structure can often be reduced to the elements of the so-called "thriller." Suspense, intrigue, mystery, murder, betrayal—these are present in some degree or other in all Greene's fiction. But the salient fact remains that in his novels they subserve a greater design, are made to contribute to the totality of significance which makes up esthetic value.

II

"His eyes, like little concealed cameras, photographed the room instantaneously: the desk, the easy chair, the map on the wall, the door to the bedroom behind, the wide window above the bright cold Christmas street." This sentence from an early "entertainment," *This Gun for Hire,* reveals in its primitive form Greene's basic method of handling focus. Here in essence is the cinematic view—the twin cameras grinding noisily away at the selective details, and these details in turn are registered and developed in a catalogue. The scene is set with swift economy recording not only the meager comforts of the prime minister's room but also the cold, calculating attitude of his killer, the hare-lipped teenager Raven, whose bitterness is reflected in the ironic adjectival arrangement of the final phrase, "bright cold Christmas street." The technical machinery here can be heard to creak, but the creaking is a happy one for the critic who would find there in crude form what begins to function smoothly in the later novels. In these the craftsman becomes artist not through a change in technique, but through its refinement. One would expect to find then: the carefully considered angles for the scene, the selective catalogue of informative details (most often arranged rhythmically in groups of three), and a choice of language alternately stripped and affective. The list of isolable elements runs to considerable length, but these must suffice, for they are basic to Greene's method of setting a scene, establishing character, and creating atmosphere.

When Greene sets a scene, he carefully chooses an angle of vision that allows him to shift rapidly from the long panoramic view to the closeup, using the catalogue to take in those representative parts which suggest the whole to the imagination and frame the action. The technique is cinematic, bringing into sharp relief those elements that serve a dramatic or thematic (that is, moral) function in the scene. Every author, of course, must select his details, but morality can be tedious, so Greene relies on the catalogue for pace and effectiveness. Its economy does not clog the narrative development, and it generates a high emotional charge through the rhythmical impact of impressions in a series. In essence, the method is synecdochic, and Greene has refined it for maximum effectiveness. The esthetic stakes are high: the wrong tone, the least unhappy phrase, even the single word improperly chosen can shortcircuit the entire catalogue.

Still, these are not poems that Greene writes, but novels, but to that genre he brings the same strict discipline of close attention to each word and its particular function as does the poet. The consistency with which he communicates what James called "felt life" and the overall unity of design in his novels are due to this discipline. Flat inexpressive words are held to a minimum; dramatic and imagistic verbs are used whenever possible; verbs of "being" and "saying" —often merely perfunctory verbiage—are dropped altogether when comprehension is not lost as a result. Whatever cannot serve in some way to render emotion, idea, or information necessary to the author's purpose tends to be scrupulously avoided. To achieve this unity, the author maintains firm control, picking and choosing, dramatizing or commenting as he deems best. The eyes that view may be those of Pinkie, Ida, the whiskey priest, Scobie, Bendrix, or Fowler, but the unifying presence is always there carefully controlling, selecting, directing.

The explosive opening scene of *Brighton Rock,* the first of his novels to be defined explicitly by a Catholic scheme of values, shows to good advantage how Greene establishes relationships through the catalogue and charges the narrative with dramatic verbs. The first sentence provokes suspense through the line of action; then the catalogue follows:

Hale knew they meant to murder him before he had been in Brighton three hours. With his inky fingers and his bitten nails, his manner cynical and nervous, anybody could tell he didn't belong—belong to the early summer sun, the cool Whitsun wind off the sea, the holiday crowd.

Packed into the second sentence are not only the distinguishing traits of the victim Hale, who though he is killed in the first chapter motivates the resultant action, but also the season and sea, the day and the type of crowd to locate us quickly and memorably in time and place. It is a typical short catalogue even to the use of repetition of the key word *belong,* which serves both for transition and emphasis. What Hale does not *belong* to is, then, graphically depicted by a selection of verbs which enforce his aloneness by contrast. The crowd "rocked down . . . stepped off . . . paint sparkled . . . houses ran away . . ." and with the race, the music, vanishing clouds and an "aeroplane advertising something for the health" a very riot of life serves as a glittering foil for the doomed Hale. The setting is one of motion and fluidity and suggests little to be hoped for in the way of stability and permanence. Further, Greene communicates by stylistic devices his feeling toward the vacuity of modern society. Intent on pleasure, indifferent to or even oblivious of the religious values posited by Pinkie, Greene's hero *manqué,* the roiling crowd will find collective expression in Ida Arnold, the hedonistic avenger who hounds Pinkie to his death. This contempt for the mass, for things and pleasures public is evoked stylistically in the first paragraph through setting and is repeated whenever crowds gather.

At the racetrack on another Brighton holiday as Pinkie betrays Spicer, a member of his gang, to Colleoni's rival mob, the vivid verbs of locomotion again animate the scene. People "poured" in, "stood packed deep" on the trams that are "rocking down" to their destination where they finally "surged . . . up and down the front." The mass of humanity, its noise and confusion, all are caught and rendered in a panoramic sweep with the focus operating alternately at long and short range between the large scene and the close familiarizing details—a negro, some children, a blind band "walking in the gutter." Two successive catalogues in the favored rhythmical pattern of threes add to the growing

confusion: "stout goalkeepers padded like armadillos; cap-
tains discussing tactics with their lieutenants; junior girls
running amuck in the bright day," and those whom the
buses wouldn't hold, "plodding . . . kicking . . . eating." (p.
142) The effectiveness of the scene depends upon the alternation between the long and short view, and Greene accomplishes this with disarming facility by the characteristic device of seizing on an object, a sound, or a light which in itself
has motion or is already moving when introduced, and using
it as the post of observation. Our vision is then anchored
to it and travels above the scene for a kaleidoscopic survey
or drops down with it for a close intimate view. Or the
focus may be transferred from one vehicle to another until
the scene is set. Then the viewpoint comes to rest with the
character who functions as the center of the immediate
action.

Thus we follow the music of the "blind band," soar in a
panoramic sweep above the school grounds, look down on
the "plebian procession," and from the steep hill up which
come the "crammed taxicabs," we look down on the milling
scene: "It was as if the whole road moved upwards like an
underground staircase in the dusty sunlight, a creaking,
shouting crowd of cars moving with it." Then our attention
is drawn to a scarlet racing car, "caught" by the sun, in
which there is a woman sitting on a man's knee singing
something about "brides and bouquets." We move now
with her song as the words blow "back along the dusty road
to meet an ancient Morris" and come through the "flap, flap,
flap of the old top to the Boy's ears." The song functions
as the vehicle to carry us to Pinkie and Spicer, whose perspective we need for the scene of double betrayal at the
racetrack. In itself the method would seem mechanical
were it not for the fact that the singing of the woman (Ida)
about "brides and bouquets" ties the present to past action.

Hearing the words, Pinkie is reminded ironically of Rose, whom Pinkie later feels he must marry for his own protection.

Functioning together, the catalogue, the vivid verbs, and the alternating focus create a tension which impels the reader on at what has been called a "breathless pace." To achieve the density and pace he desires, Greene avoids long narrative and descriptive passages. To get from one place to another or from scene to scene in a conventional novelistic manner is for him too flat and expensive. That is to say, within the story's frame (its theme, characters, and situations), each line must maintain the suspense and tension on which the ideas rely for their emotional impact. Traditional novelistic constructions at points where the action is in part suspended would tend to dissipate the tension, and, given Greene's unique situations, disbelief might set in and the novel fail. Therefore, the focus must operate dramatically at all times. It shifts back and forth between characters when each has something of importance to divulge or, more simply, for a desired effect. The shifting in itself is not disturbing because the viewpoint, even though the center of consciousness is one of the characters, remains ultimately with the author. This is a salient fact and one that has usually been ignored or overlooked by Greene's critics.

Consider the scene in which Brewer is slashed by Pinkie for not paying "protection" to the gang. The limited omniscience which has filtered the scene through Pinkie's mind ("He felt as a physically weak but cunning school boy. . . .") becomes objective in the talk between Pinkie and the anxiety-ridden mobster Spicer, whom Pinkie is shortly to kill. We should like to know what is going on in Pinkie's mind; yet we are unaware that comments have been suspended, the omniscience turned off, for the questions raised by Spicer and parried by Pinkie increase the tension. However, note what happens to the point of view after Pinkie cuts short the conversation.

"You be off with you Spicer, and take things easy."
    "If that girl Rose knew who put the card . . ."
    "She'll never know. Turn out the light and get."
    The light went out and the moon went on like a lamp outside, slanting across the roofs, laying the shadow of clouds across the downs, illuminating the white empty sand of the racecourse above whitehawk Bottom like the monoliths of Stonehenge, shining across the tide which drove up from Boulogne and washed against the piles of the Palace Pier. It lit the washstand, the open door where the jerry stood, the brass balls at the bed end. (p. 82)

Since Greene never completely gives over the vantage point to one of his characters, he can shift to another; or if the swing is away from characters altogether, a moving object, a sound, or as here moonlight, acts as the natural vehicle to round out the scene at a point of suspense. This method allows him to make a smooth transition in his change of focus without blurring the effect. At the same time the action is enforced through complementary or symbolic setting against a broad and suggestive milieu. Thus in the passage above we take a brief catalogue journey that reflects the spiritual wasteland of Brighton, before returning again to Pinkie's room to note his symbolic sterility in the series ending climactically with the "brass balls at the bed end."

In these novels the perspective is never wholly that of a single character, but that of several characters plus author. In *Brighton Rock* the characters know and do not know while the omniscient author, who does know "all," comments along with them but withholds some information. In itself this procedure is reminiscent of James and does little to isolate Greene's practice. It is not withholding of information that makes the difference but the way in which it is withheld. To James, for example, our knowledge and information may be limited by a "central intelligence"—what he does not know, we cannot be told—in Greene, the consciousness of a character and the author's omniscence are merely turned off. No exigencies of the plot are sacrificed; the method serves to heighten suspense by exciting the reader's curiosity. He is forced to recall and to reconstruct a character's role in the action from repeated and significant details. In terms of esthetic unity the on-off omniscient pattern performs its greatest function by creating a deliberate psychic distance between the reader and characters at points where overfamiliarity with any one of them might simplify or otherwise distort a book's complex issues. This results in *Brighton Rock* in an intentionally ambivalent attitude toward both Pinkie and Ida Arnold. Our response to these characters is made to fluctuate from scene to scene so that we cannot be sure about them until a completed action reveals them and the attitudes they represent. Ida is presented bit by bit through song and a hearty laugh as a pleasant, warm fun-loving creature, even a mother image. Pinkie is first introduced as "the Boy" with ageless eyes and veins full of venom; in contrast to Ida and because we are kept at a distance from him, he appears as an unsympathetic character. Later, when his identity as Pinkie Brown is established and we become more familiar with his tortured world, we are whisked from his side for a more detached view, and he again becomes merely "the Boy."

This sometimes omniscient, sometimes objective point of view is not, as in the modern French novel, due to an existential epistemology, where the author's human limitations make him despair of omniscience in his fictional world. In Greeneland the shifting focus is a necessary concomitant to the episodic structure of his novels. The catalogue is indispensable to it, concealing the art while allowing economy of treatment. The method is synecdochic, as Greene comments in *Another Mexico*, saying how one can best describe a city: "Even for an old inhabitant it is impossible; one can present only a simplified plan, taking a house here, a park there as symbols of the whole."

His next novel, following *Brighton Rock, The Power and the Glory,* which grew out of his experiences in Mexico, provides a further example of this technique. The novel opens with Mr. Tench, the dentist, coming out into the blazing Mexican sun to claim his ether cylinder from the newly arrived boat. He wrenches up a piece of road and with a "faint feeling of rebellion," throws it at the buzzards squatting on a roof above him.

One of them rose and flapped across the town; over the tiny plaza, over the bust of an ex-president, ex-general, ex-human being, over the two stalls which sold mineral water, towards the river and the sea. It wouldn't find anything: the sharks looked after the carrion on that side. Mr. Tench went across the plaza.

A brief and literally a bird's-eye view, sandwiched in quite smoothly with what the dentist takes in on his way to the landing, suggests the wide area for the action. It is significant too at this point that the carrion bird roams freely over it all, a barren exhausted land with little to suggest the presence of anything but what might be called the remnants of human effort. And within the catalogue the designative terms for the bust—ex-president, ex-general, ex-human being—run down climactically to ironic *absurdum.*

For the purpose of contrast—the freedom that lies with the sea and the oppression on the land, shrouded in darkness—the point of focus drops away from the dentist to the ship as the land recedes. We are placed on the ship by the use of the indeterminate pronoun "you" (which Hemingway often employs in the same way): "When you looked back you could not have told that it had ever existed at all." The darkness that covers the land is obviously symbolic of its spiritual loss, and being a natural symbol, the darkness can be repeated unobtrusively for emphasis, by using it as a reference to shift the perspective from the ship—"There was an enormous sense of freedom and air upon the gulf, with the low tropical shore-line buried in darkness"—to the land where the whiskey priest is: "Far back inside the darkness the mules plodded on." By the juxtaposition of two different perspectives within two paragraphs, the contrast is underscored dramatically and our interest consequently heightened. We watch the land slip away but only for one necessary moment; then we are plunged into its dark interior with the central figure of the novel, the whiskey priest who is the unwilling bearer of light.

Indeed, these two paragraphs which conclude the first chapter, in their spatial and temporal conjoining for effect by contrast, reflect in miniature the pattern that structures the book. Each scene is devoted to a character and a situation; each is separate yet part of the overall action, functional in itself but dependent for its total meaning on the irony effected through an immediate juxtaposition with another. Consider, for example, the contiguity of these scenes in Book I, chapter four: Tench, the dentist; Padre José, the turncoat priest; the romantic legend of Juan; the education of Coral; the Jefe and the Lieutenant. The dentist is inured to pain as part of his profession: a memory stirs him briefly, of a hunted priest and an undelivered ether cylinder and then melts away. The fear of pain and reprisal palsies fat and married Padre José—"If I could," he said, "my children . . ."—and he turns away from the supplications of the funeral party. The easy acceptance of pain in the romantic hagiography of Juan read by the mother instructing her children points up the tortuous trials of the whiskey priest in the next scene. The awful way of real martyrdom offers an ironic parallel in the priest's "education" of Coral Fellows, the precocious daughter of the plantation owner. The chapter closes and comes full circle with the symbolic tooth paining the Jefe, and with the bitter austerity of that modern Javert, the police Lieutenant. Each scene is vivid, alive, and suspenseful, and furthers the action. Infinite strands of complexity are dramatically laid to intersect and interconnect as the novel proceeds to its ultimate, fated close.

If the scenic method frames the book's structure, it is worthwhile to examine the making of a single scene by approaching it through point of view. Almost any scene will do, but the one which ends the third chapter is representative of the objective rendering of the priest's plight through setting and dialogue for a telling irony of circumstance. The entire chapter is short, and its purpose is to present the fugitive priest from different angles, to dramatize a character whose traits and peculiarities, if more directly presented, could very well result merely in a caricature. And yet to see him from three different perspectives in a short space may also defeat the purpose by fragmenting the focus. For we look at the priest first through the eyes of self-satisfied Captain Fellows (the owner of the banana plantation where the priest has wandered), then through the eyes of his daughter Coral (who befriends him with food and wine), and finally we see the priest from a new angle amid the squalid surroundings of a tiny village in his former parish. Even though the priest is the connecting link for the scenes, a certain jerkiness, an esthetic wrenching, would result if the point of view were as diverse as it appears to be. *Appears* not *is*, for the action in the first two scenes of the chapter, though presented through Fellows and Coral, is controlled by the author: in observations made through images, "You cannot control what you love— you watch it driving recklessly towards the broken bridge, the torn-up track, the horror of seventy years ahead"; by the repetition of rhythmical patterns of expression—phrases, clauses, and sentences balanced in units of three; and above all, by a consistency of tone. Thus Greene can shift from one center of focus to another without a blurring of effect, for if the angle of vision is changed the controlling center remains constant: it is with the author.

Consequently in the final scene, although the viewpoint to all intents and purposes seems to become objective, pattern and expression echo the earlier scenes at the plantation where the vision was framed by father and daughter. An old man is tagged as an identifying post of observation, but the setting is described as in a play—meager, suggestive.

Half a dozen huts of mud and wattle stood in a clearing; two were in ruins. A few pigs rooted around, and an old woman carried a burning ember from hut to hut. . . . Women lived in two of the huts, the pigs in another, in the last unruined hut, where maize was stored, an old man and a boy and a tribe of rats. The old man stood in the clearing watching the fire being carried round: it flickered through the darkness like a ritual repeated at the same hour for a lifetime. White hair, as white stubble, beard, and hands brown and fragile as last year's leaves, he gave an effect of immense permanence. Nothing much could ever change, living on the edge of subsistence. He had been old for years.
The stranger came into the clearing. (pp. 56-57)

Since the point of view has been ultimately with the author, there has, in effect, been no shift to a new focus. He has merely changed his vantage point while continuing the accretive process through observations; the main character is still viewed from the outside. His fundamental traits are dramatically rendered through dialogue and action.

The old man said softly: "It would be a pity if the soldiers came before we had time . . . such a burden on poor souls, father. . . ." The priest shouldered himself upright against the wall and said furiously: "Very well. Begin. I will hear your confession." The rats scuffled in the maize. (p. 59)

Hunted, starved, and exhausted, the priest ministers to this abject old man, significantly with his back to the wall and those suggestive rats scuffling in the maize. The scene then ends with the old man ironically entreating the others to confess: " 'Come,' he said. 'You must make your confessions. It is only polite to the father.' " Three brief scenes, three different points of focus with the priest always viewed objectively to reveal a little more, to add something to the growing stature of this mysterious creature chosen against all logic to be God's agent. To this end the scenes function as a dynamic unit since there is no dislocation or change of values. The moral base of each scene, the pity and self-sacrifice that motivate the entire novel, are the standards prevailing throughout.

It was eight years before Greene's next novel appeared, and *The Heart of the Matter* shows a modification of style in the use of a longer, more flowing sentence, frequently periodic in structure. The basic type of sentence that marks the earlier novels—the subject-verb-object pattern with its hammering effect—has not disappeared but is used alternately as a change of pace to underscore emotional moments. A catalogue comes early in the book with the introduction of Major Scobie, who is being pointed out to Wilson, the secret agent from the home office and Scobie's nemesis. With economy, through statement and symbol, the author foreshadows the coming conflict between the two. A close examination of the entire paragraph is necessary to give us an opportunity to consider both the catalogue and the point of view.

A vulture flapped and shifted on the iron and Wilson looked at Scobie. He looked without interest in obedience to a stranger's direction, and it seemed to him that no particular interest attached to the squat grey-haired man walking along Bond Street. He couldn't tell that this was one of those occasions a man never forgets: a small cicatrice had been made on the memory, a wound that would ache whenever certain things combined—the taste

of gin at midday, the smell of flowers under a balcony, the clang
of corrugated iron, an ugly bird flopping from perch to perch.
(p. 6)

Greene's devices are self-evident, and one is tempted to
overlook them on this account, or to find fault with them
for being too slick or pat. The authorial statements, the
deliberate foreshadowing seem at first glance to be an
imaginative way of preparing the reader for what the author
cannot render dramatically. The gin and the flowers, after
all, though they serve as points of reference, are flat and
descriptive, obvious details to fill in the realistic background
of the action. Are they functional though only at a superficial level, so that other compatible details could be substituted to serve as well? Perhaps not. For the gin and
flowers which seem to carry little significance in themselves
help to create tension through their flatness by being
juxtaposed with the vulture that alighted, a few pages earlier,
above Wilson's head. "Harris said, 'Look at Scobie,'" and
the vulture "flapped and shifted," and "Wilson looked at
Scobie." The identification is made naturally and dramatically—Wilson must be imagined shifting with the vulture—
and the graphic verbs produce an image emotionally charged
by the vulture's significance. Flat statements contribute to
the emotional tension because they undercut it through
their assertions. When the paragraph closes, the catalogue
quite naturally completes the description with the bird,
which at an ironic variance with the peaceful setting of gin
and the smell of flowers, again produces the tension and
an emotional response. The author is having it both ways,
through statement and suggestive detail, and this, one feels,
is why the reader does not resent authorial intrusion.

The language Greene employs in his descriptions and
settings is seldom static and then only by design. It is
perhaps a commonplace that a rapid style is one in which
the words are primarily referential in large units of meaning

which further the narrative and the action but call little attention to themselves. If the attention is directed to the individual unit rather than to the larger pattern of meaning, then the pace, it would seem, would be slow. By common agreement Greene's critics grant him rapid, almost breathless narrative pace, but the significant fact is that Greene achieves this rapidity through, not at the expense of, a precise and concrete diction. Wilson's "pink knees thrust," "tin roofs sloped," "corrugated iron . . . clanged and clattered," "schoolboys had swarmed," a "vulture flapped and shifted": all these details taken from the opening pages of *The Heart of the Matter* are typical Greene. The words are not only referential but realistic and dramatic. In his descriptive and narrative passages where the pace might falter, rapidity is achieved by the use of catalogue and its truncated phrases, by the alternation of staccato rhythms with longer sentences, by a varied language of learned and common words, even by a unique system of punctuation stops and pauses calculated to enhance meaning and effect. Thus even when the words, phrases, or images are in themselves arresting, the phraseology and the cumulative effects of these devices produce a rapid sense of movement.

In either descriptive or introspective paragraphs, each unit is balanced in a careful construction to form a rhythmical rise and fall. It is here that Greene is most likely to assert what he calls the author's prerogative and to comment. The paragraphs begin with a loose sentence, develop a rhythmical flow through a succession of descriptive details, and culminate in an aphoristic sentence or flat statement. They are in a sense pauses in the action, a place for marking time while some necessary information is being given or repeated incrementally, adding new detail to what was known. The pause in the action allows the mind to take in the description while the forward movement is served by the rhythm of the paragraph until the action itself sweeps onward. A representative illustration is the description of Scobie from the second scene of the book which opens: "Scobie turned up James Street past the Secretariat," and continues with personal facts about him and the series of disorders that defeated policemen of lesser hardihood and principles. The paragraph ends with the flat assertion, "The patient was always right."

There follows a longer paragraph similar in pattern and principle.

> Scobie climbed the great steps and turned to his right along the shaded outside corridor to his room: a table, two kitchen chairs, a cupboard, some rusty handcuffs hanging on a nail like an old hat, a filing cabinet: to a stranger it would have appeared a bare uncomfortable room but to Scobie it was home. Other men slowly build up the sense of home by accumulation. . . . (p. 8)

The inventory of Scobie's office continues until the photograph of his wife Louise reawakens old memories and raises the specter of his domestic responsibility. The paragraph concludes flatly: "He had formed her face." Here the symbolic use of detail under the guise of objective description enforces Scobie's sense of commitment, while the rhythmic rise and fall of the phrases and sentences that comes to a momentary rest in the final statement contributes to the sense of weariness.

A paragraph that can be treated more fully, and which will serve as a final example, deals explicitly with the novel's theme of pity and responsibility. It follows the hospital scene where Scobie first meets Helen Rolt.

> He went restlessly out onto the verandah, closing the netted door carefully behind him, and a mosquito immediately droned towards his ear. The skirring went on all the time, but when they drove to the attack they had a deeper tone of dive-bombers. The lights were showing in the temporary hospital, and the weight of all that misery lay on his shoulders. It was as if he had shed one responsibility only to take on another. This was

a responsibility he shared with all human beings, but there was no comfort in that, for it sometimes seemed to him that he was the only one who recognized it. In the Cities of the Plain a single soul might have changed the mind of God. (p. 126)

The initial descriptive sentence has a neutral tone, but the drone of the mosquitoes which changes to a deeper roar increases the tempo and charges the atmosphere, thereby underscoring the theme of pity and responsibility. The pitch has been raised and is sustained for a moment at this level. In the long sentence on responsibility to human beings it begins to taper off, coming to a slow close with the note of finality in the mournful clause, "the only one who recognized it." The falling rhythm tends to round out the passage and give it a sense of completeness. But there still remains the real close which, when it comes, has the emotional force of understatement through the contrast between falling rhythm and the rhetoric of the concluding statement.

The perceptive reader will also have noticed another basic characteristic of all Greene's novels: the progression of ideas by association. By this method Greene moves suddenly away from or close to a background, a person, or an object. Taking a word or phrase pregnant with meaning, he spawns a series of associations which are expanded and explored through metaphor or statement to a final resolution. The effect is one of spontaneity and immediacy, suggestive of live thought. The absent photograph of Scobie's wife, Louise, in the example cited earlier for instance, recalls "the handcuffs on the wall," and leads to a further assertion of Scobie's responsibility which sets off the abrupt series of statements: "Fifteen years form a face, gentleness ebbs with experience, and he was always aware of his own responsibility." The imaginative association then continues until it exhausts itself: "He had led the way: the experience that had come to her was the experience selected by himself. He had formed her face." In the other passage the mosquito's sound suggests the "dive-bombers" which recall the war, naturally bringing in the hospital and the "weight of all that misery [which] lay on his shoulders." The word *weight* leads to Scobie's consideration that he alone among men seems cognizant of the burden of responsibility. The awful implications of this recognition, the real burden, is what touches off the Biblical reference of the concluding statement: "In the Cities of the Plain a single soul might have changed the mind of God."

At its extreme, this method of progression through associative evocation allows a freedom from strict logic which lies perhaps behind Mary McCarthy's stricture that Greene introduces "words with churchly connotations" to awaken in the reader religious sentiments having no justification in the action of the novel.[14] The justification however lies in Greene's method, for the absence of a strictly logical sequence of ideas (and a diction in keeping with the logic) does not argue in a novel that a haphazard construction and an arbitrarily imposed rhetoric will result. If the ideas in the passages under fire proceed out of each other associatively, then that is their logic and their justification.

A typical case in point is the scene at the dinner party where Scobie's feeling of guilt and responsibility over his mistress is compounded by the imminent return of his wife. He fingers her telegram in his pocket as the talk turns to the case of Richard Pemberton, the young assistant at an outlying station who has committed suicide.

> Scobie with his fingers on the telegram remembered the letter signed "Dicky": the immature handwriting: the marks of cigarettes on the chairs: the novels of Wallace: the stigmata of loneliness. Through two thousand years, he thought, we have discussed Christ's agony in just this disinterested way. (p. 211)

This passage would seem to bear out Miss McCarthy's point, for, quite arbitrarily it seems, the members that follow the initial statement conclude with a phrase of "churchly connotations." The handwriting, cigarettes, and novels have an immediate reference to the dead Pemberton, whose case Scobie investigated, and are justified in the larger context of the conversation. But why "the stigmata of loneliness"? One answer lies in the fact that the reference to Christ's passion and the identifying characteristics of Pemberton were both prepared for earlier in the description of the bungalow. Also, with the receipt of Louise's telegram, Scobie "had pondered the chaos of his own life," contemplated suicide, and wondered if God would forgive him. For after all, he rationalized, "Christ had not been murdered: you couldn't murder God. Christ had killed himself: he had hanged himself on the cross as surely as Pemberton from the picture rail." But to leave it at this is to skirt the main issue by hasty retreat through the side door. The real justification for "the stigmata of loneliness" lies in the associative logic of the sequence, a psychological train of thought completely in keeping with Scobie's character and triggered off by the telegram. Louise's pet name for Scobie, "Tickie," and its association with "Dickie," is of course as obvious as the recall of the handwriting, the cigarettes, and the novels. But to account for the "stigmata" one must note that these three traces of Pemberton all share one common element—marks. Marks made on a paper, in a book, on a chair; and given Scobie's obsession with pity and responsibility and constant ruminations about that Other, what could be less arbitrary and more meaningful than the awful "stigmata of loneliness"?

There is a tension in these passages, entirely characteristic of Greene's style, effected by a merger of thought and expression that arouses the reader's expectancy for a final resolution only to frustrate it. Descriptions and ideas keep him in a state of suspension by sprouting new clusters of associations which in turn may sprout others to be explored and expanded in successive resolutions. Spontaneity, vitality and a sense of immediacy are the result. And what should be explained at this point is the stylistic function of the punctuation—especially of the colon, for it seems literally to pepper the pages of his novels. The colons set off from each other a series of succeeding clauses, but also tie them to the initial statement so that in themselves they have the simple force of a concluding statement and, in their succession, the added force of their syntactical combination. By using punctuation in this manner, Greene can strip his narrative of articles and connectives, vary the cadence by the number or the length of members in a sequence, and free the internal elements for unexpected interpolations.

Dramatic illustrations of single stylistic principles are easily culled from any of Greene's novels, but brief extracts are seldom satisfying. The paragraphs offered below, though they may not combine all the characterizing features, illustrate enough of them, including the punctuation, to justify previous generalizations. They are especially pertinent, too, in displaying, in its most basic form, progression through the expansion of the potentialities of a single patent word.

"None I heard of," the barman said. "He wasn't a Brighton man. No one knew him round these parts. He was a stranger."
A stranger; the word meant nothing to her: there was no place in the world where she felt a stranger. She circulated the dregs of the cheap port in her glass and remarked to no one in particular: "It's a good life." There was nothing with which she didn't claim kinship: the advertising mirror behind the barman's back flashed her own image at her; the beach girls went giggling across the parade; the gong beat on the steamer for Boulogne—it was a good life.

(*Brighton Rock*, 102)

"You'd better come home."
Home: it was a phrase one used to mean four walls behind which one slept. There had never been a home. They moved across the little burnt plaza where the dead general grew green in the damp and the gaseosa stalls stood under the palms. It

lay like a picture postcard on a pile of other postcards: shuffle the pack and you had Nottingham, a Metroland birthplace, an interlude in Southend. Mr. Tench's father had been a dentist too—his first memory was finding a discarded cast in a waste-paper basket—the rough toothless gaping mouth of clay, like something dug up in Dorset—Neanderthal or Pithecanthropus. It had been his favorite toy: they tried to tempt him with Meccano: but fate had struck. There is always one moment in childhood when the door opens and lets the future in. The hot wet river-port and the vultures lay in the waste-paper basket, and he picked them out. We should be thankful we cannot see the horrors and degradations lying around our childhood, in cupboards and bookshelves, everywhere.

(*The Power and the Glory*, 15)

"In the the future I must do better than that."

In the future—that was where the sadness lay. Was it the butterfly that died in the act of love? But human beings were condemned to consequences. The responsibility as well as the guilt was his—he was not a Bagster: he knew what he was about. He had sworn to preserve Louise's happiness, and now he had accepted another contradictory responsibility. He felt tired by all the lies he would sometime have to tell: he felt the wounds of those victims who had not yet bled. Lying back on the pillow he stared sleeplessly out towards the grey early morning tide. Somewhere on the face of those obscure waters moved the sense of yet another wrong and another victim, not Louise, not Helen. Away in the town the cocks began to crow for the false dawn.

(*The Heart of the Matter*, 175)

III

IF AN AUTHOR's style is his vision, Greene's vision results from a singular approach to the world of experience and is oblique. What accounts for his vision and style is not alone the bulwark of Catholicism. His personal psychology apart, it is a striking out against delusion—the delusion that any value, trust, or belief that remains unexamined can satisfy for long under the stress of *la condition humaine*. Satire and irony expose the fatuous and the complacent; guilt and pain inform the agony of others, those whose tortuous journey leads falteringly yet unerringly towards Calvary or Satan's place. But the irony in Greene is double-edged. If sardonic laughter attends the fumbling pleasures and skillful disguises of the deceived, its echo mocks the believers. Pride is their delusion and knowledge their failure (Scobie says: "We Catholics are damned by our knowledge"). For God, they must discover, is not paying off in this world. Misery is the only reality; masochism, the temporary pleasure. The Saints await beyond the spheres.

But our central concern is with style, and in *The End of the Affair* and *The Quiet American* one need read no farther than a single page to see that the style has not changed. This is not to say that there has been no development and refinement of technique, but one still finds here those stylistic features—namely, handling of focus, catalogues descriptive and analytic, and variations of sentence patterns which define his narrative method. Greene's fundamental change is from omniscient author to first person narrator, and this warrants consideration both for its limitations and for the rigorous narrative control it exacts from the author. As everyone knows the fictional world circumscribed by an inside narrator allows the delineation of but one state of mind. The limitations must work for the author rather than against him if he is to succeed; details and events must be rigorously ordered to achieve dramatic effectiveness and esthetic unity. The rewards are proportional to the difficulties involved, and Greene's talent lies in the skillful control of narrative. Of *The Quiet American* Morton Dauwen Zabel has said, "This is one of his most brilliant feats of dramatic narration."[15] Indeed, Greene overcame obstacles which Lubbock praises James for avoiding in *The Ambassadors* by using Strether as the "center of consciousness" rather than as narrator. For to have done this would be to let us into every secret without delay, or his exposition is plainly misleading . . . he could not hold back, he could not heighten the story of his thought with that touch of suspense, waiting to be resolved, which stamps the impression so firmly on the onlooker. In a tale of murder and mystery there is one man who cannot possibly be the narrator, and that is the murderer himself; for if he admits us into his mind at all he must do so without reserve, thereby betraying the secret that we ought to be guessing at for ourselves.[16]

The point lies in the essential difficulties of what Lubbock calls the autobiographical approach. Obviously the novelist must resort to the use of several devices to maintain the mystery (if that be the case) and suspense, and depend upon the power of his narrative, evocative details, and characters to sustain them. To maintain mystery and suspense Greene again employs the scenic method, withholds information through the narrator's soul-searching and by the dramatic reenactment of the past, and in *The End of the Affair* uses the devices of discovering a diary and having a novelist-narrator recording his experiences as a novel.

Setting aside for the moment the relation of point of view to these structural elements, consider first whether there has been a change in basic stylistic features. In *The End of the Affair* the catalogue, although modified to some extent, is still very much in evidence setting scenes with an economy of expression, describing characters, recording details, and creating atmosphere. There are few particularly pure illustrations since the narrator through his own analyses is free to take over the suggestive function of the catalogue. One occurs in the third chapter, which sets and leads into the scene recalling the first "meeting" between the narrator Bendrix and Sarah Miles.

How can I disinter the human character from the heavy scene—the daily newspaper, the daily meal, the traffic grinding towards Battersea, the gulls coming up from the Thames looking for bread, and the early summer of 1939 glinting on the park where the children sailed their boats, one of these bright condemned prewar summers? (p. 26)

Note how the arrangement, rhythmically paced to culminate rhetorically with the antithesis of "bright condemned" summers, evokes a nostalgia of loss. The varied length of the members, repetition of the definite article, the partial balance through the participial construction, "grinding towards," "coming up," "looking for," "glinting on," give a smooth forward rhythm to the series. But typical of Greene's extended periods, the balance is violated, here by a shift in tenses, "children sailed," to give greater force to the last statement and lead into the dramatic reenactment of the past.

What a modified descriptive catalogue contributes to the atmosphere and the emotional moment can be illustrated more dramatically by excluding it from a crucial discussion about Sarah between Bendrix and her husband, Henry.

"Why did she leave you?"
"Because I became a bore and a fool too. But I wasn't born one, Henry. You created me. She wouldn't leave you, so I became a bore, boring her with complaints and jealousy."
He said, "People have a great opinion of your books."
"And they say you're a first-class chairman. What the hell does our work matter?"
He said sadly, "I don't know anything else that does," looking up at the grey cumulus passing above the south bank . . . "I wondered why you hadn't been to see us all that time," Henry said.

The scene is a significant and important one, for it comes in the middle of Book Two which ends the preliminary section of Bendrix's narrative: the clandestine meetings with Sarah, the telephone calls, and making love on the floor beneath her husband's bedroom. In this scene which is prompted by Sarah's rejection of her lover in accordance with her promise to God, patient Henry, trusting and slow

of wit, has an illumination: he discovers the truth about
Bendrix and Sarah. Melodrama is inherent in the situation
as the cuckold confronts the lover with the truth. However,
it is the hurt and bitter Bendrix who lashes out against
Henry in his attempt to despoil the past. The unexpected,
here an ironic reversal, is manifested still further through
the details (withheld above) which are interspersed between
Henry's remarks.

He said sadly, "I don't know anything else that does," looking
up at the grey cumulus passing above the south bank. The gulls
flew over the barges, and the shot tower stood black in the
winter light among the ruined warehouses. The man who fed
the sparrows had gone, and the woman with the brown paper
parcel; the fruit sellers cried like animals in the dusk outside
the station. It was as if the shutters were going up on the
whole world; soon we would all of us be abandoned to our own
devices. "I wondered why you hadn't been to see us all that
time," Henry said. (p. 80)

Henry's realization of his wife's infidelity would be enough
to support so short a scene, which includes an additional
turn of the screw in Bendrix's vicious remark, earlier: "You
pimped by giving opportunities." But the images and details
of abandonment and ruin have only an oblique reference
to Henry. The real loser is Bendrix. Hate does not assuage
the desolation and the loss, but like a mirror sends back its
own image. What the modified catalogue offers is one of
those dramatic pauses in which an imaginative truth is
searched for behind a moment of emotion.

Although Greene uses an inside narrator for his point of
view, these examples show his technique to be that of the
omniscient novels. The apparent difference is only in the
freedom with which the narrator can now comment on the
action. This is not to confuse the narrator with the author
but to emphasize a salient feature common to all Greene's
novels. As in the example above, each of Greene's novels

makes use of the paragraph to stall the forward movement of the action. Within this unit narrative time is suspended for atmospheric effects or comment and then advanced rapidly through action and pungent dialogue.

The comment takes the form of an aphorism, and the opportunity for such a statement within a paragraph structure of clauses in long periods and short associative sentences is unlimited. Action gives rise to reflection or reflection to action with somewhere in between a general truth arising that colors the movement.

There is always one moment in childhood when the door opens and lets the future in.
(The Power and the Glory, 15)

Point me out the happy man and I will point you out either egotism, selfishness, evil—or else an absolute ignorance.
(The Heart of the Matter, 128)

It needs a God outside time to remember when everything changes.
(The End of the Affair, 180)

We are too small in mind and body to possess another person or to be possessed without humiliation.
(The Quiet American, 153)

It would be simple to compound the number of such statements and their similarity would attest to the singular vision that marks Greene's style.

Greene also resorted to the inside-narrator in *The Quiet American,* and if it shows surface changes in his material, his leading stylistic features are still in evidence. The handling of the point of view, since the narrator Fowler is the most directly responsible for the American Pyle's death, is ingenious. "You recognise him?" the French police officer Vigot asks over Pyle's refrigerated body, and Fowler answers:

"Oh, yes."

He looked more than ever out of place; he should have stayed at home. I saw him in a family snapshot album, riding on a dude ranch, bathing on Long Island, photographed with his colleagues in some apartment on the twenty-third floor. He belonged to the skyscraper and the express elevator, the ice-cream and the dry martinis, milk at lunch, and chicken sandwiches on the Merchants Limited. (p. 16)

Because the intent is to satirize through caricature the American, whose naive protestant concepts of "good" create havoc wherever he goes, the descriptive clichés are meaningful. The series, relevant as a train of thought in the narrator and thus naturally interjected, keeps us on tenterhooks by delaying the forward movement: the point of view supports the catalogue and the slow revelation of Pyle's character. Here and throughout the novel it is Greene's ultimate task to frame a dramatic image of Pyle so that the reader himself must determine the various degrees of guilt and where responsibility lies. To do this he must withhold information and fill in the background while maintaining the suspense.

Perhaps I should have seen that fanatic gleam, the quick response to a phrase, the magic sound of figures: Fifth Column, Third Force, Seventh Day. I might have saved all of us a lot of trouble, even Pyle, if I had realized the direction of that indefatigable brain. But I left him with the arid bones of background and took my daily walk up and down the rue Catinat. He would have to learn for himself the real background that held you as a smell does: the gold of the rice fields under a flat late sun; the fishers' fragile cranes hovering over the fields like mosquitoes; the cups of tea on an old abbot's platform, with his bed and his commercial calendars, his buckets and broken cups, and the junk of a lifetime washed up around his chair; the mollusc hats of the girls repairing the road where a mine had burst; the gold and the young green and the bright dresses of the South, and in the North the deep browns and the black clothes and the circle of enemy mountains and the drone of planes. When I first came. . . . (p. 23)

This passage, an inordinately long one (and half of a long paragraph), is wonderfully contrived to serve many purposes. In the first place we begin to get an insight into another Fowler—sentient, emotionally engaged, whose observations belie the role of detached observer, the reporter as he insists on characterizing himself. For after all in what sense is this descriptive catalogue the "real" background—the gold, cranes, cups of tea, mollusc hats, the bright dresses and the deep browns—and if it holds you as does a smell, the attachment, though hardly to be called intellectual, is perhaps more powerful since it is emotional. Further, one of the involved ironies of the book is achieved through the seeming detachment of the narrator, for he betrays his personal involvement through his impressions, which signal the awareness that results in pain and guilt. The continued satire of Pyle through the "response to a phrase" is obvious enough but a final purpose of the passage and the paragraph is to engage our interest elsewhere as a means of withholding further information about Pyle. The center of focus shifts from Pyle to Fowler who, thinking of his mistress Phuong, says, "Pyle ran easily and naturally out of my mind," and so he does for the moment out of the reader's.

One of the involved ironies achieved through the first-person narrator is the discrepancy between Fowler's self-revelation through aphoristic statement, satiric comment, and nostalgic reminiscence, and his protestations of non-commitment. Following the bicycle episode and the mutilations of the explosion in the town square, Fowler reflects: "It bore no relation to the sad and heavy war in the North, those canals in Phat Diem with grey days-old bodies, in the pounding of the mortars, the white glare of napalm." The emotional coloring through the elaboration of the final phrase, a typical Greene device, is Fowler's, and in knowing this we can accept his weeping in the toilet, grief for the slaughtered civilians, sympathy for Granger and the final statement on Pyle: "Everything had gone right with me since he had died, but how I wished there existed someone to whom I could say that I was sorry." If the indictment of Pyle is the result of his being "full of passionate intensity" (to borrow a phrase from Yeats), Fowler's indictment stems from the fact that he is insight-ridden and lacks "all conviction," resulting in a moral paralysis.

Still, important consideration must be given to the change in Fowler, for there is a change. Where before the coming of Pyle he had insights that paradoxically paralyzed belief and action, he ends as a person in doubt, the doubt of a new awareness. Pyle has taught him that noncommitment is no guarantee of noninvolvement, that "suffering is not increased by numbers; one body can contain all the suffering the world can feel." What the style through the arrangements of details and ironic revelations makes clear, and if we bear in mind that the novel's action has preceded its own beginning (the novel is like a long reflection on a past action), Fowler has become as *engagé* as Pyle but with a salient difference: he has no illusions of doing "good," having proved ironically through Pyle's murder that the ends do not justify the means. That salient difference that marks Fowler and distinguishes all Greene's heroes is the tortured sense of guilt. Against actions in a world where the "blood-dimmed tide is loosed," Greene urges through *The Quiet American* a pietistic complaint.

Much has been excluded in this examination of Greene's style, and the bare bones of his technique have been arbitrarily disassociated from their larger context in the novels. In a sense they are not unlike those specks and lines representing music, which, though having a theoretical logic in their printed form, represent the heard sound, the reproduction that ultimately determines their validity. The mere formula, as one well realizes, does not of itself produce a successful overture. Without Greene's subject matter, unique themes, his episodic structure with its concommitant parts, the devices rehearsed would be mere stylistic tricks finding little justification in a serious novel. But it is the author's vision that determines the technique and gives rise to it; so, in the final analysis, the stylistics have their discovery in meaning.

David H. Hesla

THEOLOGICAL AMBIGUITY IN THE "CATHOLIC NOVELS"

WHILE IT IS NOT at all extraordinary for one of Graham Greene's characters to be tempted to resolve the complexities of his existence by means of self-destruction, the incidence of suicidal tendencies is remarkably high in that group of his works which by now has come to be called the "Catholic novels." In *Brighton Rock* (1938), Rose is prevented only at the last moment from fulfilling her part of the suicide pact with Pinkie. In *The Heart of the Matter* (1948), Dickie Pemberton hangs himself in shame and despair over his debts; Helen Rolt, Scobie's lover, ponders the possibilities of giving herself to another man, of killing herself, or of both; and Scobie commits the ultimate crime against himself in order not to be a cause of unhappiness to others. Bendrix, in *The End of the Affair* (1951), plans to kill himself by taking an overdose of sleeping tablets; but, as a gesture of spite against the woman he loves, he does not carry the plan through to fulfillment. While in these instances suicide is intentional and unambiguous, whether as pondered, planned, or actually performed, the deaths of the whiskey priest (*The Power and the Glory*, 1940) and of

Sarah Miles *(The End of the Affair)*, also are suicidal, though more ambiguously so. After having made a successful escape from a territory in which he is being hunted by the police, the priest voluntarily turns back from certain safety to return to equally certain capture and execution; and even when warned by the dying Yankee murderer, he makes no attempt to defend himself. In the case of Sarah Miles, death is the result of an illness which could have been cured by penicillin if only Sarah had permitted a doctor to attend her.[1]

A number of factors combine with one another to make self-slaughter appear to these people to be the only way of resolving the difficulties of their lives. In the first place, the world in which they live is anaesthetic, uncharitable, and barren of beauty and joy. The physical environment is gaudy, cheap, vulgar, and sordid, as in *Brighton Rock*. Or, as in the Mexico of the whiskey priest, it is river and swamp and forest, inhabited by sharks and vultures, a land desperately poor, where there is to be found only "the swamp and vultures and no children anywhere, except a few in the village with bellies swollen by worms who ate dirt from the bank inhumanly." The vultures which clatter on the corrugated roofs of the West African colony of which Scobie is the Deputy Commissioner of police seem to be the same as those which scavenge the priest's Mexican town; the air is just as stifling in the English colonial territory, the heat, if anything, even more intense and oppressive. The action of *The End of the Affair* takes place mainly in the vicinity of London; and Greene conveys the drabness, the infertility and the emptiness of the world in which the affair is finally terminated by means of the stodgy Victorian buildings and the black, leafless trees of the city common. In all four novels, nature is barren, ugly, oppressive.

The inhabitants of this nasty world are all much alike: they are adulterers, racketeers, murderers; they are cowardly, self-centered, and driven; and indeed all the significant detail of their lives represents something morally reprehensible or at least problematic. Scobie, swerving his automobile to avoid a dead pye-dog in the road, describes his world in terms applicable also to the three other novels. "Nobody here could ever talk about a heaven on earth. Heaven remained rigidly in its proper place on the other side of death, and on this side flourished all the injustices, the cruelties, the meannesses. . . ."

But it is a question whether Scobie or any of the others dwells on earth or in hell—whether Greene's is a "three-storied universe," or only two-storied: heaven, and an earth-hell.

Moreover, Greene's characters are an almost incredibly obsessed lot. Pinkie is obsessed by a desire to "show the world" what an important fellow he is; Rose is obsessed by her love for Pinkie; Ida Arnold is obsessed by her passion for Justice and Right. The lieutenant of police who pursues the whiskey priest is obsessed by his ideal for the new social order soon to be established. Scobie is obsessed by a desire not to hurt anyone and by his sense of responsibility for others. Bendrix is obsessed by his love for Sarah, and Sarah is obsessed by her love for love.

Each of these compelling drives is given an exterior and public expression in the form either of a vow, or of a kind of contract with God, or—as in Scobie's case—both vow and contract. Ida Arnold's obsessive attachment to Right and Justice leads her to vow to a neighbor, "I'm going to make those people sorry they was ever born." Rose promises Pinkie, "I'll never let you down, never, never, never"; her vow is the sign of her unflawed love for Pinkie and her absolute obedience to his will. The whiskey priest is something of an exception in this regard (the novel as a whole also evades several of the generalizations made in this essay) in that he himself is not driven by an imperious passion; but it is none the less true that he returns to the territory from which he has just escaped because he has not fallen so low as to disobey the vows of his ordination. Scobie's sense of responsibility for others and his inability to coexist with the suffering of others leads him from one extreme promise to another. At the time of his marriage to Louise "he had sworn . . . that he would at least always see to it that she was happy"; and in order to do this he promises to get the money necessary to pay for her passage out of the colony to South Africa, even though this leads him to compromise his otherwise unsoiled integrity. Later, in the presence of a child who is suffering dreadfully, Scobie enters into a contract with God. " 'Father, look after her. Give her peace.' The breathing broke, choked . . . he could see the six-year-old face convulsed like a navvy's with labour. 'Father,' he prayed, 'give her peace. Take away my peace for ever, but give her peace. . . .' " Scobie's prayer is answered: the child dies and Scobie's difficulties begin almost immediately. He takes on the responsibility of making Helen Rolt happy, as well as his wife Louise; and he is led to "swear carefully" to Helen, "I shall never again want any home without you." Sarah Miles' need to love, seemingly neurotic in its motive force, drives her into making a bargain with God as rash as Scobie's. Her passion has settled for a time on Maurice Bendrix, and when she believes that he has been killed in an air raid, she prays to God, even though she does not believe in Him.

"Dear God . . . make me believe. I can't believe. Make me . . . I'm a bitch and a fake and I hate myself. I can't do anything of myself. *Make* me believe . . . Let him be alive, and I *will* believe. . . . I'll do anything if You'll make him alive . . . I'll give him up forever, only let him be alive."

Bendrix, who has only been knocked unconscious by the explosion, returns to her; but she keeps her promise to God and leaves him.

With the exception of the whiskey priest, each of the major characters is driven by an uncontrollable passion or need, and the vows, promises, and contracts are either the public manifestation of these obsessions or the direct result of them. Whether the motive forces are understood as obsessions or as needs, they produce extreme unrest and turbulence of spirit; and it is almost inevitable that the goal which is sought above all else by each of the characters is the goal of peace. Pinkie is haunted by the strains of the *Agnus Dei*: "Agnus Dei qui tollis peccata mundi . . . dona nobis pacem." Scobie dreams of peace by day and night.

> Once in sleep it had appeared to him as the great glowing shoulder of the moon heaving across his window like an iceberg . . . Peace seemed to him the most beautiful word in the language: My peace I give you, my peace I leave with you: O Lamb of God, who takest away the sins of the world, grant us thy peace. In the Mass he pressed his fingers against his eyes to keep the tears of longing in.

Bendrix' wild jealousy for Sarah is assuaged, and he achieves peace only in the very act of sexual love; and Sarah's immense capacity to love is finally satisfied, and she has a sense of peace and love for a brief moment in a mystical apprehension of God.

Driven by unmanageable forces and lured by a dream of peace, Pinkie and Rose and Scobie and Bendrix and Sarah are impelled with an awful velocity into history, into the performance of some irrecoverable and irremediable act; and from this original act there emanate consequences which eventually entrammel the agent and bring about his spiritual or physical death, or both. Indeed, history in these novels is of such a nature that the actions which are taken by the characters either in response to an obsessive power or as a means of attaining peace are the very actions which complicate existence and exacerbate spiritual disease. The more vigorously Scobie strives to provide for the happiness of those around him (and so effect his own happiness and rest), the further he sinks into the swamp of sin, violence, and despair. To be human in this kind of world is to be engaged in existence—it is to act. But to act is to suffer; to act is, in Scobie's phrase, to be "condemned to consequences." Or again, "To be a human being one has to drink the cup." So also, the whiskey priest in pondering the body of a dead child, can ask in devout and ultimate seriousness, "Why, after all, should we expect God to punish the innocent with more life?"

Moreover, the future holds no promise for the resolution of the complexities of existence or for the assuagement of the suffering which is concomitant with living. History as time future is the locus, for Rose, of "the worst horror of all"; or of more and more uselessness and worthlessness, in the case of the whiskey priest. For Scobie, the future presents only additional occasions for causing increased suffering to his wife, his mistress, and to God. In the Mass, God is as helpless as are the two women, and as long as Scobie remains in mortal sin he not only partakes of the Host to his own damnation but he performs violence on the very Body of God. "The long chain of feast days . . . unrolled themselves like a perpetual calendar. He had a sudden picture before his eyes of a bleeding face, of eyes closed by the continuous shower of blows: the punch-drunk head of God reeling sideways." During the period when Sarah's great capacity to love is satisfied in her relationship with Bendrix, she is unaware of the future; but when this satisfaction is taken from her, the future lies before her like a desert. And Bendrix is tormented to the point of suicide by the prospect of life without his beloved.

Suicide emerges not simply as a live option to these unhappy people, but as the only possible means of escape from a world in which being human means that one must drink the cup of suffering. The logic of the situation is without flaw. To be a human being is to be engaged in existence; and this engagement is effected by some existentially decisive act. Such an act is guaranteed to Pinkie and Scobie and the others since they will either be impelled into it by the force of an uncontrollable passion or by obedience to a vow or promise, or they will be lured into it in the pursuit of happiness and peace. But to act is to initiate a train of consequences which will cause and increase suffering, both for oneself and for others. History is a process of the more or less rapid elimination of the possibilities for realizing whatever good its inhabitants long for; and this is only the more exasperating, since their longing is passionate to the point of being compulsive. Driven by obsession, lured by happiness, and frustrated by history, they seek desperately for peace, but peace is not to be found in this infernal world; and there appears to be no surcease from the insecurity and suffering of existence except in suicide.

But suicide is not simply a means of escape: it is, of course, that, but given the kind of world which Graham Greene has created to be the arena of human life and action, it is also the end result for those who attempt to lead a life that is motivated by love, by humility, and by obedience to the vows and laws of self-abnegation and charity. In the case of the latter, in the case of the saints, suicide is not an act of despair over the hopelessness or emptiness of life. Unlike Helen Rolt and Bendrix, the whiskey priest and Sarah Miles do not plan to commit suicide, they do not *plan* to escape from history; nor do they, like Bendrix, operate against the forces of history. Rather, they open themselves to suffering and they cooperate with the forces of history. They give in to destiny and to the inevitable; and in both cases they give in from nothing so much as from the sheer fatigue of leading the life of suffering love.

In Greene's novels, the life of suffering love is the life lived in imitation of Christ. It is not undertaken as a stratagem for evading the onslaught of events, for this is inevitable and unescapable. The life that is lived in imitation of Christ is rather the life which meets and overcomes "consequences" by taking them into oneself in love and to the fullness of one's capacity to endure suffering. But even the saint is mortal, and eventually the cup of his endurance is filled to overflowing and he must succumb to the woes of life: in the world which Greene has created, there can be no other end, for history offers no special dispensations of hope and possibility, whether to the saint or to the martyr of despair. But in opening himself up to receive the inevitable, in offering his own life in love and humility as a sacrifice on behalf of his brother, the saint consents to his own death, and is in that measure himself a suicide.

So whether suicide is undertaken as a means of escape from an ugly and hopeless world, or whether it is the inevitable consequence of the life of suffering love, it is the almost certain end for those who become engaged in existence.

It is a bleak and seedy and hopeless world which Graham Greene has created as a habitation for both his saints and his sinners. It is indeed so dreadfully bleak, so utterly without hope, that it is difficult to comprehend the fact that it was created by an author whose religious faith tells him that the Creation is good and that history is ruled by the providence of God. Indeed, it would appear that those critics have been in error who have tacitly assumed that, because Graham Greene is a Roman Catholic, the principles by which he has constructed his fictional world are the same as or similar to the principles which inform the Catholic doctrine of the Creation. For Greene appears to be less indebted for his cosmology to the book of Genesis, the Old Testament prophets, St. Paul, or the Fathers and Doctors of the Church than to Basilides and Valentinus and Marcion and the followers of Mani—that is, to those expositors of the condition of man who, in the first centuries of the Christian era, developed the systems of thought and myth which are called Gnosticism.

Of course, to say that there are certain tendencies toward a Gnostic or neo-Gnostic world-view in the works of Graham Greene is not at all to say that Greene himself is a self-conscious heretic. The matter under investigation here is not the nature or tendency of the artist's personal beliefs but the principles which the artist has employed in "creating" or "modeling" his artificial universe. In making this distinction, I do not mean to deny that there is or may be an intimate relation between such principles and the artist's personal belief or beliefs; I want rather simply to call attention to the way in which the structure of a work of literature may be the bearer of religious or theological meaning.

The "Catholic novels" of Graham Greene have, then, certain affinities with the ancient theological myths. For example, Gnosticism speaks of the world as being a "prison" or a "cave"; and Greene seems to favor the imagery of the swamp, the jungle, and the desert. But in either case, the world is in some fundamental opposition to the needs and aspirations of man. The world is ugly and empty of joy, and is a place where man ought not to be, or would be better off in being out of; the world, or historical existence, is hell.[2] Further, there is a real kinship between the Gnostic concept of man as possessed and used by demons and Greene's concept of man as obsessed and driven. In *The End of the Affair* this idea is more explicit than in the three preceding works. Bendrix wonders why people who believe in a personal God cannot believe in His antithesis, in a personal devil.

I have known so intimately the way that demon works in my imagination. . . . He would prompt our quarrels long before they occurred; he was not Sarah's enemy so much as the enemy of love, and isn't that what the devil is supposed to be?. . . . If there existed a God who loved, the devil would be driven to destroy even the weakest, the most faulty imitation of that love . . . the devil too may have his ambitions; he may dream of training even such a person as myself . . . into being [one of] *his* saints, ready with borrowed fanaticism to destroy love wherever we find it.

And in chasing Saráh out of her sickbed and into the streets of wintry London, Bendrix does of course just that: he is driven by his fanatical jealousy and his selfishness to destroy love. But it seems almost as appropriate to speak of the characters in the other novels as being in the grip of demonic powers as it is to speak of Bendrix in this way. Certainly neither Pinkie nor Scobie could be accurately described as being his own master; they are the slaves of demonic obsessions.

In both the myth and the novels, redemption or salvation is impossible within the terms and structures of human existence. Whatever of good there may be is to be found beyond or above nature and history; and death for the Gnostic saint is what it is for Greene's saints—the end of suffering and the beginning of bliss. In both cases, redemption is "an absolutely eschatological event." It is an event which occurs at the very end of existence, though in the myth man or the Self is released by death from imprisonment in a material body, while in the novels man is released by suicide from history and from condemnation to consequences. In both cases, man makes his appeal to and is saved by the pity or mercy of "the supreme deity," for of neither the novels nor of the myths can it be said that man is responsible for his unhappy condition. In the Gnostic tradition the world of nature is the creation not of the redeemer-god but of the demons. In Manichean and Marcionistic Gnosticism, the God of the Old Testament, Yahweh, is a different God from the God and Father of Jesus Christ. The world created by Yahweh is a material and therefore an evil world, for it imprisons the immaterial "spark," the essential Self. Yahweh Himself is an evil God, but the God of Jesus Christ is the Redeemer God and a good God, and He will have mercy on those who are abandoned in a world hostile to man. Similarly in the novels: it is difficult to believe that the world inhabited by Scobie or Sarah or the whiskey priest was made by the same God as the One to whom each appeals in his extremity. It is easier to think of that world as created by the same demons which inhabit these people and their neighbors and which drive them to self-destruction—by the same demons which lend the "borrowed fanaticism" in virtue of which Pinkie attempts to kill Rose and Bendrix destroys Sarah.

But there is a difference, at least in emphasis, between the Gnosticism of the first centuries of the Christian era and that of Graham Greene. The difference, put perhaps too succinctly and neatly, is this: that whereas in the ancient myth man was understood to be imprisoned in nature or matter or space, in the world of Graham Greene man is imprisoned in history or existence or time. (This distinction is too facile because Marcionistic or ontological dualism necessarily has as its corollary historical dualism, and the dualistic concept of matter results in a dualistic concept of time. But allowing for this qualification the generalization holds mainly true.) The having of a body is not a curse to Scobie or—finally—to Sarah; their misfortunes do not stem from the fact of corporality. Rather, they are cursed by existence in time; they are victims of a history which does not offer or even contain the possibilities for resolving in any healthful way the problems with which they are afflicted. In the ancient Gnosticism (again, with qualifications), salvation and happiness were permanently obstructed by matter, and man's problem could be defined in terms of imprisonment. In Greene's novels, salvation and happiness are obstructed by history, by the malevolence of a temporal order which provides only occasions for further entangling and complicating the life of a person who is hurled by an obsession into an existential act; and the appropriate image for this kind of world is that either of a swamp or an entangling net, to struggle against which is only to be the more completely immersed, the more hopelessly entrammeled.

Trapped in a history which promises nothing but suffering, frustration, and death, Greene's saints look to the mercy of God for salvation; and, indeed, the novels seem almost to be a series of experiments whose purpose is to determine the limits of God's gracious longsuffering. But clearly, if man himself is not responsible for his plight, if his sickness was thrust upon him by the very structures of existence, or if he is what he is because he was made that way by an evil creator-god, by "beings that by nature are no gods," there can be no justifiable limit to the mercy of the Redeemer-God. Hence one does not often come across in the novels any notion of God's justice, for if mercy is to be limited, its limitations will be determined by justice. But since the Redeemer's mercy must be infinite, it cannot be limited, and justice cannot be one of the attributes of the Deity; and the definition of God which seems to emerge from the novels is, "God is suffering love"; or—if mercy and love are identical, as they seem to be—"God is suffering mercy."

To this generalization there is one serious qualification. History does permit of the life of suffering love, and if the wrath of God is ever exercised, its object is the person who is utterly without love. It is in virtue of this consideration that the old priest can hold out to Rose the possibility of

Pinkie's salvation. " 'If he loved you, surely,' the old man said, 'that shows . . . there was some good. . . .' " And if Scobie's destination is Purgatory and not a very low circle of Hell, it is because his act was motivated by love.

But just here is the ambiguity in the doctrine of salvation by love which runs through Greene's works. Scobie's suicide is an act of desperation: he has no hope that the future can bring anything but more suffering for those whom he has contracted to protect. He contemplates suicide, and argues that, since God could not be murdered, and Christ was God, Christ too had killed himself: "He had hanged himself on the Cross as surely as Pemberton [had hanged himself] from the picture rail." The life of suffering love, the imitation of Christ, leads inevitably to this end—to suicide, or—more irenically phrased—to self-sacrifice on behalf of one's "brother." And since Scobie himself is the agent for injuring those for whom he has become responsible, the love-ethic requires him to sacrifice himself for his "brothers." And though Scobie loves God, he does not trust Him to bring about the happiness of Helen and Louise. So Scobie must impose his own will on history and make it produce the happiness which, if it were left to God, might not eventuate. The future does not belong to God; it is not the repository of the grace of God understood as "possibility in spite of." The future belongs to Scobie, and by his suicide he intends to extort from history the possibility of peace and happiness which in itself it does not contain. This means, however, that Scobie's suicide is not in fact an imitation of Christ: it is an imitation of God, for it is the usurping of God's reign over history.

But again, if the Redeemer-God is not identical with the God who created the world and whose providence is the ultimate power in history, then Scobie's suicide is not the act of rebellion which it would be under Catholic doctrine. With the exception of his part in the death of Ali, his houseboy, Scobie's every deed is motivated by charity and by his sense of responsibility for others, and this is most emphatically true of his suicide. Here is a man who is eminently the object of the mercy of a Savior-God whose concern is for those who live in and by love. But according to which set of doctrines are we to evaluate the nature of Scobie's suicide—the Gnostic or the Catholic?

The moral ambiguity which characterizes Scobie's suicide prevents easy judgment; but the moral ambiguity arises from the tension which exists in the novels between a Gnostic cosmology and a Christian ethic. This ethic in turn derives from a doctrine of the Incarnation; and it is this doctrine which, in its ethical expression as the *imitatio Christi* and in its sacramental expression as a doctrine of transubstantiation, is the only thing which prevents the novels from slipping over completely into an ontological dualism. The Incarnation, with its ethical and sacramental corollaries, is the one grip which Greene permits his Savior-God to retain on a world which, by all other evidence, He did not create and which He does not govern. The Incarnation is the one point of contact between the two worlds which are constituted by Graham Greene's otherwise unqualified dualistic ontology. Godless in Greeneland, the desperate saints attempt by imitating the historical existence of their Savior-God to supply out of themselves a measure of the holy which for two thousand years has not had on earth a local residence, except mysteriously in the Mass.

The moral order which is established by the tension between a Gnostic cosmology and a Catholic love-ethic must then manifest the same tension and the same ambiguity as does the theological order. It is impossible to say of Scobie or of Sarah or of the whiskey priest that he or she did well or ill: given a hopeless future and given the pattern of the Savior in whom they believe but do not trust, they do what they have to do. In a world that is bereft of any possibility of realizing peace and happiness, they take up the one mode of existence which enables them for a time to withstand the shocks and consequences which their engagement in history entails: they adopt the pattern of the life of the Savior-God in His incarnation—the life of suffering love.

The theological tension in Greene's fiction is to be defined, then, as resulting from the qualification of a Gnostic or a neo-Gnostic doctrine of creation by a Catholic and orthodox doctrine of the Incarnation. And yet the shards and fragments of Catholic thought and piety are sufficient to prevent the novels from lapsing wholly into Gnosticism; and they have induced Greene's critics to attempt to understand and interpret the faith which informs his novels in more or less orthodox and Thomistic terms, and to pass critical judgments on the art in which his belief is expressed in more or less traditional and Aristotelian terms. Such attempts must necessarily fail, however, since the tension between Gnostic and Catholic doctrines makes for an ambiguous moral order as well as for a precarious instability in the conditions of necessity and probability. The former is illustrated by the question of Scobie's suicide; the latter is illustrated by the fact that in both *The Power and the Glory* and *The End of the Affair* the Savior-God is "persuaded" by a saint's imitation of Christ to enter a world He either did not make or else has forsaken, and there to exercise His power in existence over the Creator-God by means of performing miracles.

The confusion and contradictoriness of the critical and theological judgments of the novels of Graham Greene may be traced in large part, it seems to me, to the fact that his commentators have failed to see the deep incoherence which is constituted by this combination of Gnostic or neo-Gnostic tendencies with classical Christian tendencies. Particularly Greene's Christian critics have made the mistake of excoriating the moral and artistic ambiguities of his art in terms of principles and doctrines which are quite appropriate to traditional Catholic thinking but which are largely irrelevant when the whole pattern of his work is complicated by an old and—it was thought—impotent heresy.

A. A. DeVitis

THE CATHOLIC AS NOVELIST:
GRAHAM GREENE AND
FRANCOIS MAURIAC

In *The Emperor's Clothes,* an attack on the dogmatic assertions of writers who make use of the stuff of religion as background and rationale for their works, Kathleen Knott says concerning the novelist who writes from a Roman Catholic point of view:

It seems to be much easier for Catholic writers who are born Catholic, for instance Mauriac, to stick to psychological truth than it is for converts. This may be because it is much easier to ignore Catholic theory when it is acquired below the age of reason. Anglo-Saxon writers probably have a special disadvantage in this respect.

Aiming her barb directly at Graham Greene and Evelyn Waugh, both converts to Roman Catholicism, Miss Knott goes on to observe that she finds the situation described in Greene's *The Power and the Glory* credible because the actions of the characters result from the interplay between a sentimental-religious education and the concrete circumstances of socialistic governmental intolerance. But for *The Heart of the Matter* and *The End of the Affair* she has no

sympathy, finding the situations described in both books
factitious:

> To be artistically satisfying the situation must be objectively
> described. The author must not imply that, for esoteric reasons,
> he knows more about the answers to the problem than the
> characters do. You can write a human book about a Catholic
> if you do not at the same time write a book about Catholic
> theories of human nature.

Indeed, Miss Knott puts her finger on the point that has
given rise to much of the controversy excited by the religious
provocations portrayed by both Greene and Mauriac in their
works.

Since the publication of *Brighton Rock* in 1938 the framework of Greene's novels, with the exception of *The Quiet
American,* has been Roman Catholicism. Writing for an
audience primarily Protestant in orientation, Greene has
faced obstacles as a novelist that Mauriac, who acquired his
religious training "below the age of reason," has not. Yet
both these novelists have been faced with an identical
problem regarding their artistic and religious integrity. For,
ultimately, both concern themselves with the capacity of
the human heart for sacrifice and greatness within a world
governed by a God who seems unreasonable, hostile, and
oftentimes indifferent; and both concern themselves with
the all-pervasive nature of grace, the incontestable mystery
of good and evil and the inability of man to distinguish
between the two. The fact, however, that both these
writers, one born a Catholic, the other a convert to Roman
Catholicism, deal with the predicaments of human beings
within a framework of morality that is labelled Roman
Catholicism does not necessarily mean that they are novelists
who allow their appreciation of the orthodoxy of their beliefs
to govern the artistic value of their works; it would be as
foolish to label Homer a Greek theologian because Odysseus
and Agamemnon are Greeks and concerned with the caprices

of the deities. Furthermore both Greene and Mauriac are conscious of the difficulties of their positions as artists and have written persuasively and perceptively on the nature of their responsibilities to both their craft and their faith. Both have been accused by their critics of "conniving" with the devil in portraying their themes.

Speaking within the defined limits of Thomistic philosophy, Jacques Maritain discusses in *Art and Scholasticism* the problem of evil in the world and the novelist's responsibility to his audience. The novelist's purpose, he says, is not to mirror life as the painter does, but to create the experience of it. The novel, of course, derives its rules of conduct from the real world; but as a work of art its validity depends on the quality of the life-experience which it creates. It becomes the responsibility of the novelist to understand with what object he portrays the aspects of evil which oftentimes form the materials of the art work: "The essential question is *from what altitude* he depicts and whether his art and mind are pure enough and strong enough to depict it without connivance. The more deeply the modern novelist probes human misery, the more does it require super-human virtues in the novelist." According to Maritain the only writer who can be a complete artist is the Christian, for only he has some idea of the potentialities of man and what the factors limiting his greatness are. The Christian writer who approaches his craft honestly portrays the universal truths which are valid within a Christian configuration of morality and ethics. If the artist finds himself in too much sympathy with misery and suffering, his pity may lead him to censure the forces of divinity which make themselves apparent in the phenomenal world. Such art becomes destructive, even self-destructive, for it defeats any moral end. It is for this reason that Maritain finds the influence of Gide pernicious, for much of Gide's work exalts a gratuitous act without consideration of its moral and ethical ramifications. But neither Greene nor Mauriac, many of their Catholic readers insist, maintains a suitable "altitude."

Graham Greene has been accused by his critics and his fans alike of conniving with the devil; he has been called a Manichaean, a Jansenist, a Quietist, an Existentialist, and other names as well. Many commentators have made an attempt to abstract his personal convictions from the world of his invention, insisting, understandably enough, on a prerogative of philosophical and religious speculation. But many of his commentators, critics, and fans have failed to understand the important fact that in his novels, and often in his entertainments, Greene describes a human condition, and that the experience of life developed within that human condition is not representative of religious bias. Greene himself says in a letter to Elizabeth Bowen and V. S. Pritchett:

> If I may be personal, I belong to a group, the Catholic Church, which would present me with grave problems as a writer were I not saved by my disloyalty. If my conscience were as acute as M. Mauriac's showed itself to be in his essay *God and Mammon,* I could not write a line. There are leaders of the Church who regard literature as a means to an end, edification. . . . I am not arguing that literature is amoral, but that it presents a different moral, and the personal morality of an individual is seldom identical with the morality of the group to which he belongs. You remember the black and white squares of Bishop Blougram's chess board. As a novelist, I must be allowed to write from the point of view of the black square as well as of the white: doubt and even denial must be given their chance of self-expression, or how is one freer than the Leningrad group?

In the novels since *Brighton Rock,* with the possible exception of *The Quiet American,* Greene creates an experience of life, to use Maritain's phrase, in which the religion of the chief actors is Roman Catholicism. Like the people of Henry James, a writer whom Greene much admires, they make a place for themselves within the experience, exciting the pity and curiosity of the reader as they move within the boundaries of a problem that often seems to admit no earthly solution. Were Greene to force his people to react to the conditions in which they find themselves, as good Catholics would, if the solution for their unhappiness were brought about in terms of the author's religious convictions, then indeed the results would be bad art. But the novelist who retains his faith as a man allows himself a point from which to explore evil. "For to render the highest justice to corruption," says Greene, "you have to be conscious all the time within yourself of treachery to something valuable." If the novelist were to glorify good and refuse to recognize the beauty of evil, the beauty that Lucifer carried with him when he fell, if the novelist were to attest only the validity of a religious dogma, he would be, as Greene says, "a philosopher or religious teacher of the second rank." The fact remains that Greene is primarily a novelist—neither a theologian nor a philosopher. "The novelist depends preponderantly on his personal experience, the philosopher on correlating the experience of others, and the novelist's philosophy will always be a little lop-sided," he says while commenting on Henry James in *The Lost Childhood.*

Ultimately Greene concerns himself with the problems of good and evil not so much as they exist within the Catholic Church but as they exist in the great world. His novels deal primarily with the fall of man, and at least two of them, *The Power and the Glory* and *The Heart of the Matter,* afford the possibility of heroic action. Although his books are filled with the stuff of religion, they do not in any way attempt to justify the activities of that religion. Greene chooses to deal with the seedy, the unlikeable, the unhappy, those in whom he feels the strange power of God. When he does choose to work with the stuff of sainthood, his work suffers, as does *The End of the Affair.* Perhaps Mauriac explains the failure when he writes in *God and Mammon:*

Why should not we portray saints just as Benson, Foggazaro, Boumann and Bernanos did—or tried to do? On the other hand it could be maintained that on this point of sanctity the novelist loses his rights, for if he tries to write a novel about sanctity he is no longer dealing purely with men, but with the action of God on men—and this may be an extremely unwise thing to try to do. On this point it seems that the novelist will always be beaten by reality, by the saints who really have lived.

When Greene is concerned with sin and the possibility of redemption, he is at his best, choosing, as he does, to create his experience of life in uncharted theological waters. But at the end of the life-experience he reestablishes his direction and relocates his port. To do this Greene uses a spokesman of the Church he happens to be a member of. The priest who comforts Rose at the end of *Brighton Rock,* Father Rank who comforts Louise Scobie at the end of *The Heart of the Matter,* Father Browne in *The Living Room:* these characters are not plot contrivances, *dei ex machina* as they at first appear. Rather, they reestablish ethical norms of behavior and a proper religious perspective after the passions of men have spent themselves. As in Elizabethan and Jacobean drama, order must be reestablished before the spectator can be released. In *Hamlet* the audience leaves the theatre with the knowledge of Fortinbras's reestablishment of order in Denmark. The trick is one that Greene learned from his study of the drama, and he puts it to capital use in his melodramatic pieces.

François Mauriac's problem, as a writer who happens to be a Catholic, has been similar to Greene's. In 1936 he wrote an account of the development of his religious convictions to refute the charge levelled at him by André Gide that he sought permission to be a Catholic without having to burn his books:

If I refuse to accept this reproach of Gide's it is not because I think I am innocent. I am probably more guilty than a man who is tugged both ways, who wants to write his books without missing heaven and to win heaven without foregoing his books. It is putting it too mildly to say that I "do not lose sight of Mammon." The fact is that I am in the front line of his besiegers. But the impossibility of serving two masters does not necessarily mean the forsaking of one for the other to the extent of losing sight of the forsaken One or losing awareness of His presence and power. And even if this sight and awareness were lost, we would still be wearing the untearable livery of the Master we had betrayed; we would still, by force or free will, belong to His house.

And he goes on to say: "Above all I liked to be persuaded by Pascal that a search was always possible, that there could always be a voyage of discovery within revealed truth." Mauriac tells his reader that early in life he became aware of the fact that, born a Catholic, he could never live outside the boundaries of his religion. This knowledge led him to indulge a tendency for criticism, and many readers detected the ambiguity of his point of view in his early works. Nevertheless, he continued to write within the borders of Catholicism, an object of mistrust and contempt to many of his fellow-Catholics: "I knew that the Christian God demanded everything. I knew that he had no part in the flesh and that the world of nature and the world of grace were two and inimical. Pascal taught me this with an almost excessive ruthlessness, and I knew it to be terrifyingly true." Catholic criticism was not, therefore, as Mauriac tells his reader, unjust in detecting and criticizing the tendency towards Jansenism and Manichaeism that is to be found in such novels as *Flesh and Blood* and *Thérèse Desqueyroux;* he admits that he too could discern the element of corruption prowling over his work, "in the way it prowls over cemeteries which are nevertheless dominated by the Cross." And he goes on to say:

I always put myself on guard against the aesthetic side of present-day Catholicism, and its emotional appeal, however sublime, at once excites my mistrust. I long with all my soul for the "consolations of religion," but I know at what price they must be bought. I know all about peace in suffering, and I know that bitterness with which past sins penetrate through present grace.

Both Greene and Mauriac then are aware of the difficulties involved in writing from the Roman Catholic point of view, but both writers are aware of the fact that to render the highest justice to God, the force of evil must be appreciated, even if at times appreciating the beauty of evil seems a questioning of the orthodox preachings of their Church. Both Greene and Mauriac are concerned not only with observing life but with creating the experience of it. They bring living people into being, complex, inscrutable, made unhappy by their lack of identity with the source of good. Both Greene and Mauriac, in a very real sense, lose their identity in the subjects of their creation; hence the charge that they "connive" with the devil. Mauriac says, "If there is a reason for the existence of the novelist on earth it is this: to show the element which holds out against God in the highest and noblest characters—the innermost evils and dissimulations; and also to light up the secret source of sanctity in creatures who seem to us to have failed." To say that in their works they stress Roman Catholic theory at the expense of psychological or artistic truth is to misunderstand completely the nature and function of their art.

II

SPEAKING OF *The Power and the Glory*, Mauriac says of Greene in *Mes Grands Hommes*:

The work of an English Catholic novelist—of an Englishman returning to Catholicism—such as Graham Greene's *The Power and the Glory*, at first always gives me the sensation of being in a foreign land. To be sure I find there my spiritual fatherland, and it is into the heart of a familiar mystery that Graham Greene introduces me. But everything takes place as though

I were making my way into an old estate through a concealed door. . . .

Mauriac goes on to point out that the French Catholic enters the edifice of his religion by the front door; that as a schoolboy he is versed in the various schisms and heresies that comprise the official history of his Church. The convert to Roman Catholicism, on the other hand, enters the edifice of his religion through the archway of his early upbringing and religious training. The religious influences felt as a child, that catechism so like and so unlike the Roman Catholic's, consciously interfere and intrude when the man makes his choice later on. Mauriac may envy Maritain and Psichari, both converts to Catholicism, for the freedom of their choice, as he tells his reader in the second chapter of *God and Mammon;* but he is nevertheless confused when reading Greene, for Greene's world seems alien to him, although its mysteries are clear. The explanation is perhaps not too difficult.

Greene's early preoccupation with evil is best described in an essay called "The Lost Childhood." His early reading, he tells us, was in Anthony Hope, H. Rider Haggard, and Marjorie Bowen, stories of violence and adventure told with gusto and emphasized by melodrama. In these works he learned that people were not all as good as Allan Quartermain or as evil as the witch Gagool. From this early reading the patterns of Greene's mature work began to emerge. "It was as if once and for all I had been supplied with a subject," he says,

. . . religion might later explain to me in other terms, but the pattern was already there—perfect evil walking the world where perfect good can never walk again, and only the pendulum ensures that after all in the end justice is done. Man is never satisfied, and often I have wished that my hand had not moved farther than *King Solomon's Mines.*

Again, in an "introduction" to *Oliver Twist*, he writes:

If, as one is inclined to believe, the creative writer perceives his world once and for all in childhood and adolescence, and his whole career is an effort to illustrate his private world in terms of the great public world we all share, we can understand why Fagin and Sykes in their most extreme exaggerations move us more than the benevolence of Mr. Brownlow and the sweetness of Mrs. Maylie—they touch with fear as the others never really touch with love.

In *The Lawless Roads* Greene writes of his growing acquaintance with evil, of his father's school at Berkhamsted, where he lived on the border, between the school dormitories and the family rooms—and the image of the border has become an important one in his work. His early religious training was in the Anglican Church, but with time he found the forms and symbols of that Church unsatisfactory to his needs. The eagle was replaced by the statue of the Virgin Mary. With his conversion to Roman Catholicism he "began to have a dim conception of the appalling mysteries of love through a ravaged world"; he began to understand the questions posed by Bernanos through his Curé d'Ars and by Péguy, who challenged God in the name of the damned.

The melodrama, the key to much of Greene's work, perhaps that very aspect that makes Mauriac feel an alien in a foreign land, was set by early reading in the romantic stories of Marjorie Bowen and Rider Haggard; and later the novels of Charles Dickens, Joseph Conrad, and Henry James taught him how to handle his themes and develop his plots. An early apprenticeship as movie critic for *The Spectator* sharpened his perceptions concerning the nature of melodrama and what could be achieved through it. Greene's conversion to Roman Catholicism seems to have been a logical step in an intellectual development; for in the teaching of that Church he found a hint of an explanation, to use his own term, for many of the problems that vexed him as a child and a man. The Catholic Church offered him some explanation for suffering and misery, although he did not always find the explanation satisfactory; hence the questioning and probing that so many readers find in such mature works as *The Heart of the Matter* and *The End of the Affair.*

Ultimately Greene is different from Mauriac in method rather than theme. For Greene writes his novels and his entertainments within the traditional forms of the English novel as defined by John Bunyan, Charles Dickens, Joseph Conrad, and Henry James. Greene's reading in Dickens accounts for many of his "seedy" characters, for his Ackys and Mintys, for his inept detectives, and for his grotesque children, his Elses and young Parkises; it accounts also for the social commentary of such works as *England Made Me, It's A Battlefield,* and *Brighton Rock,* the mixture of sentimentality and social ire. Greene's reading in Conrad and in Bunyan taught him the nature of allegory and the importance of ethical choice. Lord Jim stands behind the whiskey priest, as Axel Heyst, who cultivates pity as a form of contempt, stands behind Arthur Rowe and Major Scobie; as Conrad's antiheroes stand behind Pinkie Brown and Raven. Greene's reading in Henry James taught him concern for style, for correctness, for the dissection of human motive; James taught him how to manipulate the stuff of evil while unfolding the complexities of character:

There was no victory for human beings, that was his conclusion; you were punished in your way, whether you were of God's or the Devil's party. James believed in the supernatural, but he saw evil as an equal force with good. Humanity was cannon fodder in a war too balanced ever to be concluded. If he had been guilty of the supreme egotism of preserving his own existence, he left the material, in his profound unsparing analysis, for rendering even egotism the highest kind of justice, of giving the devil his due.

With the death of James, Greene writes in an essay on François Mauriac, the religious sense was lost to the English novel, and with the religious sense went the importance of the human act.

Furthermore Greene, unlike Mauriac, is in the unenviable position of writing his books for a predominantly Protestant audience, an audience which still nourishes a distrust of Catholicism that goes back to the English Reformation. If at times Greene seems belligerent, it is perhaps because he feels, remembering his origins, the hostility of his audience. The fact that so many British readers have seen fit to question Greene's orthodoxy is in itself an indication of the fact that he has achieved some measure of success in fabricating stories of violence and suspense within a framework of Roman Catholic belief, a belief that suggests treachery to the spiritual fitness of many Protestants, and Catholics as well.

François Mauriac, on the other hand, writes to a predominantly Catholic audience, an audience aware of the implications of Jansenism, the religious controversy between Bossuet and Fenelon, and the hundreds of years of Church influence on the hearts and intellects of Frenchmen. Mauriac has written eloquently in *Mes Grands Hommes* of the influence of Pascal, Voltaire, Rousseau, Maurice de Guérin, and others on his works. Both Elsie Pell and Gerald Moloney have recently commented on the literary sources of Mauriac's work. But in *God and Mammon* he says revealingly: "I can say with truth that no book has moved me more deeply than a simple and innocent novel called *Feet of Clay* which I adored when I was fourteen. It was the work of an old and virtuous woman called Zenaide de Fleuriot, and it was full of imagination and sensibility." Imagination and

sensibility are the keynotes of the Mauriac novels as melodrama and suspense are the keynotes of the Greene novels.
Like Greene whose indebtedness to a work of innocence
—Charlotte M. Yonge's *The Little Duke*—is testified to by
The Ministry of Fear, Mauriac's youthful sensibilities were
moved by the exploits of innocence abroad in a black and
white universe, the innocent taking the form of a freckle-
faced girl with the lovely name of Armelle Trahec. Yet
Mauriac admits in the same passage that when asked to
name the writers who have most influenced him, he replies
automatically Balzac and Dostoevsky. This is to say that a
youthful imagination, stimulated by the innocent exploits
of Mlle. Trahec, was disciplined by a rigorous training in the
classics of the French novel and the psychological analyses
of the pre-Freudian analyst, Dostoevsky, an influence that
can also be seen in Greene. In *Mes Grands Hommes* Mauriac
tells his reader that he read avidly the writings of the
iconoclastic Anatole France; that, despite Flaubert's anti-
Catholicism, that writer's skill and understanding impressed
him deeply, particularly Flaubert's liking for those who
threw themselves into extremes, perhaps as do Thérèse
Desqueyroux and Maria Cross, as do Jean Péloueyre and old
Villenave. Stendhal stands behind the partly romantic,
partly realistic love scenes of *The Woman of the Pharisees*,
as he does in those many many scenes in which the psychology of the characters seems to shape itself on the very
page. And Balzac and Zola stand behind those many novels
which are centered around the Bordeaux countryside, novels
in which the traditions of French family life, its greed and
hypocrisy, its humor and its dignity, are carefully and
poignantly developed. Mauriac is not a realist, however,
in the sense that Zola is a realist; rather, he is a realist
in a moral sense. As do the works of Balzac, the writer
who automatically springs to his lips when his literary
influences are called into question, Mauriac's works move

quietly, the observations keenly made and the scenes fully
realized, the religious and moral implications rising in-
sistently above action that might at times verge on the
sensational. Even the sensational aspects of the Desqueyroux
murder trial seem folded into the fabric of the novel in
Thérèse Desqueyroux, for there the emphasis falls on the
instinctive evil of the heroine whose face reveals the
pitilessness of her character only in moments of lethargy; a
heroine in whom, nevertheless, her author finds the germs
of spirituality, through whom the power of grace may be
felt.

The traditions of the French novel ultimately define the
method that Mauriac follows in portraying themes that are
animated by a Roman Catholic consideration of the effects
of sin on the soul, and the all-pervasive powers of grace.
No wonder he feels an alien when he first reads Greene.
The mystery may be the same, but the approach to the
mystery has been determined by the conventions of the
English novel. The similarities that exist in the works of
these two writers, obvious enough, become insignificant.

There is one more point, however, that needs to be made.
In each case it would be foolish to say that Greene has
not read the French novels that Mauriac has, and vice versa.
And in this respect it is interesting to observe the reciprocal
influences that can be seen in their works. In this case it
would seem that Greene has borrowed more from Mauriac
than Mauriac from Greene. Greene's drama *The Living
Room,* for example, shows a remarkable similarity of theme
and character with Mauriac's *The Woman of the Pharisees.*
Greene's drama concerns the efforts of Helen Browne, an
elderly and misguided Catholic, to keep her niece Rose from
abandoning her religion by giving in to a liaison with a
married man. *The Woman of the Pharisees* recounts the
exertions of a stepmother, Brigitte Pian, to impose the
precepts of Roman Catholic dogma on her wards. "Do you

know what Monsieur Calou said to Jean about Brigitte Pian," Michele says to her brother Louis, "He said that there are some people who choose God, but that perhaps God doesn't choose them. . . ." Both these characters are studies in misguided and, to some extent, unintentional hypocrisy, and they indicate the concern that both Greene and Mauriac have in similar themes. Further similarities could be drawn but would prove little more than that Greene has read Mauriac and Mauriac Greene, that both are dealing with experiences of life within a Roman Catholic framework, and that both are different because they are different people.

Both writers, dealing with individuals in their relationship to God, and, consequently, to their fellow men, develop their themes according to their own geniuses. And in this realm all comparisons prove fruitless. The point is that both novelists work within the confines of the novel as determined by their origins, their cultural traditions, and the times. From the vantage point of their religion they explore good and evil in the world. They do not write from a Roman Catholic theological point of view; rather they are novelists who happen to be Catholics as well. And one does not need to know Roman Catholic theories of human nature to appreciate their art.

Herbert R. Haber

THE END OF THE CATHOLIC CYCLE: THE WRITER VERSUS THE SAINT

One would have to be a saint. But then one could not write novels.

—François Mauriac

We are created in the image and after the likeness of God because we are capable of loving. Saints have a genius for love, but not that sort of genius which is the artist's, for example, which is the privilege of a very small number.

—Georges Bernanos

I could have become a saint, a worker of wonders. I have become a man of letters.

—Leon Bloy

At least since his essay on Henry James's prefaces, it has become virtually an axiom for Graham Greene that a novelist's poetic vision is inseparable from the craft he practices, from his discreet adherence to or responsible infringement of those "rules" which James almost single-handedly invented and Percy Lubbock later codified. James himself, Greene noted, "never hesitated to break his own rules, but he broke them with a full consciousness of his responsibility, shivering a little with the temerity of his 'exquisite treacheries'; and it remains true today that no novelist can begin to write until he has taken those rules into consideration; you cannot be a protestant before you have studied the dogmas of the old faith."[1] Even *ex cathedra,* one might naturally expect Greene to couch his commitments to the craft of fiction in the language of theology; in *The End of the Affair,*[2] however, the juxtaposition of religious and literary terms serves larger ends than metaphor, for in this novel which ends his Catholic cycle,[3] Greene demonstrates an almost unprecedented concern with certain religious imperatives which beset the believing novelist, though as befits Greene's highly personalized mode of belief, these imperatives are markedly less orthodox than those which Mauriac conjured with in *God and Mammon.* For Greene, unlike Mauriac, has never shown himself exceptionally troubled by the unwarranted effects his novels have produced, nor with imputations by the pious of blasphemy or disloyalty. In an open letter some three years before the publication of *The End of the Affair* Greene remarked:

If I may be personal, I belong to a group, the Catholic Church, which would present me grave problems as a writer if I were not saved by my disloyalty. If my conscience were as acute as M. Mauriac's showed itself to be in his essay *God and Mammon,* I could not write a line. There are leaders of the Church who regard literature as a means to one end, edification. That end may be one of the highest value, of far higher value than literature, but it belongs to a different world. Literature has nothing to do with edification. I am not arguing that literature is amoral, but that it presents a personal moral, and the personal morality of an individual is seldom identical with the morality of the group to which he belongs.[4]

Nonetheless, in *The End of the Affair* Greene raises a related question, which Mauriac did in fact touch on in *Le Roman,* that of whether the novelist who willingly or not subscribes to a religious view of the world may serve as the mediator of truth, even of that kind of poetic or empirical truth which the writer has historically claimed as his prerogative. Through Maurice Bendrix, the novelist-narrator of *The End of the Affair,* Greene puts the novelist's thirst for truth to the ultimate test, enquiring not only how useful it may indeed be, but what corrosive effects it may have on the novelist himself, if not on others. And he questions, too, whether the thousand or so technical choices the novelist makes in the process of creation, the detached existence he must needs maintain, the judgments he makes, and the pride he takes in his profession may not reflect but one more instance of some "monstrous egotism" devilishly at work, another and less than "exquisite treachery" to his own "personal morality."

For Greene's personal morality has always implied a frustrated impatience with man's egotism and a denial of conscious intellection as the ultimate means of achieving truth—though paradoxically these are the very qualities which sustain the novelist and allow him to write freely, subject only to the "rules" he chooses and his intelligent use of them:

This, [Greene noted] is the chief importance of James's prefaces: that they have made future novelists conscious: that the planned effect has been substituted for the lucky stroke. . . . We have watched James choose his point of view, work out his ironic antitheses, arrange his scenes, but the peculiar aptitude remains; even given the directions no one has equalled him.[5]

It is exactly this "peculiar aptitude" of the novelist that is on trial in *The End of the Affair,* along with its accessory before and after the fact: the novelist's tacit assumption that he can sift, order, and interpret life, reduce it to its essential meaning. And it is this trial which accounts in large part for the unity of the novel, for its narrator, Bendrix, is here both defendant and prosecutor, at once fearful of the imminent loss of his profession and the identity it has always

insured him and torn by that agonized suspicion that some
other and Omniscient Author is arranging the scenes, im-
posing a plot on his own life as he, with a now doubtful
sense of free will, imposed one on the lives of others. The
first paragraph of the novel finds Bendrix beginning his
recollections from this paradoxical position:

A story has no beginning or end: arbitrarily one chooses that
moment of experience from which to look back or from which to
look ahead. I say "one chooses" with the inaccurate pride of a
professional writer who—when he has been seriously noted at
all—has been praised for his technical ability, but I do in fact
of my own will *choose* [my italics] that black wet January night
on the Common, in 1946, the sight of Henry Miles slanting
across the wild river of rain, or did these images choose me?
It is convenient, it is correct according to the rules of my craft
to begin just there, but if I had believed then in a God, I could
also have believed in a hand, plucking at my elbow, a suggestion,
"Speak to him: he hasn't seen you yet."

In varying degrees of intensity, the stridency of this beginning carries through the remainder of the novel; here, it is
less the adjunct of some covert rejoinder to those critics of
Greene who had backhandedly praised him only for his
technical virtuosity than it is the authentic tone of despair
—that despair which Kierkegaard described in the man who
has gradually come to recognize the insufficiency of the
esthetic mode of existence.[6]

Essentially, the novel is then an account of such self-
discoveries, an accountably halting revelation of the experiences which have permitted them and of the effects which
they have had on the novelist. As such, *The End of the
Affair* bears a structural resemblance to other stories of
emergent awareness and adds itself to a significant minor
tradition of the novel in which the values and psychology
of the artist himself are critically examined. Though the
reader is almost as aware of Sarah as Bendrix, no account
of the novel which begins with her can exhaust its meaning,

for like Kurtz in *The Heart of Darkness,* she remains a less than substantial figure, seen only through the doubts and fears of the narrator who finds her (as we must, despite her diary) unaccountably motivated, and emblematic finally of some irrational capacity which the novel's author has ever found impervious to analysis. And though the novel seems at times the biography of some latterday saint, Greene is here more concerned, as Conrad was with Marlow, with the effects produced upon the narrator: with the impact here which Bendrix's witnessing of that unsanctioned and ambiguous canonization has had on his mind and feelings, on the professional code which has ordered and given a significance to his life. "There it goes again," Bendrix cries at one point, "—the I, I, I, as though this were my story, and not the story of Sarah, Henry, and, of course that third, whom I hated without yet knowing him, or even believing in him" (p. 38). But the reader is, or should be, aware that it really *is* Bendrix's story—one which Greene has been retelling in varying ways since his Liberian trek; and one which is here, so to speak, a mirror image of Conrad's own tale of Africa. It is, once again, the story of a man's stultifying progress toward that confrontation with what seems to be fanatical, perhaps even supernatural goodness, rather than as in Conrad with inhuman evil; and of its evocation of all that he has repressed in himself in the maintenance of his profession—his buried capacities for involvement, tenderness, and selfless love; his unexpected discovery of the power of his mind to believe unequivocally in the supernatural implications of what he has encountered. Moreover, it is Bendrix's reassessment of his craft and himself, in the light of such self-discoveries, that allies *The End of the Affair* in some measure with that tradition which includes, at a hazard, Melville's *Pierre,* Hawthorne's stories of artists and writers, and those of Henry James and Thomas Mann, and in some ways Gide's *Counterfeiters.* All are accounts of artists whose struggles involve them as both artists and men, who possess the dangerous habit of seeing the world through artists' eyes.

Bendrix has come to see himself as being one of them and though he long forbears to confess it, Sarah here is a fearful precedent before him, proving to him the final unimportance of Art and the artist, demonstrating an alternative that he cannot—or will not—accept, though ironically he finds himself susceptible. For even before her own "leap," she was, Bendrix recalls, uniquely capable of destroying his esthetic detachment and the long practiced habits which implemented it.

When young one builds up habits of work one believes will last a lifetime and withstand any catastrophe. Over twenty years I have probably averaged five hundred words a day for five days a week. . . . I have always been very methodical and when my quota of work is done, I break off even in the middle of a scene. . . . When I was young not even a love affair would alter my schedule. A love affair had to begin after lunch, and however late I might be getting to bed—so long as I slept in my own bed —I would read the morning's work and sleep on it. Even the war hardly affected me. . . . It needed Sarah to upset my self-imposed discipline. (p. 36)

And after her death, the memory of Sarah and all that she represents continued to hamper that self-imposed disengagement which the writer requires.

If a woman is in one's thoughts all day, one should not have to dream of her at night. I was trying to write a book that simply would not come. . . . So much in writing depends on the superficiality of one's days. One may be preoccupied . . . but the stream of the unconscious continues to flow undisturbed, . . . and suddenly the words come as though from the air. . . . But this hate and suspicion, this passion to destroy went deeper than the book—the unconscious worked on it instead, until one morning I woke up and knew, as though I had planned it overnight, that this day I was going to visit Mr. Savage. (pp. 17-18)

The visit with Mr. Savage, the detective, and Bendrix's involvement with his assistant, Parkis, and the search for Sarah's "lover" are but other occasions which inform against the writer, for in time they seem only to have revealed to him the extent to which he has fallen prey to what Hawthorne had called the "unpardonable sin": that cold-blooded researching into the minds and lives of others which Bendrix grudgingly acknowledges is his own profession as well as that of Mr. Savage (whose name in this context becomes grimly appropriate). And Parkis himself, with his dedication to the trade, is but a comically grotesque though more humanized version of himself, for Bendrix too persists in his "professional pride"—a pride of intellect. Now in retrospect, that detached pride and distrust of appearances, so useful to him as a novelist, seems to him, and he calls it as much, his personal "demon," the source of an evil to which, as Hawthorne recognized, the artist was only too liable; though Bendrix, unlike Chillingworth of *The Scarlet Letter*, has come at last to recognize the devilish nature of his inability to accept any kind of love that is more than carnal or transient, to understand the implications of his blind inertial attempt to seek out and destroy it.

I have never understood why people who can swallow the enormous improbability of a personal God boggle at a personal Devil. I have known so intimately the way that demon works in my imagination. No statement that Sarah ever made was proof against his cunning doubts though he would usually wait till she had gone to utter them. He would prompt our quarrels long before they occurred: he was not Sarah's enemy so much as the enemy of love, and isn't that what the devil is supposed to be? I can imagine that if there existed a God who loved, the devil would be driven to destroy even the weakest, the most faulty imitation of that love. Wouldn't he be afraid that the habit of love might grow, and wouldn't he try to trap us all into being traitors, into helping him extinguish love. If there is a God who uses us and makes his saints out of such material as we are, the devil too may have his ambitions; he may dream of training even such a person as myself, even poor Parkis, into being *his* saints, ready with borrowed fanaticism to destroy love wherever we find it. (pp. 67-68)

As a consequence of Parkis's successive efforts Bendrix becomes, so to speak, less the devil's disciple than the devil's advocate; for like Smythe, the scarred rationalist who is no less a foil to Bendrix than Parkis, the novelist maintains a terrible vested interest first in proving Sarah's "conversion" to be the product of a hysterically misguided sense of obligation and then in disproving her seeming sanctity and those miracles which seem to confirm it, in certifying that it was his own driving will and not that of God which took Sarah from him. He seeks, in short, to dispel the gnawing doubt that threatens his profession and his whole assured agnostic way of life, "this doubt," as Bendrix puts it, "that always comes when I begin to write, the feeling that after all perhaps she was right and I wrong" (p. 62). But that doubt is, to borrow again the Kierkegaardian terms which Bendrix himself succumbs to at the close of the novel, the symptom of an incipient rejection of the esthetic outlook, for as Bendrix later notes: "if Sarah is right, how unimportant all the importance of art is." Though Bendrix at last refuses to consent to the alternative her own "leap" suggests, his voice at the end of his narration is, as R. W. B. Lewis noticed, "thick with premonitions of leaping," for Bendrix finds himself in that exhausted state that conduces to the irrational leap to faith, that state of anxiety-ridden impatience with reason and consciousness, with self in short, which Kierkegaard called "the sickness unto death."

I said to her, I'm a man of hate. But I didn't feel much hatred; I had called other people hysterical, but my own words were overcharged. I could detect their insincerity. What I chiefly felt was less hate than fear. For if this God exists, I thought, and if even you—with your lusts and your adulteries and the timid lies you used to tell—can change like this, we could all be saints by leaping as you leapt, by shutting the eyes and leaping once and for all: if *you* are a saint, it's not so difficult to be a saint. It's something He can demand of any of us, leap. But I won't leap. I sat on my bed and said to God: You've taken her but You haven't got me yet. I know Your cunning. It's You who take us up to a high place and offer us the whole universe. You're a devil, God, tempting us to leap. But I don't want Your peace and I don't want Your love. I wanted something very simple and very easy; I wanted Sarah for a lifetime and You took her away. With Your great schemes You ruin our happiness like a harvester ruins a mouse's nest: I hate You, God, I hate You as though You existed. (pp. 235-36)

By a series of contrivances, Greene has plunged his novelist-hero into an endeavor in which Bendrix's bitter attempts at truth have only brought him closer to the brink. For Bendrix's cold insights into human nature have, in the manner of the novel's epilogue from Leon Bloy,[7] stirred within him a dim and unforeseen sympathy with humanity and an attendant desire for release from self which belief seems quick to feed on: "Sometimes," Bendrix early remarks in the novel, "I see myself reflected too closely in other men for comfort, and then I have an enormous wish to believe in the saints, in heroic virtue" (p. 6). If Bendrix is tempted to credit Sarah's sainthood—her "genius for love," as Bernanos called it—it is because she herself has been led to it only after the novelist's relentless analysis and judgment of human nature, or so she tells Bendrix in that posthumous letter he receives from her:

Maurice, dear, don't be angry. Be sorry for me, but don't be angry. I'm a phony and a fake, but this isn't phony or fake. . . . You took away all my lies and self-deceptions like they clear a road of rubble for somebody to come along it, somebody of importance, and now he's come, but you cleared the way yourself. When you write you try to be exact and you taught me to want the truth. . . . So you see it's all your fault, Maurice, it's all your fault. (pp. 178-79)

Bendrix who had tested Sarah asking her if she would make
his bed has, ironically, made hers for that last and spiritual
"affair." And the "craftsman's mind" with its cynical detachment, its propensity to steep itself in no other kind of reality
but the corporeal, leaves Bendrix at last in a paradoxical
state of despair, ambiguously tempted to escape from himself through Sarah's selfless love, yet cognizant of his unwillingness to accept or maintain that mode of love, still
fearful of the far greater sacrifice and loss of identity it
would demand of *him*.

It's all very well for you to love God. You are dead. You have
Him. But I'm sick with life, I'm rotten with health. If I begin
to love God, I can't just die. I've got to do something about it.
. . . If I ever loved like that, it would be the end of everything.
Loving you I had no appetite for food, I felt no lust for any
other woman, but loving Him there'd be no pleasure in anything
at all with Him away. I'd even lose my work, I'd cease to be
Bendrix. Sarah, I'm afraid. (p. 225)

Thus the novel which begins with Bloy's words finds both
here and in the despondent wintry prayer of Bendrix which
ends his narrative another and curiously inverted sentiment
of Leon Bloy who voiced despair at the thought that his
profession had robbed him of potential sainthood: "I could
have been a saint," Bloy once cried, "a worker of wonders.
I have become a man of letters."[8] Bendrix's narration has
been another such confession, a more attentuated and
agnostic confession of despair ending with that equally in-
congruous agnostic prayer that the God he will not believe
in will "leave me alone for ever." Bendrix would have
remained a man of letters; now he will not, or so he
flaggingly insists, become a saint, though the scar on his
leg,[9] his growing tenderness to Henry, and the weariness
of his last prayer seem to belie him. While the reader may
suspect Greene, Bendrix himself suspects that it is God
who creates such "ironic antitheses." For the story he has

told which might have confirmed the "enormous improbability" of the personal God Sarah believed in has only betrayed to him the inadequacy and coercion of the novelist's special aptitude—his ability to use his methods to separate the melodramatic contingencies of life from its more permanent meaning.[10] "I remember," Bendrix recalls, "Mr. Savage had said—a detective must find it as important as a novelist to amass his trivial material before picking out the right clue. But how difficult that picking out is—the release of the real subject. The enormous pressure of the outside world weighs on us like a *peine forte et dure*. Now that I come to write my own story the problem is still the same, but worse—there are so many more facts, now that I have not to invent them" (p. 24). Life is again, to paraphrase James, at its clumsy work; but only a God, Bendrix realizes, could see the ultimate significance that lies in the "germ" of his own story, impose upon it the comforting simplicity of a plot with some describable beginning and some foreseeable end.

Bendrix, however, cannot, and the very discontinuity of his narrative might in itself suggest that inability if Bendrix did not continue to remind us of it himself: "If this book of mine fails to take a straight course, it is because I am lost in a strange region: I have no map" (pp. 56-57). And again later: "If I were writing a novel I would end it here: a novel, I used to think, has to end somewhere, but I'm beginning to believe my realism has been at fault all these years, for nothing in life ever seems to end" (p. 179). Like Edouard in Gide's *Counterfeiters*, Bendrix feels the inability of traditional literary methods to encompass life. In one sense, then, the choppiness of Bendrix's narrative with its endless backtrackings, its digressions, its hints, reflects, even before Bendrix admits to it, a genuine fear of making some frontal attack on the evidence of his own and Sarah's lives and their potential significance. But implicit too, though less discernible, in the ruptured chronology of *The End of the Affair* is Bendrix's antagonism toward time: his recognition, invoking as it does Augustine, of that harrowing sense of transiency of thought, memory, and desire which keeps man from holding fast to *any* mode of love or truth.

This attitude of the novelist toward time has been described with some justice by Jean-Paul Sartre in his essay on François Mauriac's *La Fin de la Nuit*. There Sartre indicates that the "real [i.e. the nonbelieving] novelist is stirred by things that offer resistance; he is excited by doors because they must be opened, by envelopes because they must be unsealed." In his work, Sartre feels, such a novelist is joyously challenged by the sense of time, and it is one of his working tools. But certain Catholic writers—and Mauriac is Sartre's instance here—have none of the "real" novelist's "fondness for the Bergsonian necessity of waiting for the sugar to melt," more specifically, for describing in their novels the way in which characters *gradually* change in the course of time, how they remember and forget, how they learn, or how they sense the painful or pleasurable immediacy of the present, how they sometimes even come to anticipate or fear the yet unknown future. "To him," Sartre says of Mauriac, "his creatures's time is a dream, an all too human illusion; he gets rid of it and resolutely sets himself up with the eternal."[11]

Whatever else, Sartre's contradistinctions point up the polarities of Bendrix's transition, for the novel finds Bendrix increasingly dissatisfied with his own novelist's heightened sense of transiency and the way in which it has robbed him of Sarah's love and made him aware of his own dehumanization. For, as Bendrix says, "I never lose the consciousness of time: to me the present is never here: it is always last year or next week" (p. 57). Unlike Sarah, who seems imaginatively impervious to conceptual time, Bendrix ". . . couldn't bring down that curtain round the moment. I couldn't forget and I couldn't not fear" (p. 57). Until he discovers that he has, in an even more disconcerting sense, never lost Sarah's love, Bendrix's memories of Sarah are only bitter; they are reminders of how his inescapable sense of duration caused him to turn love into a "love affair" which in turn he had helplessly pushed to what he thought—but now doubts—was its conclusion: "Deliberately," Bendrix remarks, "I would put the caustic soda of that word 'affair,' with its suggestions of a beginning and an end, upon my tongue" (p. 64).

In his presaintly life Augustine might well have understood Bendrix's recriminations, though he later grappled with the vagaries of time in Book XI of his own Confessions, establishing categories that might give palpable immediacy to his faith in God and spiritual truths: "There are three times," he noted, "a present of things past, a present of things present, and a present of things future. For these three do somehow exist in the soul, and otherwise I see them not: present of things past, memory; present of things present, sight; present of things future, expectation."[12] That formula Bendrix accepts—but gallingly. For past memory and future expectation at best intensify his sense of loss, emptiness, and doubt, so that in spite of his denial he can perceive the present, both negatively in the recognition of his own unhappiness and more tangibly in the unrelenting pressure of his own will: "The sense of unhappiness is so much easier to convey than that of happiness. In misery we seem aware of our own existence, even though it may be in the form of a monstrous egotism" (p. 52). It is only death, Bendrix surmises, and less often physical love, that alone may annihilate consciousness and its cruel sense of time and self:

Death never mattered at those times—in the early days I even used to pray for it. . . . I have wondered sometimes whether eternity might not after all exist as the endless prolongation of the moment of death, and that was the moment I would have chosen, that I would still choose if she were alive, the moment of absolute trust and absolute pleasure, the moment when it was impossible to quarrel because it was impossible to think. (pp. 80-81)

That moment, with its unalloyed sense of release, Bendrix recalls achieving but once; and, as always in Greene's dialectical mystique, it occurred at the point of death, the instant of the bomb's concussion outside his flat:

My mind for a few minutes was clear of everything except a sense of tiredness as though I had been on a long journey. I had no memory at all of Sarah and I was completely free from anxiety, jealousy, insecurity, hate: my mind was a blank sheet on which somebody had just been on the point of writing a message of happiness. I felt sure that when my memory came back, the writing would continue and that I would be happy. (p. 82)

Barring the ultimate extinction of death, Bendrix recognizes that it is only the equally ineffable and more transient happiness of sexual love—and *perhaps* Sarah's mode of spiritual love—that can provide any release.

The words of human love have been used by the saints to describe their vision of God: and so, I suppose, we might use the terms of prayer, dedication, contemplation to explain the intensity of love we feel for a woman. We too surrender memory, intellect, intelligence, and we too experience the deprivation, the *noche oscura,* and sometimes as a reward a kind of peace. It is odd to find myself writing these phrases as though I loved what in fact I hate. Sometimes I don't recognize my own thoughts. What do I know of phrases like 'the dark night' or of prayer, who have only one prayer? I have inherited them, that is all, like a husband who is left by death in the useless possession of a woman's clothes, scents, pots of cream. . . . And yet there was this peace. . . . (p. 52)

All "memory, intellect, intelligence," it seems, even the coercion of the language the novelist feels called upon to

use and his lost hope of death, lead Bendrix back to Sarah
and the desperate alternative she and her remaining diary
represent, offering as they do proof that one may escape,
albeit painfully, from time and self. R. W. B. Lewis is surely
right when he sees Greene implying that "one must travel
again the ancient way of negation, in a steady denial of
ordinary human categories of perception and judgment."[13]
But of Sarah, Bendrix recalls that unlike himself she had
never had much faith in her own judgment or perceptions;
and in her diary he discovers that she found it hard to
follow any path *but* the straight and narrow. All she could
do in fact was cry out in the pitched accents of Augustine:
"I'm tired and I don't want any more pain. I want Maurice.
I want ordinary corrupt human love. Dear God, you know
I want Your pain, but I don't want it now. Take it away for
a while and give it to me another time" (pp. 148-49). And
all Bendrix can do now is to echo that cry in his "only
prayer," since he too feels "only the memory of desire."
Neither the novelist's insight nor his methods can relieve
the trying uncertainty of his own life.

In this respect then the first words Bendrix reads in
Sarah's diary become an ironic anticipation of his own
predicament: "I have no need to write to you or talk to you,
you know everything before I can speak, but when one
loves, one feels the need to use the same old ways one has
always used. I know I am only beginning to love, but
already I want to abandon everything, everybody but you:
only fear and habit prevent me" (p. 59). Curiously, Bendrix
also feels that need to write and, in the manner of a confession, to talk. For he, too, has begun to sense the beginnings of love. His reflections on Sarah are thus, at first at
least, a literary means of restoring Sarah, to his own mind
more than to the reader's, in some corporeal form, as something other than a shadowy memory with its fearful predica-

tion of her last and unassailable lover. But "the old ways"
fail Bendrix:

> How can I make a stranger see her . . . ? It has always seemed
> to me that in a novel the reader should be allowed to imagine
> a character in any way he chooses. . . . Now I am betrayed by
> my own technique, for I do not want any other woman sub-
> stituted for Sarah, I want the reader to see one broad forehead
> and bold mouth, the conformation of the skull, but all I can
> convey is an indeterminate figure turning in the dripping mac-
> intosh, saying, "Yes, Henry?" and then "You?" She had always
> called me "you" . . . so that I imagined, like a fool, for a few
> minutes at a time, that there was only one "you" in the world and
> that was me. (pp. 15-16)

If James's dictum to dramatize, which Bendrix has followed,
fails him here in this extraliterary purpose he would put it
to, the novelist's habit allows him at a climactic moment in
the novel to objectify his own emerging "religious sense";
to conceive what God and the saints must be like if they
exist at all, and how he may look from their point of view:

> Always I find when I begin to write there is one character
> who obstinately will not come alive. There is nothing psycho-
> logically false about him, but he sticks, he has to be pushed
> around. . . .
> And yet one cannot do without him. I can imagine a God
> feeling in just that way about some of us. The saints, one would
> suppose, in a sense create themselves. They come alive. They
> are capable of the surprising act or word. They stand outside the
> plot, unconditioned by it. But we have to be pushed around.
> We have the obstinacy of non-existence. We are inextricably
> bound to the plot, and wearily God forces us, here and there,
> according to his intention, characters without poetry, without
> free will, whose only importance is that somewhere, at some time,
> we help to furnish the scene in which a living character moves
> and speaks, providing perhaps the saints with the opportunities
> for *their* free will. (p. 229)[14]

Bendrix's description here remains, to be sure, but the
correlative of his own nagging suspicion. It adumbrates

Lewis's suggestion that in all of his novels Greene has sought to suggest that no one can "peep through the eye of God." But what of the novelist—and especially the religious novelist? Is he especially privileged, or does he not in the conscious act of creation usurp God's perfect perspective? This is the very question Sartre raises and answers in his essay on Mauriac. That essay is a critical byproduct of the larger polemic debate between equally articulate French existentialist and French Catholic writers, but since Greene has obliquely participated in both the literary and ethical issues of that argument, Sartre's essay and Greene's subsequent defense of Mauriac are relevant here, for they suggest the rationale of Greene's unprecedented use of the first person point of view in *The End of the Affair*.

Sartre's essay on the last of Mauriac's Thérèse novels points to what he feels is a ruinously obvious and dialectic use of the point of view. He cites the manner in which Mauriac intermittently invests his third person narration with the quality of omniscience, betraying at such times his commitment to a closed and static vision of reality, one which has the effect of robbing the reader of the illusion that Mauriac's heroine is free. The existentialist writer indicates those places in which Mauriac shifts between what Sartre calls *"elle-sujet"* and *"elle-objet";* more specifically, between Thérèse as a viewer and judge of reality and Thérèse as she is viewed and judged by Mauriac, between her uncritical and intuitive sense of herself and what she feels to be her "real self," which is—so Sartre discerns—that spiritually destined self Mauriac has created for her. It is clear, Sartre feels, that "for M. Mauriac, freedom differs from slavery in *value,* and not in nature. Any intention directed upwards, toward Good, is free; any will to Evil is fettered. Sartre bypasses direct discussion of "the intrinsic worth of this ordering principle." Instead, he devastatingly accuses Mauriac of falling prey to the sin of pride:

M. Mauriac has put himself first. He has chosen divine omniscience and omnipotence. But novels are written *by* men *for*
men. In the eyes of God, Who cuts through appearances and
goes beyond them, there is no novel, no art, for art thrives on
appearances. God is not an artist. Neither is M. Mauriac. (pp.
11-13)

Neither is Maurice Bendrix, and in creating him Greene
may be demonstrating that he has since felt the full impact
of Sartre's condemnation. Though Greene in a letter referring to a review of *The Quiet American* has decried the
finding of overly literal correspondence between himself
and one of his imagined characters, he had earlier defended
and still maintains the writer's privilege to impose some of
his own beliefs upon the sensibility of his character, even
and especially when that character speaks with what Sartre
called "the dizzying-intimacy of the *I*."[15] In his own essay
on Mauriac, Greene opposed the Sartrian view of the novelist,
commending Mauriac's interposing of himself between his
readers and his own characters. Mauriac's violations of the
rules of art are, Greene felt, the traditional right of the
novelist, one which writers like Joyce and Woolf misguidedly
relinquished hoping to find order in Art, and significance
in those buried psychological layers from which they felt
human behavior arises.

M. Mauriac's first importance to an English reader, therefore, is
that he belongs to the company of great traditional novelists: he
is a writer for whom the visible world has not ceased to exist,
whose characters have the solidity and importance of men with
souls to save or lose, and a writer who claims the traditional and
essential right of a novelist, to comment, to express his views.
For how tired we are of the dogmatically 'pure' novel, the tradition founded by Flaubert and reaching its magnificent torturous
climax in the works of Henry James. . . . I am not denying the
greatness of either Flaubert or James. The novel was ceasing to
be an aesthetic form and they recalled it to the aesthetic conscience. It was later writers who by accepting the technical

dogma blindly made the novel the dull devitalized form (form it retained) that it has become. The exclusion of the author can go too far. Even the author, poor devil, has a right to exist, and M. Mauriac reaffirms that right. It is true that the Flaubertian form is not so completely abandoned in this novel [*La Pharisienne*] as in *Le Baiser au Lepreux;* the 'I' of the story plays a part in the action; any commentary there can be attributed by purists to this fictional 'I', but the pretence is thin—'I' is dominated by I.

Thus, in opposition to Sartre's '*elle-sujet*' and '*elle-objet*' Greene invokes his own disjunctive mode of narration: the 'I' which is the narrator and the I which is the authentic voice of the author himself; he finds both in Shakespeare and Mauriac that those moments in their works when the " 'I' has ceased to speak" and the "I is speaking" are the most important, more important even than the characters and, in the manner of Bendrix's description of the saints, "unconfined and unconditioned by plot."[16]

Though Bendrix seems then to embody the supposition that the novelist is least of all fit to comment with any accuracy or ultimate validity on the truth of man's life or destiny, one might expect then that Greene has not altogether discarded the novelist's traditional right to comment. If indeed such moments of extracontextual intrusion do exist at all in *The End of the Affair,* they are at least as difficult to sense as they are in Shakespeare's plays, and Greene's method, at once more complex and more ingenious than that of Mauriac, is proof against the weapons Sartre brought to bear on *La Fin de la Nuit* to find the author's hand visibly and disconcertingly at work in that novel, for in this "novel about a novelist" the pretence is understandably thicker. Yet, if as Greene leads one to suspect those moments of intrusion have a significance which stands apart from the plot, the characters, and the contextual meaning of the novel, one which is well worth noting, then I imagine they occur not so much during Bendrix's discoveries of his writing practices as when the narrator despairingly confesses his distrust in human nature, in his own inescapable will, and in Art itself—just as Greene himself did in responding to the fiction of Leon Bloy.

We read with pleasure to just the extent that we share the hatred of life which prevented him from being a novelist or a mystic of the first order (he might have taken as his motto Gaughin's great phrase—'Life being what it is, one dreams of revenge') and because of a certain indestructible honesty and self-knowledge which in the long run always enabled him to turn his fury on himself, as when in one of his letters he recognizes the presence of 'that bitch literature' penetrating 'even the most naif stirrings of my heart.'[17]

Surely, one feels, at those moments when Bendrix expresses this measure of Bloy's rankling discontent, " 'I' has ceased to speak, I is speaking."

Nor should it be surprising that a writer capable of so intricately conceived and executed a novel as *The End of the Affair* should yet respond to Bloy's indictment of 'that bitch literature' and its desiccating effects on the emotional springs of human love. Jacques Maritain noted that this kind of despair which permeates the novel has been a chronic symptom in Catholic writers.

Dealing with this particular situation of the novelist, and the relationship between his work on the one hand, and, on the other hand, his own soul and the souls of others, but especially of his own soul, Mauriac wrote: "Il faudrait être un saint . . . Mais alors on n'écrirait pas de roman." "One would have to be a saint. But then one would not write novels."

Thus the question is posed by Mauriac in terms of the supreme perfection of human life, or of *sainthood*. For Leon Bloy it was obviously posed in these terms. "If Art is part of my baggage," he said, "so much the worse for me! My only recourse is the expedient of placing at the service of Truth what has been given me by the Father of Lies." To one degree or another, we find the same sort of anxiety in Bernanos, in Graham Greene, still more in Julian Greene.[18]

By his own admission and the less tangible evidence of this novel, Greene has shown that he subscribed in some measure to Bloy's suspicion of the demoniac presumptuousness and desensitizing effects of Art. Has he also, one wonders, come to share Bloy's disposition to place his Art at the service of the Truth of his faith? R. W. B. Lewis suspects that he may have, that in his Catholic novels and plays Greene has of late been attempting to "befuddle" his readers and audiences, seeing to it that "Doubt is gradually shed over the whole *human* order of discourse and experience, until it is annihilated as a meaningful and valuable order: inducing in us a desperation of the senses until we, too, can . . . make the leap and desperately infer the divine perspective from the ruins of the human."[19] Clearly, that suspicion seems to be borne out by Greene's ambiguous "miracles" which in these later works are more indigenous to the plot and meaning than they are in *Brighton Rock* and *The Power and the Glory;* and in *The End of the Affair* by having those "miracles" recounted by what seems at first an angry nonbeliever, one who baldly states on the first page of the novel that "this is a record of hate far more than of love," only to have him end his narrative with that last doubt-filled prayer which he has long withheld from his readers:

I write at the start that this was a record of hate, and walking there beside Henry toward the evening glass of beer, I found the one prayer that seemed to serve the winter mood: O God, You've done enough, You've robbed me of enough, I'm too tired and old to love, leave me alone forever. (p. 237)

That Greene has led his narrator into doubt and toward the brink of belief less by those miracles which Bendrix angrily dismisses as coincidences than by Sarah herself and his own

discontent with consciousness and unrelieved bitterness, that
he leaves the novelist with at least the narrowest of choices
in committing himself to that extrahuman kind of love may
indicate that if Greene has truly fallen prey to didacticism,
he has, at least in this novel, not altogether succumbed to
bootlegging the ideals of his adopted creed in the manner
Mary McCarthy imputed to his plays.[20] For in this novel
Greene is yet somewhat closer to his French counterpart,
Georges Bernanos, who also recognized, as Bendrix and
Greene seem to, that

miracles overwhelm the mind but harden the heart because they
give the impression of an ugly summons, a kind of violation of
judgment and conscience by a fact which is, in appearance at
least, a violation of order. . . . Coercion for coercion, it would
have been so much easier to hold us once and for all by recon-
ciling the human will to the Divine Will, in the manner of a
planet spinning around its sun. But God didn't want to make
us irresponsible, by which I mean incapable of love, for there is
no responsibility without freedom, and love is a free choice or
it is nothing at all. (pp. 227-29)

If Greene has in some more complex way than Bloy
hopefully intended to make his later Catholic novels and
plays the handmaiden of the Truth of his faith and attempted implicitly to coerce others as well to make the leap,
either blindly or by choice, he has, I suspect, made few
converts—a fact which is testified to by Miss McCarthy's
outrage at *The Potting Shed* and the subreligious titillation
she claims to have sensed in the play's audience. One may
only surmise, of course, whether or not Greene did indeed
have in mind some extraliterary intent in these works, and
if so what that intent was. Against Miss McCarthy's re-
sentful suspicion of his plays and Lewis's assertion that
Greene does in fact have some other than dramatic purpose,
I offer another hypothesis, one that is in keeping with
Greene's stated claim that far from trying to provide edifica-

tion he has sought in his fiction only to dramatize a personal morality, which bears but a coincidental resemblance to that of Catholicism. I suggest that Greene, in the manner Rayner Heppenstal once described, has been testing that personal morality of his against what he may continue to feel is the spongier morality of the civilized world. The sophisticated technique of Greene's works often blinds one to the primitive notions which underly them; they may blind us as well to the essentially childish (an adjective Greene would never find offensive, nor is it here meant to be) function they seek to perform, a function, which, as Heppenstal implies, yet ties him in some prophetic way to that "sinless empty graceless chromium world" his writings only intermittently disconcert:

A fiction is the testing of a myth, a lie told by a child wishing and yet fearful to gain general acceptance for its private fantasies. A novel is a lie put about by an author to test the credulity of the world around him. That even the most extravagant lies are widely believed is the cause of momentary exaltation and then of anxiety and fixed depression in authors. A fiction is a personal myth, a myth not generally applicable. It is a masquerade and an act of defiance. Let us not be taken in by the general pronouncements of Bloy, Bernanos, Mauriac, Greene. Or rather let us accept the seriousness of their attachment without ever supposing that their works are anything but anti-social in origin. Their potency as novelists is increased by their religious adherence. The defiance and misleading of a world in which you do not believe offers little excitement.[21]

If Greene continues to allow his plays to propagate those lies, it may be that he has found in the theatre a larger and more impervious audience to test his personal myth, the drama itself a quicker vehicle. But whatever genre or vocabulary he chooses to express it in, Greene's vision, with its denial of complacent notions of human nature and the ultimate worth of human intelligence, with its insistence on the complementary necessity of gratuitous love in the face of man's almost inescapable egotism, is one that *ought* to persist in testing us. For the alternatives, so Greene maintains, are death or despair, and the bait of Greene's antisocial lies may, like those of Freud, snare a carp of truth.[22]

Robert O. Evans

THE SATANIST FALLACY OF
BRIGHTON ROCK

Brighton Rock, THE sordid tale of an adolescent
gangster, Greene's first essay in the religious, as opposed to
the secular, vein, presents many obstacles to understanding
and appreciation, some mirrored by the critics. For example, H. R. Haber has written, "Given Macbeth's conscience and social stature Pinkie might also be re-enacting
that blood drenched drama in modern dress."[1] Though
Haber is quite aware that Pinkie Brown, aged seventeen,
almost totally lacks those qualities requisite for a tragic
hero, he nevertheless finds reasons to call the book "a kind
of tragic drama," and R. W. B. Lewis would seem to agree,
for he has said, "*Brighton Rock* betrays an initial confusion
between what Greene calls an 'entertainment' and what he
finally offers as tragedy,"[2] and later, "the tragedy is Pinkie's
... its action is defined in advance by the book's motto, from
the *Witch of Edmonton,* with overtones of *Macbeth*—'This
were a fine reign: / To do ill and not hear of it again.'"[3]

With respect to that motto the critics, Haber as well as
Lewis, are perhaps mistaken, for in the first place the *Witch
of Edmonton* is not tragedy at all but rather a tragicomedy,

and Greene's reference at the beginning of the book, clearly calculated to reveal something of the ensuing plot structure, may be to that fact—that the book is intended as a sort of tragicomedy. In the play by Dekker, Ford, and Rowley, Thorney marries Susan Carter, for low motives, and subsequently murders her. In *Brighton Rock* Pinkie marries Rose for equally reprehensible motives—so that she cannot testify against him—and presently attempts to murder her, by persuading her to enter a suicide pact. In both cases the overtones from *Macbeth,* excepting the blood which is ever-present in melodrama, are accidental. And an interpretation of Pinkie Brown as a tragic hero is untenable; he has none of the necessary qualities. To claim that he does distorts otherwise brilliant analyses of the novel, but Greene, like Milton, has come to suffer his Satanist fallacy.

Perhaps both critics are overly influenced by the fact that the first American edition of *Brighton Rock* announced the book as an "entertainment." They seem to imply that Greene develops, in a sense, organically, somehow feeling his way from "entertainment" to "novel," a view not subscribed to by John Atkins in his book *Graham Greene.* Greene himself made the initial mistake of first calling *Brighton Rock* an "entertainment," and it does not seem to have helped much to change the designation. One reviewer, perhaps encouraged by what he read on the preliminary page, called the book "a masterpiece of horror," suggesting an inability to distinguish it from Greene's other "entertainments." The point may not, after all, be a very important one, for Greene nowhere pretends that his "entertainments" are potboilers, as Faulkner did of *Sanctuary.* Greene has said that he has a horror of "books, written without truth, without compulsion, books to read while you wait for the bus, while you strap-hang . . . a whole industry founded on a want of leisure and a want of happiness"— like prostitution.[4] Whatever *Brighton Rock* is, it is not that, whether it began as an "entertainment" because Greene had accepted a large advance from his publisher and needed a success or whether it began as something else. Despite the label on the first American edition, I should contend that *Brighton Rock* was conceived as serious literature, that it was carefully planned from beginning to end, that it executes the author's intention satisfactorily, and—what is more—that one can demonstrate as much by close analysis of many passages in the book. While not entirely subservient to James's ideas, Greene is nevertheless quite capable of weaving a pattern into the carpet and leaving it there for us to discover.

To begin with Pinkie Brown is a precocious juvenile delinquent and, as Haber recognizes, lacks virtually all the conventional attributes of a tragic hero. With such a subject Greene faced a serious artistic difficulty. The book is about human struggle on the ethical and spiritual plane, about evil in the human soul. How was he to bring his reader to recognize its meaning without writing tragedy, for with Pinkie at its center tragedy was impossible if not preposterous? Doubtless there are ways Greene might have compromised, but he did not try. Instead he marshalled an array of impressive devices to make his meaning clear. For example, he employed a pervasive allegory.[5] He uses what one might call an "allusive structure." Lewis has pointed out that, in a sense, "Greene's novels [he is talking about *Brighton Rock, The Power and the Glory,* and *The Heart of the Matter* particularly] reverse the direction of the greatest religious trilogy, *The Divine Comedy,*"[6] and to Haber we are indebted for an analysis of the seven sections of *Brighton Rock* as inversions of the seven sacraments.[7] All of these varying readings reinforce the contention that Greene's intent here was serious. Moreover, Greene manages to create a sense of tremendous historical perspective and spatial extension,[8] which add a distinct dimension to his meaning, by attempting, like T. S. Eliot, to fuse disparate areas of experience into an organic, meaningful unity, and, thereby, to emphasize the kind of religious truth with which the book is concerned. Lewis has said, rather ambiguously, that "*Brighton Rock* belongs with the early and late medieval tradition, the tradition now again in fashion,"[9] and he might have added that it points forward to eternity. Still, if the contention is at all correct, it should end criticisms of Greene that see him as decadent or claim that his work is "pessimistic . . . in the last degree unhopeful and, as a result, unhelpful,"[10] for it is impossible to write seriously of religion in this fashion and remain unhopeful and unhelpful. One might as well apply such strictures to *Paradise Lost*.

In fact Greene's task is, in some respects, similar to Milton's: how to write of a protagonist with a difficult nature and maintain the serious artistic stature of the work? Perhaps Greene borrowed a page from Milton to guide his treatment of his central character, for Pinkie Brown, progressively perverting the sacraments, surely descends in stature throughout the work, until at the end he is damned for all eternity. As Sean O'Casey has said rightly of Pinkie, but wrongly of Rose, "The roman catholic girl of sixteen and the boy of seventeen, respectively, are the most stupid and evil mortals a man's mind could imagine."[11] And again, "If one can be sure of anything . . . Pinkie Brown is damned."[12]

In fact Pinkie, like Milton's Satan, gathers exactly what he has sown. It is worth pointing out that if he were a real tragic hero, in a work with a well-constructed plot, the reader ought not to come to that conclusion. But with *Brighton Rock* it proves more interesting to investigate the means by which Greene conveys his serious intention, given the conditions with which he has decided to work. For one thing Greene finds some of his answers for a means of linking disparate experience—medieval Christianity with modern Brighton with eternal damnation—in modern poetry. He may have read Pound's "A Few Don'ts by an Imagiste"; at any rate he employed a mode of communication in which a complex idea is presented instantaneously, yielding an effect of "sudden liberation, that sense of freedom from time and space limits."[13] A common example of this method cited from *Brighton Rock*, usually with the intention of illustrating Greene's cinematic technique, is the scene in the cars going up the hill out of Brighton towards the race track.

However Greene developed his esthetic, his acquaintance with Eliot is surely clear enough. The images in *Brighton Rock* "owe a good deal to Eliot's *Waste Land*: the broken window, the ouija board, the Cosmopolitan Hotel, death by water."[14] A French critic, Paul Rostenne, has argued that Greene had no "edifying purpose" in writing, and Lewis has cited his authority to support his contention that "the very design of the book shifts and reforms,"[15] but when one recognizes Greene's indebtedness to Eliot, it begins to seem less likely that he allowed the characters to run away with the book, changing it, as it were, from "entertainment" to "novel." In fact Eliot almost rings the theme of the book himself in "The Fire Sermon," especially when he quotes from Verlaine, "*Et O ces voix d'enfants, chantant dans le coupole!*"

There are other allusions even more specific than the images cited; for example, "A secretary trotted a little way behind him, reading out from a list. 'Bananas, oranges, grapes, peaches. . . .' 'Hothouse?' 'Hothouse.' 'Who's that?' Ida Arnold said." Who indeed but T. S. Eliot? "The waiter brings in oranges, bananas, figs, and hothouse grapes." It is typical of Greene's style that he forces the reader to answer Ida Arnold's question and, thus, recognize the allusion. The literal answer to the question "Who's that?" is, of course, the gangster Colleoni, a minor character whose name is borrowed from James's *Aspern Papers*, but the repetition of the word *hothouse* surely makes the reader associate the passage with Eliot. If anything Greene may be forcing the allusion; the device is, of course, quite deliberate. The connection is for the benefit of the reader; Ida Arnold could not have made it, for her reading tastes ran to Warwick Deeping, a writer whom Greene considered to be "without truth or compulsion."

Greene might not agree with Turgenev that a writer's worst sin is not to write well, but he certainly writes well himself, at least in a technical sense. He is an accomplished craftsman; *Brighton Rock* is the work of a trained artist with several good books under his belt. In it Greene pays the closest attention to verisimilitude, probability, and structure. Haber has described what he called his allusive structure, but a simpler analysis of structure is also rewarding. Greene begins the plot with focus on Fred Hale, the initial victim, and to a lesser extent on Ida Arnold, the avenger, rather than on Pinkie Brown, the central character. It would seem that Greene deliberately wanted the first crime to be committed before concentrating on Pinkie so that the downward progression could go on uninterrupted. He did not choose to show Pinkie before the crime in a state his audience might mistake for relative innocence. Pinkie is already on the path to damnation by the time the focus shifts to him.

When Greene turns to the job of uniting disparate areas of experience and vast perspectives of time, he employs a series of devices, few of which are in themselves notable. The first to which I should like to call attention is a minor image, which is repeated in the novel. It deals with birds, one of Greene's favorite images, but this time not his favorite species: "A seagull flew straight towards him between the pillars," he wrote, at a moment when the gangster, Spicer, overcome by fear sought in an irrational flight to evade the inexorability of his punishment (i.e. space and time): "Like a scared bird caught in a cathedral, then swerved out into the sunlight from the dark iron nave." The image is a metaphorical complex, at its simplest level comparing the gull with a frightened bird (presently I shall suggest a sparrow) and with Spicer himself, who is, in the slang of the streets, literally a "frightened bird." It may have been encouraged by a reference to the *Waste Land*, to "Death by Water," where Eliot wrote of a sort of surrender where "Phlebas the Phoenician, a fortnight dead, / Forgot the cry of gulls, and the deep sea swell / And the profit and loss." The situation could appropriately be applied to Spicer, who has indeed forgotten all the cautions of life. In a moment he will allow himself to be photographed by a street photographer, an incident which will lead directly to his death. But the image is much more complicated, for it suggests that life is a sort of cathedral, an edifice of precious value, and one who takes life—Spicer, too, was a murderer—is trapped in an iron prison, a cathedral with no exits (as Sartre might have said). Spicer had good reason to be afraid; if the law did not catch up with him, through the efforts of Ida Arnold, the gang would, and when they discovered his fear they would slay him as relentlessly as they had Hale. Furthermore, as the passage progresses there is a suggestion, psychologically correct, that fear leads to remorse, and thus to repentance, or conversion (in *Brighton Rock*, it seems to me, they amount to much the same thing). The main concern of the novel is the pervasive potentiality of this repentance.

Thus what we find actually operative in this small, seemingly insignificant passage is something akin to Cassirer's principle of symbolic forms. One is reminded of Virginia Woolf's contrasting of the lower temporal world with a moment of vision in *To the Lighthouse*. There she manages to attain something epic, or timeless, much as

Greene in his sordid, seedy world stretches out towards eternity. Lewis has said that the rhetoric of the book progresses by "a series of oxymorons, or seeming contradictions, which sometimes appear as strained or perverse but often arresting similies,"[16] used, he says, largely to destroy conventional morality. So it is with Greene's literary allusions. In this image the sordid milieu of the backstreet is connected with a great cathedral—iron, it would seem, not only to symbolize Spicer's imprisonment in the condition in which he finds himself, but also to show that life is a sort of prison and true morality a hard business. Conduct for Greene is always a serious matter. The purpose of the image is to relate the disparate reality of a modern, brutal world to the ideals of Christianity. This subject is of vital interest to the writer: "Today our world seems peculiarly susceptible to brutality," he said in *Journey Without Maps.*[17]

Unlike the earlier Eliot allusion, which is less hidden and is more typical of Greene's technique, this image is handled with such delicacy that its significance to plot and theme may escape all but the most careful reader. An oversight would not be fatal, however, for the image is primarily devoted to an explication of Spicer's predicament, and Spicer is only a minor character. There is no doubt anyhow that he did not die in a state of grace; it would constitute a violation of verisimilitude if he had. Why, then, trouble to include such a subtle image at all? Lewis has argued that Greene uses a stylistic technique "which may be best defined as a technique of befuddlement and concerning which one has the uneasy suspicion of mere cleverness."[18] When Greene is being cinematic, the stricture is sometimes appropriate, but for this particular image (and others like it elsewhere in Greene's work) it is not difficult to construct a separate rationale. Greene is using it to contrast the transitory nature of life with eternity and thus relate a minor incident to his theme, to indicate the possibility of salvation which is always open to all men. After all, that is what the book is about; Greene tells us so time and time again. He is also preparing the reader for something he wants to say about a far more important character than Spicer, about Pinkie himself; thus shortly he repeats the image, slightly altered, in a passage in which he describes an old man walking along the shore: "The gulls which had stood like candles down the beach rose and cried under the promenade . . . a gull dropped from the parade and swept through the iron nave of the palace pier, white and purposeful in the obscurity: half vulture and half dove."

Now the image is even more complex than before, and rightfully so because of its intensified relationship to Pinkie. A preamble has been added in which the gulls stand like candles on an altar, appropriate when one remembers that the essential difference between Pinkie and Spicer is that Pinkie was reared a Catholic. The flight has become "white and purposeful," as the journey through life should be for a Catholic. Nevertheless, the bird (and, one presumes, the man it symbolizes) remains "half vulture and half dove," strongly suggesting the dualistic vision of life to which Greene seems to subscribe. He may have found the concept in Plato or St. Augustine, or even in T. S. Eliot.[19] Where it comes from is not important. What he does with it is what matters, for the unfolding of the book is revealed by it. Greene is not so much dualistic in a metaphysical sense as he is in a special theological one. He posits the existence of separate principles of good and evil in the world but insists on their interconnection. As Plato did, he holds a notion of a medium connecting, one could say, "the eternality of being with the fluency of becoming."[20] With perfect aplomb he quotes, *Corruptio optimi est pessima.* Hence Pinkie becomes evil though he began, we are told, with aspirations towards the priesthood. Literary critics have made much of this aspect of Greene's metaphysic, usually failing to recognize that the position is not especially uncommon to Catholics. It depends on the doctrine of Immanence.

In the revised version of the image the street, which was the abode of Spicer, is changed to the Palace Pier, possibly for distinction of the characters, but we cannot forget the connection of a pier with water, and, as the old hymn says, of water with the Word. Thus Pinkie is deliberately revealed to rest closer to possible salvation than Spicer, because he is a Cátholic, though at the same time he runs a greater risk of damnation. A paradox is implicit in the image: that the Catholic is closer to God and at the same time closer to Satan. Greene, however, does not rely on this passage to make that point; he says so plainly.

At the instant Greene invokes the image of the gull Pinkie is rested on the verge of what might have been a selfless action. It is a significant instant in the narrative: as Blake said in *Jerusalem*, "Events of Time start forth & are conceived in such a Period / Within a Moment." The image appears just at Pinkie's instant of crisis; it is immediately followed by a discussion (and explanation) of his proposed marriage to Rose, who personifies innocence (not absolute good, for innocence itself is not an active virtue, despite Greene's remark, "What was most evil in him needed her; it couldn't get along without her goodness").

Greene has been said to derive remotely from Kafka,[21] and perhaps there is a sign of that derivation in the illogicality of this situation. Pinkie is prepared to marry Rose to prevent her from testifying against him, but he seems to believe that the marriage would prevent her testifying against the rest of the gang as well. The passage is vitally important, for the marriage is the last positive action Pinkie takes in the entire narrative that might have set him on the road to salvation. If it had been a selfless act (as the reader wishes) it might turn Pinkie from a life of criminal violence; it might even lead him back to the church. But Greene never gives the marriage a chance, and indeed in the eyes of the church there is no marriage at all. Pinkie and Rose are living in sin. To make the point meaningful Greene suggests that any action in life, especially on an ethical plane, has two possible interpretations; it is half vulture and half dove. In such a view of reality Greene's edifying purpose, which Rostenne could not discover at all, lies. Accordingly, I believe he is making a serious attempt in *Brighton Rock* (as in the other serious works) to come to terms with ethics in the modern world. However, unsatisfactory the solution may seem to the reader, it is certainly not unique in literature. Conrad offers a somewhat similar ethic in *The Heart of Darkness;* notice Marlow's lie to obtain rivets (bad, though effective) compared with his lie to obtain peace of mind for Kurtz' fiancee (good, though possibly not very effective). It was for this knowledge—that it was not the action that mattered so much as the intention that lay behind it—that Marlow went to Africa. And with Greene, beyond the point of the marriage, once Pinkie acted from the wrong motives, there was nothing that could save him, except of course the omnipresent possibility of repentance: "Between the stirrup and the ground" any man *can* be saved.

Salvation, however, requires a conscious effort of will, and Pinkie finds that in the instant of death there is no time, though for him there has always been plenty of time to make an effort of will directed towards evil. The metaphysic of *Brighton Rock* requires an act of will for both good and evil. Greene deliberately says so, though he sometimes states his case negatively: "You could lose vice as easily as you lost virtue, going out of you from a touch."[22] The touch that threatens Pinkie is Rose's, and he is careful not to allow it to become effective. Throughout the book Pinkie is hellbent on damnation, and it is this fact that gives rise to a 'satanist fallacy' and prevents his being a tragic hero.

In Pinkie's situation there is almost unbearable irony in the fact that one who is aware of and perhaps in touch with the whole history of corporate Christianity, perhaps eternity as well, cannot spare a moment for God. It is the dilemma of the bad Catholic, but it is not necessarily tragic. Moreover, Greene never allows any real possibility of saving Pinkie. As a moralist he could not do so, and in the end Pinkie gets what he deserves. As Greene leads up to the ending, he tries to destroy any stray sympathy for Pinkie that the reader may retain by prodding him from one obscenity into another. Moreover, his crimes become more and more meaningless. He slays Spicer and plans to murder Rose when any selfrespecting, adult gangster would be occupied with plans for wiping out the rival mob. Greene very lightly conceals this idiocy (for verisimilitude, one presumes) by suggesting that Pinkie is committing one murder to cover for another. There is nothing new in that; it is part of the melodramatic machinery of the detective story. Pinkie is a difficult character to manage, and Greene cannot afford to make him into an obvious blunderer nor into a desperate criminal, bent on commiting one crime after another to avoid detection. What he required at the end of his book was a serpent (a problem analogous to Milton's), and, as many critics have noted, the record he made for Rose, which outlasts him, accomplished that much. "God damn you, you little bitch," he spoke into the microphone, "Why can't you go back home forever and let me be?" For the sheer force of its evil I know of nothing to equal this passage short of Milton's Satan: "Hate stronger, under shew of Love well feign'd, / The way which to her ruin now I tend." So relentlessly Pinkie drives himself to damnation, and Greene, perhaps unwittingly, to his own Satanist fallacy.

By its metaphorical associations—sometimes direct and sometimes paradoxical—the image of the gull, for one thing, helps make Greene's intention clear. Of all his works *Brighton Rock* (with possibly *The End of the Affair*) comes closest to Catholic apologetic. It is easier to recognize that fact when one realizes that the gull image is a lightly veiled literary allusion, not only to Eliot but to a memorable passage from the Venerable Bede as well, though of course Greene does not depend on the image as his sole means of explication. The passage from Bede to which I refer—the reader may already have remembered it—is the one relating to the conversion of King Edwin: "The present life of man, O King, seems to me, in comparison to that time which is unknown to us, like the swift flight of a sparrow through the room wherein you sit at supper in winter . . . If, therefore, this new doctrine contains something more certain, it seems justly to deserve to be followed." As rhetoric this image is now seen to serve Greene's purpose admirably by linking the ancient past with the present, the age of Bede (the beginning of Christianity) with that of Eliot (the modern dilemma), while maintaining direct focus on the theological issue.

It might be argued that an allusion so far removed in time could be quite accidental if it were not for the fact that Greene seems deliberately with the image to have been attempting to capture a moment of vision, an esthetic category whereon he might hang part of the meaning of the work. Moreover, the passage from Bede was surely familiar to him; if he did not remember it from his school days, he certainly must have from *King Solomon's Mines*, though Haggard there put it to little effective use: "Like a storm-driven bird at night we fly out of Nowhere; for a

moment our wings are seen in the light of the fire, and, lo,
we are gone again into the Nowhere. Life is nothing. Life
is all."[23] Just the sort of passage to appeal to Greene and set
him thinking—but no multiplicity of sources is necessary to
demonstrate that the reference is not accidental. Greene does
that by weaving the image into the structure of his narrative.
Of course he has altered the passage; the sparrow has become
a gull, perhaps in interests of locale and perhaps to suggest
The Waste Land. The hall has become a cathedral. But
the basic symbolic associations remain the same. Moreover Greene must have welcomed, if he did not seek, a
means of pulling together the centuries of Christian history into a moment of time. He had considered the idea
before, in *Journey Without Maps*: "There must have been
scenes very like this, I thought, in the last days of pagan
England, when a story about a bird flying through a lighted
hall played its part in the conversion of a king."[24] It is not
surprising he adopted the story, as an image, for *Brighton
Rock,* where it becomes a key, a sort of Jamesian pattern
in the carpet, to the significance of the whole book. The
ideas of repentance and conversion (Greene scarcely distinguishes between them) lie close to the central intention
of the work. And the image clearly illustrates his edifying
purpose, directed at Catholics, on the one hand, as repentance, and at non-Catholics, on the other, as conversion.

The question of Greene's double audience bears some
relation to the fallacy of considering Pinkie Brown as the
tragic hero of *Brighton Rock. Brighton Rock* is much more
than allegory lightly clothed in melodrama, though it is
that, too. In the book two structures parallel each other,
the immediate story of Pinkie and Rose, and the other story
of ageless religious conflict within the human soul. The
structures—they might even be called plots—cross and re-
cross each other, in a manner similar to the film technique

of "parallel montage."[25] Actually both are highly symbolic, for even the immediate story, it has been argued, is a saint's life in reverse.[26] Part of Greene's art is to set up a tension between the two structures, thereby achieving what we might in esthetic terminology call spatial form. It becomes desirable, however, to unite these structures now and then; otherwise tension may evaporate as the reader forgets one meaning in favor of another. That Greene does not wish to run that risk is clearly shown by examination of such cruxes as the gull image, one of the points of synthesis. Although it is easy enough to read *Brighton Rock* without being aware of Greene's bistructuring technique, the device plays a very important part in that work and in *The Power and the Glory*, a more important novel,[27] and in much of his serious writing. Indeed it has been said that most modern symbolic novels make some use of an esthetic concept of spatial form.[28]

Of course, to reveal the ethic and metaphysic of *Brighton Rock*, Greene employs other methods which serve to prevent serious distortion of the meaning (though to judge from the critics they have not always proved sufficient). One of these, also rhetorical, is the repetition of a theme in the form of a truncated phrase from the Ordinary of the Mass: *"Agnus dei, qui tollis peccata mundi,"* sometimes followed by *"Dona nobis pacem."* In either case the first quotation lacks a proper response, which is *"Miserere nobis."* The Catholic reader may, of course, supply it automatically. As this response is, in a sense, an ambiguous statement of the major theme of the book, the pervasiveness of God's mercy, it might have been desirable for Greene to have stated it outright. But it is one of his peculiarities to appeal separately to Catholic and non-Catholic readers.

Furthermore, he cannot afford, in terms of his characterization, to allow Rose or Pinkie, both backsliders, to re-

member their religious training too exactly. Too clear a
memory of religious training might interrupt Pinkie's plunge
to perdition and impinge on the probability of his evil
actions.

One critic has argued that the intention of *Brighton
Rock* is "to evoke the far, faint light of an incomprehensible
divine mercy."[29] While agreeing in substance, one might
rightfully demand qualification of the adjectives *far* and
faint. Greene states his theme plainly enough, though ironically, through the lips of the old priest to whom Rose
repairs for confession, at the very end of the book: "'You
can't conceive, my child, nor can I or anyone—the . . .
appalling . . . strangeness of the mercy of God.'" (Ellipsis
Greene's.) Nowhere is Greene more explicit; the old priest
cannot understand the extent of Pinkie's degradation, nor
can he take the measure of Rose's love. He is useful primarily to state this theme. He cannot even believe in
Satanism, and of course he did not know Pinkie, nor had he
heard his creed: *"Credo in unum Satanum."*

When Rose is contemplating suicide, the priest tries to
comfort her with a parable about a man who did unspeak-
able evil because he could not bear the idea of sinners being
damned. He wished to take their punishment on his
shoulders. He became a saint. In suggesting the Christ
image to Rose, though the reference is actually to Péguy,
the priest is implying that Pinkie may have been such a
one. Once before in *Brighton Rock* Greene has deliberately
suggested a Christ image, when Pinkie killed Spicer and
the 'cross' of wooden railing was placed on top of his body.
Both cases are of mistaken identify. It is perhaps regret-
table that Greene included them, for they seem to have
led some critics to believe that Greene is working from
an entrenched Jansenist position which denies free will.[30]

As I have pointed out, Pinkie wills his own damnation.
Rose, too, must will her fate, though the reader is not per-

mitted to know the outcome. Though her situation is indeed dismal, there is no reason to believe it hopeless. She must still face her trial when she plays Pinkie's phonograph record, but already she has taken a substantial step in the direction of salvation, as any Catholic will understand, by going to confession. It is true she cannot understand the priest, nor does he understand her. She is far too innocent; doubtless that is why she is called Rose. Innocence is an asset, but Greene never pretends it is any assurance of virtue. He remembers quite well that it supplied no very substantial protection for Eve. But innocence has kept Rose from selflove, an effect on character of Jansenism, and accordingly there is very real hope she will find salvation. She must, however, earn it.

At the end of *Brighton Rock* the focus of the work has shifted from Pinkie to Rose. Greene rightfully makes the shift; not many people, after all, are concerned with creating their own damnation, and it is really salvation that interests Greene. Besides he does have an edifying purpose. I believe the sexual imagery also supports such an interpretation. Pinkie is perverted; at only one instant in the story is he capable of normal sexual activity. Though Greene leaves uncertain Rose's premonition that she carried life, it is worth considering that Pinkie's evil has again backfired. This conception in fact gives Rose something to live for, rather than sinks her deeper into the trap of life. Such a view would be consistent with her selfless character and her innocence. Thus, there are at least two major considerations which encourage the reader to believe that Rose will find her salvation.

One further point requires mention; salvation is the subject of the novel. God's mercy is an all-pervasive possibility, not really difficult of attainment. In order to avoid it one must will to do evil. Greene carefully directs the reader to the belief that mercy is always there for the taking: *"Miserere nobis, miserere nobis."* So much mercy is offered throughout the book that the outcome should not be pessimistic, though doubtless life is very hard. To epitomize Pinkie's struggle and Rose's potential, one is tempted to recall the words of another Catholic writer, whom Greene in some respects resembles, Francis Thompson: "All things betray thee, who betrayest Me." Pinkie has fled Him down the nights and days and successfully evaded Him. But Rose and the audience, Catholic and non-Catholic—theirs is another story. Poor innocent Rose comes to the final page cherishing the illusion that she was loved by Pinkie as she loves the child in her womb. Will she learn better? "Ah, fondest, blindest, weakest, / I am He whom thou seekest!"

Kai Laitinen

THE HEART OF THE NOVEL:
THE TURNING POINT IN *THE*
HEART OF THE MATTER

THE FINNISH CRITIC and translator, J. A. Hollo, has
written an essay entitled "The Turning Point in Great
Novels."[1] As in plays, he says, in great novels there is often
a turning point, which sometimes may seem slight and
hardly noticeable. "Nevertheless, it is important for fully
understanding the work and its author. It constitutes an
elevation from which the reader may view the total land-
scape, examining the series of events both forward and
backward." (See the volume of essays, *Kohtaamiani*—"Some
of Those I Have Met.")

Even at my first reading of Graham Greene's novel,
The Heart of the Matter, I had a strong feeling that the
focal point in it was Chapter One of Book Two, where
Scobie arrives to receive the shipwrecked from the French
colonial area, for the first time meeting his future beloved,
Helen Rolt, and happening to witness the death of a little
girl. A closer look shows that in this chapter all the central
threads of the novel intersect. The text is more compact
than elsewhere; decisive events occur that motivate the later

happenings in the novel or start them off. This is the heart
of the novel, its turning point in the sense in which Hollo
uses the expression in his essay.

This chapter comes a little less than half way through
the novel. At its beginning Major Scobie has behind him
three significant events: his wife Louise has gone on leave
to South Africa, he has borrowed money for this trip from
the Syrian trader Yusef, and he has been investigating the
suicide of Pemberton, the Assistant D.C. He is pleased
to have fulfilled his wife's dream, for her trip has enabled
him to gratify also a desire of his own by giving him a
moment of peace. But he is likewise aware of having paid
dearly for all of this by having become beholden to Yusef.
Pemberton's suicide indicates where such dependence on
another may lead, what may happen if one fails to keep
one's affairs in order and has to bear the burden of loneliness. The events in this chapter take place out of the city—
the only time when this occurs in the novel—at a remote
border station where the freedom of movement of the members of the British colony comes to an end: beyond the river
a forbidden, hostile country begins. Both of the factors
limiting the existence of the characters in the novel, the
tropics and the war, are thus concretely present. The stage
is narrowed and the *dramatis personae* are all concentrated
into the same place as in a play. Of the principal figures
of the novel, Louise only is absent, but her presence is not
indispensable: Scobie's relationship with her does not
change appreciably throughout the novel. Her absence, on
the other hand, is structurally necessary: only in this manner can Scobie be placed in a sufficiently complex test situation. Distance makes him feel detached from her and less
strictly obliged to consider her in his decisions than before.

The initial section of the chapter already makes clear
that Scobie has made a mistake in following Yusef's hint:
the matter with the parrot is seen to be a trap laid by Yusef

for his rival Tallit. True, Scobie has committed no offense against the law, his conscience is clear in this respect, and he has in his possession the tangible trophy of the first diamonds which the police have succeeded in confiscating. But morally the situation has become more complicated, and the return to the original state of affairs now is far more difficult. The first concession has been made; it is consequently fully understandable that more concessions are to be expected. The ground on which Scobie moves has been dangerously shaken. This is important, since the novel is essentially the story of Scobie's lapse into loneliness, away from men. Step by step those persons of his environment disappear whom he might have regarded as friends; that is, those whom he may *trust*. Louise is lost, Helen proves to be weak, and eventually even the priest, Father Rank, and the servant Ali betray the hopes placed on them. Even though the mysterious, double-faced Yusef, friend as well as tempter, stays close to Scobie, his action has torn a serious gap in the net of Scobie's human relationships.

In departing, Louise has left emptiness: "Now there was nothing to listen for." Although Scobie has experienced some relief, he now misses the presence of a person close to him for whom he might sacrifice himself. He does not know how to live without shouldering responsibility. But this gap is filled. Scobie is immediately seized with pity when he sees the sick company of the shipwrecked, more particularly the little girl in her mortal illness and the utterly exhausted young widow, Helen Rolt. By certain turns of phrase, the author underlines the importance of these matters for Scobie with more emphasis than usual: "Scobie *always remembered* how *she was carried into his life* on a stretcher grasping a stamp album with her eyes fast shut" (my italics). The reader who has taken these hints, from now on closely follows the way the relationship between Scobie and Helen develops and already at this stage realizes the important part Helen is to play in the novel. When Scobie later gets ever more deeply entangled in this new love, he actually only remains true to the memory of this first meeting and to the pity it stirred in him. When he in the following chapter surprisingly runs into Helen in the refugees' shack, that event at once occurs to him: ". . . a river . . . early morning . . . a dying child."

The stamp-album, symbol of Helen's childlike nature and immaturity, plays an important part in their relationship. It is the leitmotiv of their love—exactly as the vultures on the streets of the town constitute a motif akin to death. That album is mentioned five times in the chapter in question, and later it always comes to the fore when something decisive happens to Scobie and Helen. Scobie brings stamps to the girl when their relationship starts; he opens the album, attempting to meet her for the last time before his suicide. No wonder, then, that the author in this preparatory chapter refers to it time and again. The pages of the album wordlessly carry the story of Scobie and Helen's love.

There are other indications, too, anticipating Helen's significant part in the novel. Hers is the first name of the women tourists mentioned, already before she herself appears on the scene. Exactly as Gide in the first part of his *Faux-monnayeurs* flashes the visiting card of Victor Strouvilhous, the character who later proves so essential, Greene, too, presents the name of his heroine before she actually appears. In the hospital Scobie examines the girl with particular interest, viewing the expression in her face: "Like a fortune-teller's cards it showed unmistakably the past—a voyage, a loss, a sickness. In the next deal perhaps it would be possible to see the future." And, "I knew a policeman once—in our town," the girl half-unconsciously mutters. Scobie opens the stamp-album, sees Helen's father's inscription, and feels his pity grow. He likewise sees the colorful stamps with the pictures of parrots, but the matter of Yusef's parrot does not occur to him. He already has turned his back on the past.

The next phase consists in the growth of suspicion among the bystanders. Losing his patience, Wilson for the first time links the names of Scobie and Mrs. Rolt, suggesting that they have something in common. If this idea has not occurred to Scobie before, he now has it implanted into him. This annoyed outburst of Wilson's is important in other ways, too: his hatred of Scobie and his falling in love with Louise now become fully manifest. Wilson himself shows his hand; Scobie now knows for certain that Wilson is covetously scrutinizing him and is the first to gather evidence against him. Later Wilson becomes Helen's neighbor and even starts prying into Scobie's love life. Throughout the novel Wilson is quite deliberately used to counterbalance Scobie; by placing him in a variety of situations, the author demonstrates how he outwardly performs his job more blamelessly than Scobie, but inwardly he is a person of much less worth. Wilson is of the same type as Pyle in *The Quiet American,* "innocent" and immature, and never in any doubt as to the righteousness of what he is doing. "Nobody had yet marked on his face the lines that make a human being."

In the hospital two significant events occur which are important for Scobie and the way he subsequently develops. The first of these is the death of the child, a little girl like Scobie's own dead child, Catherine. She immediately becomes identified with Catherine: "When he looked at the child he saw a white communion veil over her head: it was a trick of the light and a trick of his own mind." The death of Scobie's daughter is the heaviest loss he has had to bear in his life. It was the event which probably closed for him the way back to his country and made him stay where he was. But he had always drawn comfort from the fact that he did not have to see it himself. Now the situation is super-

ficially actualized—the girl calls him father, and he has to
assume a father's part. "He had been in Africa when his
own child died. He had always thanked God that he had
missed that. It seemed after all that one never really missed
a thing. To be a human being, one had to drink the cup."
Thus Scobie comes painfully to reexperience that event
which more than anything else has estranged him from his
wife—a fact which Louise senses and expresses with bitter
perspicuity. As that experience now is repeated, he again,
more distinctly than before, realizes the chasm separating
him and Louise. His way to Helen becomes easier and
simpler. The scene is of importance also in another respect,
from the point of view of the religious problems of the
novel: he prays for peace for the dying girl at whatever
cost. "Take away my peace forever, but give her peace."
His part as a vicarious sufferer is reinforced. The same
argumentation is used by him at the end of the book as one
of the weightiest motives for his suicide. Concluding his
days in a state of deadly sin—and so actually becoming
twice guilty of deadly sin—he believes his peace is gone
forever and that he has no way left of regaining it. But
he has the power to give peace to others by taking himself
out of the way, by buying it at the cost of his life. So
foreign has all selfseeking become to him.

Another notable scene is that in which Scobie reads to
the boy in the hospital. He has chosen at random from the
mission library a book, the title of which happens to be
A Bishop Among the Bantus. The book strikes him as
tedious reading for a boy of school age, and he invents a
story of greater interest to the youngster: the Bantus, he
says, are pirates, and Bishop is the man's name who comes
to them in disguise as a government agent, but "he falls
in love with the daughter of the Captain of the Bantus and
that's when he turns sloppy." The scene is interesting for
many reasons. For one thing, it is one of the few comic

passages in the novel: a policeman reading a story about pirates from a pure-minded missionary's book! Secondly, it is vividly illustrative of Scobie's character: we again see how powerfully pity, the desire to do good to others, governs his actions. It makes him invent fantastic tales and brings out hitherto unfamiliar aspects of him. Thirdly, some of the plot quickly improvised by him reveals symptomatic features. Scobie assigns to his imaginary hero *a double rôle*: in other words, the kind which he has begun to play himself after borrowing money from Yusef and in which he will be fully absorbed when Louise returns home earlier than expected. The love motif is likewise noteworthy: the hero of Scobie's imagination falls for the captain's daughter; that is, a person whom he ought not to love and who makes it difficult for him to carry out his original task and probably will keep him from completing it. The situation is— *mutatis mutandis*—precisely analogous to Scobie's own situation at the end of the novel. Scobie is not spinning his yarn for the boy only; he knows Helen is listening, too. The continuation of the scene where Scobie begins to "read" the fairy tale he has invented is no longer so symbolic in this respect. But it is comedy of a high order and shows how consistently he keeps the course he has chosen. The same consistency dictated by pity is shown by him at the end of the book when he falsifies his diary, simulating a heart ailment.

In the essay on the turning point in novels, Professor Hollo points out as one of the characteristics of the device that "the artist himself often makes his appearance in it, addressing us more directly than elsewhere in his story." But Greene does not belong to those writers who take the floor in their own name in the middle of the tale; he addresses the reader indirectly by dropping significant hints or leaving signs in the text. A few such hints were already included in the sentence telling of Helen's arrival on the stretcher; an almost unnoticeable but real anticipation of later events ("Scobie always remembered") and the stress laid on the importance of the matter for Scobie. Another sign appears in Scobie's diary. There for the first time an exact date is given: the fifth of May. On the following day, May sixth, Helen arrives. Since we also know the date of Scobie's suicide, November fifth, the duration of the love affair between him and Helen is precisely defined. In the earlier part of the novel, time is indicated vaguely; we only know that it is Sunday in the first chapter and that according to the bank manager, it is "the end of the month," so probably the end of March. With Helen, exact dates appear in the novel. From then on Scobie's days are literally numbered.

The third sign is in the title of the novel. In the text it appears only once, so far as I know, namely when Scobie for a moment stops outside the jungle hospital and goes to visit the dying child:

The lights inside would have given an extraordinary impression of peace if one hadn't known, just as the stars on this clear night gave also an impression of remoteness, security, freedom. If one knew, he wondered, the facts, would one have to feel pity even for the planets? if one reached what they called the heart of the matter?

Security, freedom, peace are mere delusions for him who knows. All lights carry news of suffering. If one looks at things this way, the only possible attitude is one of despair or pity. Scobie experiences despair, but also knows that it is of no use. His pity, on the other hand, reaches universal proportions; it is akin to love.

The characters of the novel may be divided into two groups according to whether they do or do not "know." The former includes, in addition to Scobie, partly Father Rank, the old Commissioner, and Yusef, perhaps also Helen after Scobie's death; the latter group consists of Louise,

Wilson, Harris, and all the rest. Louise and Wilson see the same things as Scobie, but their pity and feeling of responsibility are not stirred the same way. Scobie, for his part, feels responsible for everything he encounters.

The lights were showing in the temporary hospital, and the weight of all that misery lay on his shoulders. It was as if he had shed one responsibility only to take on another. This was a responsibility he shared with all human beings, but there was comfort in that, for it sometimes seemed to him that he was the only one who recognized it.

Scobie does not feel any strength being instilled into him from behind the stars; on the contrary, he feels as though he had to bear the responsibility even for the stars and had to offer his pity to everything everywhere. He "sees," he "knows," he is unable to close his eyes before the misery of existence. In a somewhat modified form, the same train of thought stirs in him as he recalls Pemberton's death:

What an absurd thing it was to expect happiness in a world so full of misery. He had cut down his own needs to a minimum, photographs were put away in drawers, the dead were put out of mind: a razor-strap, a pair of rusty handcuffs for decoration: but one still has one's eyes, he thought, one's ears. Point me out the happy man and I will point you out either egotism, selfishness, evil—or else an absolute ignorance.

These quotations, all from the same paragraph—the third of the chapter—that in which the child dies, deeply illuminate Scobie's character. We know a few things about him from the earlier chapters, but only now do we see distinctly how powerfully pity, clearsightedness, and loneliness are intertwined in him. When later in the novel his faults and, on the other side, as a counterweight, the happiness of others are placed on these sensitive moral scales, it is clear that he has to reach a decision taking him out of the way. Besides, suicide is no new idea with him: ever since Pemberton's farewell letter, the signature "Dicky" in the letter and his own nickname "Ticki," identified in his feverish ravings, have been echoing together in his mind. Later in the novel his suicide is given a religious motivation; in this chapter it is motivated in a human fashion which impresses even the religiously indifferent reader.

The title of the novel appears for a second time in its motto, a fragment from Charles Péguy in which the sinner is said to be at the very heart of Christianity ("au coeur même de chrétienté")—the same as the saint. The point at which sinner and saint meet has always interested Greene. In most of his novels he blends features of both in his heroes, making black melt into white until it is impossible to tell their dividing line. The hero of *The Power and the Glory* is a degenerate priest whose life derives its significance from his loyal adherence to his mission: he is the representative of God, a worthless medium of worth who grows with his task. In *The Heart of the Matter* there is no such strengthening factor; religion is not defeated with Scobie, he represents none but himself. This difference is brought out vividly by the way these two characters die. The priest is shot in bright daylight, whereas Scobie dies at midnight, alone, and by his own hand. It is as if Greene had removed from the moral structure of his Mexican novel one of its supports (as well as its outward element of suspense: the pursuit) and tried whether it will still stand without collapsing. In *The Quiet American* he takes a further step, concluding the settling of accounts by making the principal character take not his own life but that of another person.

In other words, the problem is that of the conflict between letter and spirit, between dogmas and situations in real life. Such conflicts Greene finds most frequently there where conditions are still unsettled: in the tropics and the exceptional situations created by war. In such conditions the customary moral laws no longer prevail or seem wrong,

like clocks showing another local time. This is precisely
the way in which the central predicament characteristic
of Greene's novels comes about: a predicament in which
basic values have to be reevaluated and people have to
shoulder the full responsibility for their actions, seeking
under the pressure of conflicting factors for the solution
most valid by human standards. Scobie breaks the rules
of the Church, although he acts in the spirit of Christianity.
In the final chapter Louise, criticizing his suicide, sees the
rules but not Scobie's motives. She does not "know." She
has not experienced that all-pervasive pity reaching to the
heart of the matter, to which Scobie dedicated himself in
the darkness of night before the jungle hospital and at the
deathbed of a strange child. Father Rank, perhaps weak
as a priest, but still understanding the situation, sees both
Scobie's faults and his motives. "The Church knows all the
rules. But it doesn't know what goes on in a single human
heart," he says in the final dialogue of the book, which in
places has much the same ring as the conversation between
Scobie and Father Clay after Pemberton's suicide. In order
to break Louise's opposition, Father Rank also presents his
most peculiar but perhaps also his most weighty argument:
"And do you think God's likely to be more bitter than a
woman?"

The novel naturally has more turning points than only
Chapter One of Book Two; from the point of view of its
religious problems the last pages, of course, are of first
importance. Furthermore, all the letters quoted in the book
are significant in one way or another. The Portuguese
captain's confiscated letter to his daughter causes Scobie
to break the regulations—from pity—and to burn it; Pemberton's letter brings the important suicide motif into the
novel and anticipates the essential meeting with Yusef; the
letter Scobie sends to Louise in South Africa shows in a
veiled manner that his love for Helen is already well under

way; Harris's draft of a letter to the paper of his old school, again, is an incomparable example of the empty life led by him and his like; Scobie's letter to Helen is a desperate promise of love and, in the hands of Yusef, becomes a fatal instrument of blackmail; Scobie's last love message to Helen, the sentence scribbled on the portrait of George VI, is a drowning man's ringing cry for help. All these letters are like lenses concentrating the problem pattern of the novel into one point. In any significant novel a number of philosophical, structural, and stylistic factors cooperate. In Greene this unity is especially compact; everything depends on everything else and even the slightest happening essentially affects the total picture. In *The Heart of the Matter*, for example, each turn of the plot is exactly calculated, depending both on outward conditions—the tropics and the war—and on the characters, particularly those of Scobie and Louise.

At no point in the novel, however, do we see such wide perspectives open as in Chapter One of Book Two. This is the novel's watershed. Scobie arrives there as a relatively free person; he seems to have several possibilities to choose from. Yet by the end of the chapter he has taken the decisive steps on the way leading to death. He has met the woman whom he cannot force himself to leave and because of whom he gets involved in an irreconcilable conflict both with his wife and with his Church; he has seen Wilson's hostility burst out openly; he has prayed at the child's deathbed for peace for others at the cost of his own peace. This experience of belonging together and of responsibility which he undergoes in the darkness of night in front of the jungle hospital, this profound universal pity which in him is intensified to passion, henceforward always stays with him like the ballast in the bowels of a ship.

John Atkins

ALTOGETHER AMEN: A RECONSIDERATION OF *THE POWER AND THE GLORY*

DEATH! DEATH! DEATH! What a way to start a novel! And what a way to continue it! But that's what he wanted—it was certainly no accident, for Greene doesn't make slips, except intentional ones—and death's ubiquity is the slogan he drives home, like a particularly beastly nail. As literary drumming, *The Power and the Glory* ranks very high indeed.

Just see what he accomplishes in the first fifty pages or so. He begins with an epigram from Dryden, describing death closing in hourly. The first paragraph firmly reminds us of the existence of vultures, carrion, and sharks. If I felt in statistical mood I would count the vultures in the novel as a whole; as it is, I'll just take all comers that vultures lead the field in this particular animal stakes. The town is clearly dead, the boat is plainly dying. As a variant on death we are given failure, a never-ending interest with Greene. The air of failure is as insistent as the solar heat which beats the characters in the novel as remorselessly as the image of death beats the reader. In Greeneland,

Mexican Province, heat crushes to death instead of stimulating the sex drive, as it frequently does elsewhere—in Faulkner's South, for instance. "Heat stood in the room like an enemy": it did not embrace like a lover. When we first meet the priest "he had the air, in his hollowness and neglect, of somebody of no account who had been beaten up incidentally, by ill-health or restlessness." It didn't take long for Mr. Tench to be reminded uncomfortably of a coffin by the priest's dark suit and sloping shoulders; and when he looked in his visitor's mouth, the focal point of the world's interest for him, he saw death in its carious lines. There is no emotion in all this, nor does Greene think there should be. We know this (he never makes a slip except on purpose), for he brings on a child to tell the priest that his mother is dying, with the same degree of feeling with which he would announce the passing of a train.

Who made death so unexciting, so acceptable, so dull? Certainly no regime has the power to do it. One with the resources of the World Controller in *Brave New World* might make a shot at it, but a barely fledged revolution in the least efficient of states cannot do it. Greene makes his death, gives it a personality, and then implies it is someone else's foundling. Literary sleight-of-hand, really. The lieutenant is introduced now. He hated the very idea of life; he believed in the final vacancy, animals without purpose. It looks like he might be a villain. Capt. Fellows, stupid Anglo-Saxon as he was, felt happiest in the wild (nature's version of desolation) with the vultures flopping overhead. He was reminded of war-torn France. That's what this wretched band of Protestants, atheists, agnostics, and fruit-drinkers really long for, the good and simple virtues of No-Man's-Land, the modern bathroom, so long as it's clean. Mrs. Fellows knew that death was coming nearer, and that she lived in a cemetery everyone else had left. She didn't like it but she was in it, and there's a pretty firm implication that you don't stay in a place if you really dislike it. Trixy was far gone, anyway, and had to be with a name like that—Greene doesn't bestow names for nothing. She didn't like to hear the word "life," it reminded her of death. Is this loading, or is it not?

Now Greene has a right to load, as has every novelist. No novelist could create his particular hell (and it is the hells which interest us and prevent the novel from its own decease) without drumming, hammering, and loading to some extent, but it is over the extent and nature of the drumming, hammering, and loading that we are entitled to exercise our capacities for judgment. One hint of excess lies in the use of the pathetic fallacy. Greene does not neglect it. Apart from his treatment of the sun he can be far more explicit, as when he writes of the rain coming down perpendicularly, "as if it were driving nails into a coffin lid." Who sends the rain? God or the Revolutionary Government? The latter can't win. Personally, I would hate them to win but, in my Anglo-Saxon simplicity, I enjoy a fight to be vaguely fair.

Death is the condition of this novel: It is its ambiance, its air, its food and drink, its matrix, its lover, its demiurge, even its priest. What is the opposition? Are we to believe that Greene, his Church, and his whiskey priest, are offering life? If so, one feels for the first time a little sympathy for those occasional idiots who have, through history, shouted Long Live Death! Of course, Greene, Church, and priest assert fervently that they offer life, but we have got used to examining that one. There are no louder shouters for the richness and fullness of life than the concentration camp designers. Greene is at pains to put God in the hands of a worthless drunkard. He was greatly applauded for this; it was so audacious—but too many critics have allowed the audacity to overawe their judgment. For did the priest really carry God? While we say, What a magnificent conception! How ironic! Glory be! we forget to ask whether it is true. The boy Luis's welcoming of the new priest in the last sentence proves nothing. The worst causes have their heroes and martyrs—remember Horst Wessel? The succumbing of the modern intellect to the perverse allure of Greene's whiskey priest is comparable, if not on the same level.

Greene has never sounded a happy Catholic, which is why I distrust his claims. There is no doubt about his literary skill—it is that that makes it necessary to resist his claims. His unhappiness is probably the major contradiction in his work—he writes for joy and wine and sex and the wonderful civilisation of the past, yet never does he make them attractive. He writes against the puritan yet manages to wrap his phrases in a cocoon of disapproval that would have impressed a seventeenth century dissenter. Is there a single admirable character in the whole of Greene's output who enjoys his wine? Could you imagine any young man thinking sex was anything but a compulsive bind from reading Greene? Greene is not so simple as that, you see, that's all Chesterton and old hat, and anyway, that's not his particular line in satisfaction. We ought to enjoy our wine, he says, and hints at orgies of pleasure beyond the covers of his books, but we never taste them—our teeth are bad, our breath smells, digestion is hopeless, the wine is synthetic.

I get the impression that Greene is aware that he hasn't the best of cases. As a propagandist for the Catholic Church he is not very persuasive. For every masochistic intellectual he gains he must lose them a dozen cricketers and philanderers. He tells us one thing and implants resistance by his way of telling it. Of course, he is not trying to be a propagandist and would rightly feel insulted if we suggested that that was his role—but incidentally every writer must express some kind of creed. Perhaps it doesn't matter what the creed is but it will help if it possesses intellectual solidity. We get a glimpse of Greene's difficulty when the priest, in the course of one of his reminiscent moments about the comfortable old days that have gone beyond recall, thinks of the better school he had planned at Concepción. It is hardly a fortunate choice, for the Roman Church has never been associated with wholehearted educational programmes. In fact, the despised new regimes have shown much more energy in this direction, even if we dislike their motives— and you cannot separate good and bad in an educational programme. God and devil are worshipped with the same instruments. But if you ask what could have replaced education you see Greene's difficulty. Health, social service, adequate wages, holidays with pay—it's the devil who provides them. Isn't this exactly why the priest was on the run? Perhaps he did carry God, but couldn't God be a little less austere? Couldn't He actually provide a little fun in-stead of endlessly talking about His love of fun, and His contempt for those who couldn't agree about the best way to provide it?

Greene's well-known virtues are present in profusion. In fact, *The Power and the Glory* is one of the most care-fully worked out of all his novels. Not an image and scarcely a word is superfluous. But the assault on the reader's allegiance is much more violent than in, say, *The Heart of the Matter* or even *The End of the Affair*. This novel can make us uncomfortable in the same way as his play, *The Living Room*. Unorthodox and sometimes irrele-vant opinions on theology and sex are thrust at the reader. At the same time, the more mechanical processes of mystery and suspense are heightened by methods which are not al-ways acceptable. For example, the priest is reintroduced into the narrative again and again as an apparently new character, who is described (obliquely) anew until we recognise him. But surely, once we have been introduced to the priest we are entitled to know him on arrival, instead of repeatedly going through the process of reestablishment. As technique it is on a par with describing Byron by his foot or Chesterton's irritating repetitions of Father Brown's external appearance. Perhaps Greene did take something from GKC, after all.

Even the parallel readings of the children seem to be heavy-handed twenty years later. (It's strange how one's feelings about a book can mature and settle down just through the passage of time.) Luis and his martyr, Coral and her War of Independence, can certainly create the desired atmosphere, but they cannot survive a critical glance. It is this critical glance that Greene deprecates, calling it death or vacancy, but the alternative is to accept any trick the author cares to play. Even the priest's girl is less credible than she used to be. "My dear, tell me what games you play," says the priest. "The child sniggered. He turned his face quickly away and stared up at the roof, where a spider moved." Quintessence of the 1940 Greene. We know what the priest thought (the spider settled it, anyway), but the girl wasn't thinking that. Either she wouldn't think of sex as a game, or if she did she wouldn't see any reason to snigger. For a moment we are back in Brighton. But the humanity of the child has dwindled away. She is now a prop. Within ten pages the lieutenant says she is worth more than the Pope in Rome and the priest says she is more important than a whole continent. It is perhaps inevitable that they should speak in this way. What is depressing is that for Greene she is little more than a shuttlecock. The Pope is getting the worst of it.

The priest wanted to die but hadn't sufficient grace to die. The land about him, the society he moved in, were dying without grace. Here and there he uncovered pockets of grace and helped them with the grace bestowed on him, not generated within him. There is a disagreeable sense of defeat, of irremediable human defeat, not the defeat of a religious sect, about this novel. The truth is, we resent it. It is not simply because it is defeat, for we have learnt to accept defeat in Hardy, even to love our defeat. But Hardy's fate was imposed by God, by fate. Greene's appears to be willed by the author. It is a joyless acceptance of this is Hell nor am I out of it—thank God!

Miriam Allott

THE MORAL SITUATION IN *THE QUIET AMERICAN*

When *The Quiet American* appeared in 1955 it was described on the jacket as "a modern variant on a theme which in the last century attracted Mark Twain and other writers: a study of New World hope and innocence set in an old world of violence," a statement which places it in a literary tradition with which it has some important elements in common. We are likely to do it more justice, I suggest, if we look at it in the context of sophisticated moral analysis of the kind associated with some later 19th century English and American fiction than if we begin by relating it to certain types of contemporary existentialist thinking.[1] In its concern with the nature of effective moral action, its feeling for the anomalies which surround most human attempts to achieve this, and its assertion nevertheless of certain enduring human values, it reminds us particularly of James and Conrad (both writers with whom Greene is especially familiar). At the same time, in spite of its non-Catholic central characters, it gives a fresh focus to themes which Greene explores in his 'Catholic' novels and, as we might expect, it shows a close emotional and intellectual kinship with these books. For a 'correct reading' of this novel all these factors ought to be considered.

The notion that active intelligence rather than simple good intentions is necessary for the successful ordering of human relationships barely emerges as an explicit theme in the English novel until George Eliot; and even here the sober vision which this theme encourages is not yet of the kind to instill serious misgivings about the moral consonance of ends and means. Although George Eliot feels that "heroic Promethean effort" is required to achieve ultimate moral good, she places the effort within the limits of human ability and tries to free it from those limitations of temperament to which she is otherwise particularly sensitive. It is clearly no part of her purpose to unsettle her Victorian readers by suggesting that action directed towards "ultimate moral good" can be contaminated by the evil which it is designed to overcome. A more unflinching reading of experience is offered by her successors in the next generation, who confront more squarely than she does the fact that in an imperfect world choice lies between greater and lesser evil rather than between clear right and wrong. Conrad puts forward his 'few simple ideas' concerning fidelity and honour, and then shows in his characters' fated lives, and with the help of Marlow's brooding commentaries, that a code of behaviour based on such ideas is at best no more than a fragile defence. James takes the argument several stages further in his own analysis of the moral life. In characters such as Isabel Archer, Maggie Verver, and Milly Theale, innocence is equated with immaturity, and it is through their experience of betrayal and treachery that these people arrive at a fuller moral vision and come at last to understand the situation into which they have been drawn as much by their own limitations as by their adversaries' selfwill and ambitious cunning. Determining now to retrieve this situation, they take up the instruments whose use they have just learned. So Maggie resorts to deceit in order to counteract the deception practised on herself and her father by the Prince and Charlotte, and Milly Theale relies on the "cunning of the serpent" rather than "innocence of the dove" to make her way through the labyrinth which Kate and Merton, Lord Mark, and Mrs. Lowder, have prepared for her (it is this 'cunning' which ultimately helps to bring about Merton Densher's moral awakening and his final separation from Kate).

Graham Greene's handling of his central characters in *The Quiet American* displays a similarly ironical criticism of life, the main difference being that Pyle's naive good intentions and their disastrous consequences carry James's theme of simple good faith divorced from wisdom into a wider area of social reference, while Fowler's behaviour extends the relevance of James's statement about the corrupting effects of experience to a more urgent and far-reaching 'international situation' than any which he could foresee. Some prominent nonexistentialist French writers also share Greene's concern about the high price in personal integrity which may be paid by anyone aiming at efficient moral action for the general good, and they explore in a comparable way the ambiguous relationship between 'intelligence' and 'goodness.' Albert Camus, who firmly opposes Sartre's existentialist beliefs, reminds us in *La Peste* that those who dedicate themselves to the conquest of violence find it hard to escape infection by this 'pestilence.' Again, in Anouilh's *Antigone*, we find Creon depending on violence and trickery to restore order in his troubled kingdom; his destruction of Antigone is forced on him because, in the society which he must hold together by compromise, backstairs intrigue, and the ruthless suppression of criticism, her inflexible—and in this case noble—innocence can only make for disaster.

Graham Greene's kindred themes point to the contemporary relevance of much of his thinking, but the reader of *The Quiet American* is bound, I suppose, to be more immediately struck by its Jamesian affinities, which are especially noticeable in its dramatization of what is primarily an Anglo-American 'international situation'; its quasi-metaphorical juxtaposition of representatives from the 'New' and the 'Old' worlds; and its probing concern both with the motivation of treachery and betrayal and with the nature of an innocence which is dangerous because ignorant. There is a further similarity in the close interdependence of its tragic and its comic elements. It is after he has exhausted the more direct possibilities for social comedy in his 'international situation' that we see James beginning to explore differences between the 'New' and the 'Old,' less as a Balzacian social historian than as a moralist for whom the two worlds are convenient illustrations for universally opposed systems of value. The people who find themselves at odds with each other in *The Golden Bowl* or *The Wings of the Dove* illustrate general moral dilemmas of a kind with which contemporary sensibility is still deeply engaged. Yet at the same time that James locks together his victims and victimizers, his betrayed and betrayers, in their mutually destructive embrace he still manages to surround them with a strong flavour of irony. Similarly Pyle and Fowler, the two principal figures in *The Quiet American* who represent the New and the Old worlds, sometimes appear to stand for conflicting systems of value which cut across the artificial boundaries of nationality and race; at the same time they also succeed in conveying their author's strong feeling for comic incongruity. Pyle and Fowler at cross purposes are often as entertaining as, let us say, Sarah Pocock and Madame de Vionnet in that historic confrontation at the Paris hotel; and in association with the delightful and uncomprehending Phuong, whom they both love, they also demonstrate their author's skill in mingling the funny and

the sad, a quality which gives special distinction to some
of James's most intelligent achievements from the 1890s
onwards.

This ironical temper also links Graham Greene with
earlier writers than James, a point which he emphasizes
himself by his choice of passages from Byron and Clough
as epigraphs for his story. The lines from Byron occur in
Don Juan, Canto I, stanza CXXXII.

> This is the patent age of new inventions
> For killing bodies and for saving souls,
> All propagated with the best intentions.

Like the description of armies attacking from the air in
Rasselas, the passage can arouse amusement and surprise
in a modern reader, who sees in it a longer reach of irony
than the author originally intended. However, a little more
may be said about its appearance in this new context without straining its significance too far. As it happens, it follows
immediately after a stanza in which Byron indulges in some
high-spirited satirical junketing at the expense of America.
Along with even more libellous statements, Byron suggests
that it might be a good thing if the population of America
were to be thinned

> With war, or plague, or famine—any way,
> So that civilization they may learn.

It is hard to ignore the bearing of this remark on Greene's
presentation of Alden Pyle, which is also in keeping, both in
theme and tone, with Byron's frequent emphasis in his
satirical verse on the connection between 'good intentions'
and, so to speak, the road to hell. In *The Quiet American*
Alden Pyle, setting out equipped with simple humanitarian
'good intentions' and a totally untutored moral intelligence,
ends up helping General Thé to bomb civilians with explosive bicycle pumps, one of the age's newest "inventions

for killing bodies." The epigraph from Byron thus underlines Greene's sardonic commentary on a combination of
qualities now distressingly prevalent: i.e., the high development of technical skill combined with the low development of moral intelligence, so that the skill too often
gets used for 'killing bodies' instead of helping to make
them good and happy. Alden Pyle, then, has to carry the
burden of representing this combination of qualities, while
Fowler, as the knowing observer who is intelligent enough
to see the menace in Pyle but refrains from taking preventive
action until it is almost too late, illustrates the more complex
aspects of Greene's argument about moral responsibility.
"Innocence is a kind of insanity," Fowler says, thinking of
the way in which Pyle is "impregnably armoured" against
knowing his own power for harm "by his good intentions
and his ignorance" (pp. 213-14). Like the spokesman of
Don Juan, Fowler inhabits a mental region which is sit-
uated at some distance from Pyle's "psychological world of
great simplicity," where one heroically asks trusting questions of one's rival in love. "You'd play straight with me,
Thomas, wouldn't you?" Pyle asks, but Thomas Fowler
knows that human behaviour, whether in love or war, demands more complex formulations than this. In the consequent disenchantment of its tone his narrative has in fact
much in common with Byron's wry amusement, his distrust
of cant, and his admiration for the civilization of the Old
world as against that of the New.

What it does not have, however, is Byron's vigour. Here
one sees the relevance of the quotation from Clough which
appears above the lines from Byron at the beginning of the
book. The passage is taken from *Amours de Voyage* (Canto
II, stanza XI) and the spokesman this time is a young
man, Claude, who suffers from that paralysis of the will
and the emotions which is a continuing theme in 19th century European literature and which owes so much to the

'other' Byron—the Byron, that is, of the verse tales and
Childe Harold. It unites Russian Hamlet-figures, like the
heroes in Pushkin and Lermontov, with Flaubert's Frédéric
Moreau, and it even emerges as late as "The Beast in the
Jungle," Henry James's short story about the man whose
destiny it is to be someone "to whom nothing on earth was
to happen." But the major factor in Claude's predicament
is the sort of scepticism which we associate particularly with
the movement of ideas in mid-19th century England. His
creator is an expert on the crippling effects of this kind
of doubt and is also skilled in aiming his best ironical effects
at his own indecisiveness. It is almost certain that Greene
intends us to place Fowler in this context and see him as
a 'doubting Thomas,'[2] who is endowed with moral sensibility and yet fears, or is too lazy, to act, these characteristics meanwhile providing constantly renewed resources for
the free play of his own ironic sense. Clough's hero does not
like 'being moved,' we are told in the lines which Greene
quotes:

> I do not like being moved; for the will is
>   excited; and action
> Is a most dangerous thing; I tremble for
>   something factitious,
> Some malpractice of heart and illegitimate
>   process;
> We're so prone to these things, with our
>   terrible notions of duty.

Fowler does not "like being moved" either, and he goes out
of his way to assert his lack of involvement. "You can rule
me out," he says early in the story, though it is already
apparent that he is protesting too much:

"I'm not involved. Not involved," I repeated. It had been an
article of my creed. The human condition being what it was, let
them love, let them murder, I would not be involved. My fellow
journalists called themselves correspondents; I preferred the title
of reporter. I wrote what I saw; I took no action—even opinion
is a kind of action. (p. 27)

For all his assumed air of disengagement, however, Fowler cannot permanently refrain from action. Face to face at last with "the malpractice of heart and illegitimate process" which Pyle is led into by his "terrible notions of duty," he finds that he too has his 'notions of duty' and must act upon them. One of the various ironical implications here is that these 'notions of duty' again lead to 'an illegitimate process.' The tragicomic temper of this writing sees to it that Fowler's decision to act, which is founded on a sense of moral outrage and the desire to prevent further violence and suffering, should nevertheless result in betrayal, murder and—as the result of yet another ironical twist to the plot—considerable material advantage to himself. As we pursue the windings of the story it also becomes apparent that the author's tragicomic method acts as a necessary distancing device for certain strongly obsessive emotions.

Here it is necessary to take into account Fowler's relationship with Phuong, for one's judgment of the book depends to a great extent on what is made of this part of it. In the first four lines of the stanza from Clough's poem (Greene gives only the last four) Claude tells us,

> There are two different kinds, I believe, of
> human attraction.
> One which simply disturbs, unsettles, and makes
> you uneasy,
> And another that poises, retains, and fixes
> and holds you.
> I have no doubt, for myself, in giving my voice
> for the latter.

Fowler 'gives his voice' for it too. Phuong—who is charmingly drawn: the elegance and economy of the style are nicely adjusted to the subject—represents the attraction which "poises, retains, and fixes and holds. . . ." She is totally different from "the girl in the red dressing-gown" of Fowler's earlier love affair. Sometimes, he tells Pyle, she seems "in-

visible like peace," while the girl of the old affair stands for
the other kind of human attraction which "disturbs, un-
settles, and makes you uneasy."

"I was terrified of losing her. . . . I couldn't bear the uncer-
tainty any longer. I ran towards the finish, just like a coward
runs towards the enemy and wins a medal. . . . Then I came east."
"And found Phuong?"
"Yes."
"But don't you find the same thing with Phuong?"
"Not the same. You see, the other one loved me. I was afraid
of losing love. Now I'm only afraid of losing Phuong." (p. 131)

For a reader interpreting the book in existentialist terms
it is naturally hard to believe that Fowler "loves" Phuong.
"Fowler lives with Phuong because she prepares his opium
pipe and satiates his sexual appetites" is one of the views
expressed in the essay referred to in the footnotes; but
this is a simplification which may lead to our misjudging
both the quality of Fowler's feelings for Phuong and the
function of Phuong herself in the structure of the story.
Through her, and through the reactions which she arouses
in Fowler, the author succeeds in making us see how
inevitable Fowler's ultimate commitment really is. Fowler,
we realise, acts as he does because he has never, in any
real sense, managed to remain uninvolved. His feelings
for Phuong help to explain why. They are complex and,
if we may judge by the general effect of his novels, they
are also fairly typical of Greene's own feelings about humanity. They mingle tenderness, selfishness, compassion, pain,
respect for human dignity, and a bitter sense of the limitations of human faith and love. A passage like the following,
even though it is supposed to voice the thoughts of a nonbeliever, could have been written by no one but this particular novelist.

Why should I want to die when Phuong slept beside me every
night? But I knew the answer to that question. From childhood
I had never believed in permanence, and yet I had longed for it.

Always I was afraid of losing happiness. This month, next year, Phuong would leave me. If not next year, in three years. Death was the only absolute value in my world. Lose life and one would lose nothing again for ever. I envied those who could believe in a God and I distrusted them. I felt they were keeping their courage up with a fable of the changeless and the permanent. Death was far more certain than God, and with death there would be no longer the daily possibility of love dying. (pp. 49-50)

A strong ingredient in these complex feelings is pity, an emotion which afflicts Greene's characters like a disease. Fowler's clipped reporting does not disguise from us— though it may do so from the imperceptive Pyle—the intensity with which this feeling can work in him. It is present when he recalls the vulnerability of Phuong as he saw her first, dancing with lightness and precision on her "eighteen-year-old feet" and living on simple dreams about security and happiness; when he seeks emotional relief by describing the grey drained bodies of men caught in a crossfire and filling the canal at Phat Diem as "an Irish stew containing too much meat"; and when he thinks of the peasant woman holding in her lap and covering "with a kind of modesty" what is left of her baby after General Thé's bombs have exploded in the square.

It is this suppressed but inextinguishable emotion which binds Fowler indissolubly to his fellow creatures and makes it impossible for him to remain not involved. It is this, too, which finally separates him from Alden Pyle, whose 'York Harding' liberalism encourages belief in large clean abstractions like Freedom and Honour which exist on a plane safely out of sight of "the fury and the mire of human veins." It is true that this belief can promote Pyle's daring cloak-and-dagger enterprise in saving his rival's life under fire because this "is the right thing to do," an act of heroism which stands beyond criticism. And yet nothing in the belief is capable of bringing home to its possessor the enormity of what has happened when General Thé's bombs go off in the square. "I dealt with him severely," Pyle says afterwards, and he speaks "like the captain of a school-team who has found one of his boys breaking his training" (p. 229). His continued association with Thé does not present itself to him as needing any kind of moral justification. The General is "the only hope we have" in the struggle for power, and the Vietnamese he sees as too childlike and uncomplicated to nurse any resentment against the violence which he and Thé will continue to inflict on them so long as the struggle for power goes on. It is just after Pyle has uttered these shattering statements that Fowler finally commits himself. He moves to the window and gives to the waiting trishaw driver the signal that Pyle must die. "Sooner or later," he has been told earlier by Heng, a man who will help to bring this death about, "one has to take sides. If one is to remain human" (p. 227). In spite of his hatred of political action, he joins at last in Pyle's cloak-and-dagger game, ranging himself in the name of humanity beside Heng and his undercover gang against Pyle and *his* fellow-plotters.

It is at this point, I think, that one becomes aware of the thematic continuity linking this book with Greene's 'Catholic' novels, where the author is occupied with the allied problems of pain and of how far man is justified in risking damnation for the sake of relieving the suffering of his fellow creatures. These stories are haunted by memories of "the curé d'Ars admitting to his mind all the impurity of a province, Péguy challenging God in the cause of the damned." It is Péguy of whom the priest speaks in *Brighton Rock* when he seeks to console Rose after Pinkie's death.

"He was a good man, a holy man, and he lived in sin all through his life, because he couldn't bear the idea that any soul should suffer damnation. . . . He never took the sacraments, he never married his wife in church. I don't know, my child, but some people think he was—well, a saint."

Scobie, in *The Heart of the Matter*, risks damnation by committing suicide to save his wife and mistress from further suffering, and the whiskey priest in *The Power and the Glory*, praying for the salvation of his corrupted child, beseeches God, "Give me any kind of death—without contrition, in a state of sin—only save this child." Like Ivan Karamazov, who challenges Alyosha on the subject of divine justice and can find no justification for innocent suffering, these people find no escape from the ravages of their sense of pity. The extra turn of the screw in their case is their full consciousness of the spiritual peril into which they have been led by their compassion.[3]

This theological dilemma is absent in *The Quiet American*, but the moral and emotional predicament is essentially unchanged: indeed since the author is now depicting man without God, it is possibly even more urgent in its presentation. We sense this urgency when we realise that Scobie's feelings about suffering lead him to incur the risk, but not the certainty, of damnation, while the effect of comparable feelings in Fowler is to make him take on a burden of guilt from which he cannot be set free. For Scobie and his Catholic fellow-sinners there is always the hope of grace; the point of light may appear at the end of the tunnel, the glimmer of dawn may rise in the night sky, the hand of God may reach out to stay their free fall from "the stirrup to the ground." For Fowler, enacting his Judas role, there is guilt and a happiness stained with remorse. A certain emotional resonance in Greene's treatment of this situation calls to mind Tarrou's question towards the close of *La Peste*: "Can one be a saint without God?—that's the problem, in fact the only problem, I'm up against today."[4] Obviously we cannot say of Fowler, as the priest in *Brighton Rock* says of Péguy, that he may be "well, a saint." And yet it is also obvious that among the characteristics which Fowler shares with these Catholics who challenge God in the cause of suffering is his willingness to take the responsibility of wrong-doing for the sake of diminishing human pain.

He also shares with these Catholic characters the longing for peace which is one of the consequences of their burden of pity, especially their pity for the suffering of children. Like Scobie at the bedside of the shipwrecked child and the whiskey priest praying for his daughter—and like Father Paneloux in *La Peste* watching a child's protracted death from plague or Ivan Karamazov torturing himself with stories about cruelty to children—Fowler experiences with the growth of this anguish the growth also of an angry despair. All victims of suffering—the men in the canal at Phat Diem, the young soldiers in the watch-tower—arouse these feelings in him. But it is memories of the child in the ditch ("one shouldn't fight a war with children . . . a little curled body in a ditch came back to my mind") and of the mangled baby in the Saigon square, which trigger off his decision to take measures against Pyle. His desire for peace is accentuated by these feelings about human suffering, and its existence is in itself a measure of how deeply, after all, he has always been 'involved.' He identifies Phuong with 'peace' and loves her for her stillness and serenity, while death seems to him to be 'the only absolute value' because it puts a stop to despair. "There can be no peace without hope," thinks Rieux in *La Peste*, as he meditates on the death of Tarrou, the man who had wondered whether one could be 'a saint without God.'

> Tarrou had lived a life riddled with contradictions and had never known hope's solace. Did that explain his aspirations towards saintliness, his quest of peace by service in the course of others?
>
> (Part IV, Chap. iii)

Fowler's life, too, though lived at a lower emotional temperature, is "riddled with contradictions" and he has "never known hope's solace," while "service in the cause of others" does not bring him peace any more than it really does to

Tarrou. On the contrary it gives him cause to long for it all the more. Peace remains the *princesse lointaine* of his dreams, and his author may well intend this longing to be felt as an expression of the love of God. The desire for peace seems to pursue Fowler as the nameless 'something' pursues Pinkie in his last despairing drive through the dark. Like Tarrou, Fowler appears to be one of those people who, as Rieux puts it, "desired reunion with something they couldn't have defined, but which seemed to them the only desirable thing on earth. For want of a better name, they sometimes called it peace." (*La Peste*, Part IV, Chap. iv)

Fowler himself finds another explanation for his longing, seeing it simply as the manifestation of his own selfish egotism. When Pyle at the risk of his own life brings members of the patrol to his rescue, Fowler refuses their aid until they have attended to the young soldier whose moaning (it is now stilled because he is dead) had filled him with a sense of anguish and guilt harder to bear than the pain of his wounded leg. He totally repudiates Pyle's admiring interpretation of this behaviour. Pyle sees him, one understands, as another Sidney at Zutphen, but Fowler merely remarks that he "cannot be at ease (and to be at ease is my chief wish) if someone else is in pain, visibly or audibly or tactually." He goes on: "Sometimes this is mistaken by the innocent for unselfishness, when all I am doing is sacrificing a small good—in this case postponement in attending to my hurt—for the sake of a far greater good, a peace of mind when I need only think of myself" (p. 146). There is, of course, some truth in this, for Fowler, as I have said, is by no means a saintly figure: largely, he illustrates the ordinary selfregarding emotions of the *homme moyen sensuel*. Yet the revelation that his peace is contingent upon the peace of others only succeeds in further emphasising how inescapably involved he is in the human situation. Moreover his remark about "sacrificing a small good . . .

for the sake of a far greater good" acquires an impressive
irony when it is applied to his betrayal of Pyle. The possibility of repose recedes even further into the distance once
he has sent to his death the man who is at once the pre-
server of his life and his rival in love. In the earlier part of
his story he explains that the human situation "being what
it is" he has never been able to experience the "peace of
mind when I need only think of myself" (it is only in his
opium-sleep that he manages to approach this state): in
the later part of his story he indicates that his own actions
have done little to bring the experience any nearer.

It is also in this later part of the story, as we should
expect, that the possible religious significance of his longing
for peace presses itself more noticeably on our attention.
It is especially apparent in his final interview with Vigot,
the intelligent Roman Catholic police officer at the Sureté,
who keeps his copy of Pascal at his side like a manual for
living. Vigot is in charge of the investigations into Pyle's
death, and the verbal fencing which characterizes his ex-
changes with Fowler, although far less elaborate, is not unlike the dialectical duelling which takes place between
Raskolnikov and the examining magistrate in *Crime and
Punishment*. Fowler certainly shares with Raskolnikov a
compulsive desire to unburden his conscience. The similarity in their situations also draws attention to the enormous
contrast between Raskolnikov's intensity of feeling and
Fowler's cooler response. He does not give himself away,
but he comes near to it in the interview which at last closes
his association with Vigot.

. . . "I've got nothing to tell you. Nothing at all."
"Then I'll be going," he said. "I don't suppose I'll trouble you
again."
At the door he turned as though he were unwilling to abandon
hope—his hope or mine.
"That was a strange picture for you to go and see that night.

I wouldn't have thought you cared for costume drama. What was it? *Robin Hood?"*

"*Scaramouche,* I think. I had to kill time. And I needed distraction."

"Distraction?"

"We all have our private worries, Vigot," I carefully explained.

It was strange how disturbed I had been by Vigot's visit. It was as though a poet had brought me his work to criticise and through some careless action I had destroyed it. I was a man without a vocation . . . but I could recognize a vocation in another. Now that Vigot had gone to close his uncompleted file, I wished I had the courage to call him back and say, "You are right. I did see Pyle the night he died." (pp. 222-23)

The dialogue here has the allusive understatement which serves its author well in his plays. Even the film-titles carry their ironic overtones. The make-believe world of *Robin Hood,* where a gay and gallant solution is found for the problem of wrong and injustice, and the mischief-making buffoonery of *Scaramouche*—Fowler provides himself with an alibi for the last hours of Pyle's life by sitting through this film—underline the contrast between sober reality and the boy's adventure-story world in which Pyle had so touchingly and yet so dangerously believed. There is a similar telling allusiveness in Fowler's throwaway remark about 'hope.' In the unwillingness on Vigot's side "to abandon hope—his hope or mine," especially when it is taken in conjunction with the references to Vigot's 'vocation' and Fowler's desire to confess, one sees the police officer assuming at this point in the story the function in Greene's Catholic novels which is often fulfilled by his priests. The reader is surely intended to remember here Fowler's earlier conversation with the Catholic priest whom he encounters at the top of the church tower in Phat Diem.

He said, "Did you come up here to find me?"

"No. I wanted to get my bearings."

"I asked you because I had a man up here last night. He wanted to go to confession. He had got a little frightened, you see, with what he had seen along the canal. One couldn't blame him."

"It's bad along there?"

"The parachutists caught them in a cross-fire. Poor souls. I thought perhaps you were feeling the same."

"I'm not a Roman Catholic. I don't think you would even call me a Christian."

"It's strange what fear does to a man."

"It would never do that to me. If I believed in any God at all, I should still hate the idea of confession. Kneeling in one of your boxes. Exposing myself to another man. You must excuse me, Father, but to me it seems morbid—unmanly even."

"Oh," he said lightly, "I expect you are a good man. I don't suppose you've ever had much to regret." (p. 57)

The unconscious irony of the priest's reply is brought home to the reader when Fowler, now with something momentous to regret, wishes he has the courage to obey his impulse, recall Vigot and confess the truth.

Although this wish is not fulfilled, it seems on the face of it that Fowler's story will nevertheless have 'the happy ending' which Phuong has tried so hard all along not to seem to want: his job is secure; his divorce will come through; he will be able to marry Phuong; she will stay with him now that Pyle is dead. But the shadow of Pyle remains. Even when the wonderful telegram arrives and Phuong knows that she is to have the security which she had earlier sought with Pyle, the shadow is still there. Pyle's copy of York Harding's *The Role of the West*—another title obviously chosen for its ironical effect—stands out from Fowler's bookshelves

like a cabinet portrait—of a young man with a crew cut and a black dog at his heels. I could harm no one any more. I said to Phuong, "Do you miss him much?"

"Who?"

"Pyle." Strange how even now, even to her, it was impossible to use his first name.

"Can I go please? My sister will be so excited."

"You spoke his name once in your sleep."

"I never remember my dreams."

"There was so much you could have done together. He was young."

"You are not old."

"The skyscrapers. The Empire State Building."

She said with a small hesitation, "I want to see the Cheddar Gorge." (p. 247)

These nicely adjusted lines of dialogue at the close of the novel, their hinted regrets signalizing new areas of sensitivity in the relationship between Fowler and Phuong ("'It's like it used to be,' I lied, 'a year ago'") show Fowler ruefully admitting that the memory of Pyle will be difficult to discard. As we see him last, Pyle is still on his mind.

I thought of the first day and Pyle sitting beside me at the Continental, with his eye on the soda-fountain across the way. Everything had gone right with me since he had died, but how I wished there existed someone to whom I could say that I was sorry.

Pyle may not always stay in his mind, one feels, but what has mattered in Fowler's story is that he is capable of feeling this pity and sorrow for the lost young man; that as an ordinary, nonpolitical, moderately selfish, but intelligent human being he is moved to act against violence and stupidity; and that he is impelled towards such action above all by his insight into human suffering, especially the suffering caused by war and political conflict.

It is easy to mistake the nature of Greene's achievement in this novel, partly because its extreme economy disguises both the range and quality of its feeling and the reach of its ideas. Perhaps it is also true to say that it illustrates how far this author's obsessive themes make for weakness as well as strength. Pity is one of the most urgent of these themes and it is a dangerous one for any artist to handle. It requires stringent distancing devices, and although the author's careful understatement and the operation of his irony go a long way towards supplying these, there are times when one feels that he may be near to an unbalancing subjectivity. All the same, the theme enables him to present with necessary dramatic intensity issues which it would be perilous to ignore. He succeeds in reminding us that we need Pyle's courage and none of his ignorance, Fowler's moral intelligence and none of his indecisiveness, if we are to find a way out of the alarming difficulties which as nations and individuals we are most of us nowadays required to face. He takes us a long distance, I feel, from the moral position implied in a good deal of modern existentialist writing.

John Atkins

THE CURSE OF THE FILM

THE FILMIC QUALITY of Greene's fiction has frequently been pointed out and as often praised.[1] In fact,
it is his worst work which invites the film comparison.
Novels like *A Gun For Sale* could easily be filmed (and
were) and remain secondrate literature. Later Greene was
to learn that excellence in one particular art depends on an
adherence to the rules of that art. It cannot be approached
through another.

"Unlike the heroes of classical tragedy," wrote Mlle.
Marie-Beatrice Mesnet in *Graham Greene and the Heart
of the Matter,* "or at least to a much greater extent than they,
Greene's characters need an 'aura' of images and sensations
to give them reality, to compensate, as it were, for their
failure in self-creation. Their personality is not sufficiently
developed for them to rise above their 'situation' in the
world." This very modern characteristic is exemplified by
the demand for a 'gimmick,' first of all by 'TV Personalities'
(who are usually not personalities as the word was once
understood) and subsequently by film 'stars' who cannot
act. Fame, popularity, and reputation depend not on the
essence or being of the person concerned but on some trick

or gagline. Greene's characters belong to this world. They are created by their environment. The inevitable result is that they tend to be regarded as inferior to the environment, as emanations and therefore illustrations of it. The classical heroes were emphasized by environment. Now the character emphasizes the world he lives in. There is no doubt that the general standards of art have been greatly debased in modern times by press, film and radio. Most serious novelists fight *against* this development. Greene, on the contrary, accepts it and uses it as a background. Unlike Kafka, with whom he shares many qualities, he has eliminated the allegorical element in his portrayal of the contemporary world. Yet he cannot avoid distortion because his characters have no powers of self-creation. They are merely the products of their environment, something important is left out. The result is, to quote Julian Symons ("Of Crisis and Dismay: a Study of Writing in the Thirties," *Focus One,* edited by Rajan and Pearse), "a world without faith, where men exist simply as the hunter, strengthened by hardness and emptiness, and the hunted, tragically weakened by a disturbing sense of guilt, where sexual relations are unsatisfactory because they are exclusively carnal (something like Auden's view of love as 'wrong') and women exist merely as corollaries to men, helping or hindering some vital masculine action, the whole a compound of violence, terror and a bewildered search for some form of faith." When Greene attempts to fill the emptiness he has recourse to dogma.

It is not surprising that Greene became a film critic. From 1935 to 1939 he was responsible for weekly reviews in *The Spectator* and during the latter half of 1937 in the short-lived humorous paper, *Night and Day.* He also collaborated with Walter Meade in writing the screen play and dialogue for Galsworthy's *The First and the Last,* which could not have been much to his taste. In 1938 he contributed his views on "Subjects and Stories" to *Footnotes*

to the Film, edited by Charles Davy. He began by taking
a text from Chekhov, who said of his fellow novelists: "The
best of them are realistic and paint life as it is, but because every line is permeated, as with a juice, by awareness
of a purpose, you feel besides life as it is, also life as it
ought to be, and this captivates you." I have no doubt
that Greene believed he was painting life as it is—he was
probably unaware of his distortions. (They were not un-
genuine; he was not a Babbitt.) But so far there had been
no signs of any vision of life as it ought to be. This was to
come later, and as the result of definite intention. Both the
stage and the popular novel had ceased to represent life
as it is, he went on. They gave us nothing more relevant
than a snapshot, and their vision of the future did not go
beyond sexual or financial happiness. He then quoted Ford
Madox Ford approvingly to the effect that in 1911 the
only vitality remaining to the stage was to be found in the
music hall. The cinema had killed the music hall. Had it
absorbed its virtues or "the sinister forms of morality" still
existing in the theatre?

The cinema must be popular yet it must also serve a
critical purpose. There is an element of satire in all dramatic
art (life as it is, life as it should be). Searching for a film
that adequately performs this role, he rejects the specious
though much praised *Man of Aran* and selects Basil Wright's
Song of Ceylon, in which two distinct ways of life are contrasted in a way that only the film could do. But *Song of
Ceylon* was not intended to be popular and never would
attract large audiences. And here we come up against the
chief challenge to the film: it must be as popular as the
drama of Webster and bear-baiting once were, and at the
same time it must never relinquish its critical role. "We
have got to accept its popularity as a virtue, not turn away
from it as a vice." So-called popular art today has lost the
quality that gave the music hall its vitality, viz., vulgarity.

It has become refined, muted, private and soothing. A good, popular film should give the sense of having been made by its spectators, not merely shown to them. Examples are few, and most are farces: *Duck Soup*, the early Chaplins, a few Laurel and Hardys. Serious films of the kind are even rarer: perhaps *Fury, The Birth of a Nation, Men and Jobs*. Unfortunately the censorship will not allow certain subjects to be treated at all. We in England, for instance, could not treat human justice as truthfully as the Americans did in *I Am A Fugitive From the Chain Gang*. This means we are driven back to the "blood" and the thriller, which is not altogether a bad thing. But our thrillers have been too polite, too middle-class, too much concerned with Raffles and gentlemen cracksmen. We need to dig deeper—in fact, to uncover the Ravens and even the Anthony Farrants, who shame their class. (Raffles, of course, was applauded—he showed that a gentleman could beat a thug at his own game if he only tried.) And so we are given the recipe for a good film story: it must be popular in the true sense, not mock-popular as are the novels of J. B. Priestley, but of the people, *ex populo*, as are the entertainments of Graham Greene. We must recover the level of *The Spanish Tragedy* and then develop in subtlety and thoughtfulness.

Having summarized his argument, it will now be worth our while to consider some of his actual criticism. First of all from *The Spectator*. His method of contrasting the simple if crude honesty of documentary with the pretensions of so many big feature films was illustrated when he wrote of a film called *Abyssinia*: "It leaves you with a vivid sense of something very old, very dusty, very cruel, but something dignified in its dirt and popular in its tyranny and perhaps more worth preserving than the bright slick streamlined civilization which threatens it. I don't refer particularly to Italy, but to the whole tone of a time whose popular art is on the level of *The Bride of Frankenstein*." This is

familiar enough—Abyssinia replaces Liberia, and the Hollywood monstrosities, real and imaginary, do duty for the
gangsters. He was tempted to call *Boys Will Be Boys,* based
on a fantasy of Beachcomber's, realistic. The morality of
Narkover was only slightly removed from that of the public
schools. It bears the same relation to the truth as *Candide.*
(Dramatic art will always have an element of satire.)

Greene's power as a critic, both of books and of films,
derived almost entirely from his faculty of apprehending the
significant symbols. His mind is not an analytical one, and
his attempts at intellectual process are never impressive.
But he can *feel* his subject more intimately than anyone
else writing in England today. His criticism is that of the
creative writer, the sort of thing I came across once before
in a slapdash article on Hemingway by John O'Hara. The
following perception, for instance, is perfectly obvious once
it has been pointed out to you, but it could not possibly
come from the analytical mind of a Desmond McCarthy or
an Edward Sackville-West: "There was something about
floods which appealed to the Victorian temperament (only
Herr Freud could explain why), not the gigantic floods of
China or Mississippi, but little domestic floods which gave
opportunities for sacrifice and the ringing of church bells
and drenched golden hair." But there was a growing tendency to be irritated by films in general, to criticize shortcomings that might be almost invisible—in fact, to nag. He
welcomed Asiatic actors in one film because they didn't
express their emotions so garishly as Europeans—a "faint
flicker across the broad rice-white surface" was sufficient to
indicate love, pain, or tenderness. The film version of *A
Midsummer Night's Dream* upset him because it seemed to
have been written "with a grim determination on Shakespeare's part to earn for once a Universal certificate." And
although he was impressed by the colour of *Becky Sharp*
he could not help wondering if it would be subtle enough

for Greeneland: for the "machine gun, the cheap striped tie, the battered Buick and the shabby bar . . . the suit that has been worn too long, the oily hat."

These were the sober, barely noticeable beginnings of a vendetta which Greene came to wage against the American film industry. His fury found expression in attacks on two targets: film actresses and Americanism in general. While reading the film criticism in chronological order one is impressed by the change that develops in his attitude to beautiful actresses. At first he is full of admiration. One of them is "lovely to watch and to listen to; she has a beautiful humorous ease." Claudette Colbert is "always pleasant to look at and in the right part she is an able actress." He mentions the "loveliness of Miss Loretta Young who has never been more lustrously, caressingly photographed." He tells us that he has seen "few things more attractive than Miss Neagle in breeches"—which perhaps contains a warning tone of irony. But Graham Greene was a highly-sexed young man. Soldiers who attach their lusts to pin-ups occasionally go berserk. The actresses were beautiful but inaccessible. Slowly the admiration turns to frustration, chagrin replaces delight, and actresses were American, or had at least been groomed by the American film industry, they come to play the part of symbols for something towards which Greene was beginning to feel an uncontrollable animosity. America was the absolute antithesis of Liberia. It provided the apotheosis of the kind of existence that fascinated him, and which he loved to write about, exercising his mingled emotions of love and hate. He began to abuse America and all things American, and in return the Americans hit back. The result was a conflict which has only recently been resolved.

Greene's first shot seems to have been fired at Cecil B. DeMille. "Richard Coeur de Lion, in Mr. DeMille's pious and Protestant eyes, closely resembled those honest simple

young rowing men who feel that there's something wrong
about sex." Here there is a link between the anti-American
animus, Greene's dislike of people who retreat from sex, and
his peculiar view of Protestantism (to be developed to an
exaggerated degree in *Brighton Rock*). There follows a
passage that is worth quoting whole (the film is *The Cru-
sades*):

Neither of the two principal players, Miss Loretta Young and
Mr. Henry Wilcoxon, really get a chance in this film. The
programme says all there is to be said about them. Mr. Wilcoxon
is "six feet two inches tall, weighs 190 pounds. He was nick-
named Biff as a child." Miss Young is "five feet three and weighs
105 pounds." The information is not as irrelevant as it sounds,
for the acting can roughly be judged in terms of weight. Mr.
Wilcoxon leads over the hairy hermit, played by Mr. Aubrey
Smith, by six pounds, and Miss Katherine DeMille, who has an
agreeably medieval face, as Alice of France beats Miss Young
by ten pounds. (To quote the programme again, "She avoids
starches, sugars and fats; eats all greens and only enough meat
to get the necessary proteins.")

After this, sexual, carnal images begin to erupt in
Greene's prose in such a way as to suggest libidinous agita-
tion. "The wealthy woman in pyjamas swaying her munifi-
cent hips along the shore in pursuit of the famous conductor
is followed by the camera behind a close-up frieze of enlarged feet stuck out towards the lens, of fat thighs, enormous backs, a caricature of ugly humanity exposing pieces
of itself like butchers' joints in the sun." With *Arms and the
Girl* we are referred back to "the simple rather adolescent
American manner which seems insolubly linked with high
cheekbones, fraternities and curious shoes." Then comes a
comprehensive attack on the industry, in which he proposes
that certain actors and actresses should be confined to one
annual performance—in the same film, of course, to get it
over and done with. The all-star cast would include Pat
O'Brien, George Arliss, Herbert Marshall, Jack Hulbert,

Cicely Courtneidge, Carl Brisson and Penelope Dudley Ward. "A nightmare, do you say? But I like to rationalize my nightmares."

It will be seen from the foregoing list that Greene's growing irritation with the Americans had not blinded him to the shortcomings of British films. His first review for *Night and Day* was a withering attack on a British film, and again I propose to give a long extract which will serve as an illustration of his method:

The best line to cheer in *The Frog*, an English thriller, is "I must get John Bennett's gramophone record if I am to save his life." The dialogue otherwise goes rather like this: "My name is Bennett—Stella Bennett." "No, not really? Stella Bennett? What a charming name! I very much hope we shall meet again one day soon." "Must you really go? Goodbye then." "What, Stella! Are these gentlemen still here?" "We were on the point of leaving, sir." "This is my father, inspector. May I introduce Inspector Elk of Scotland Yard?" "Goodbye, Miss Bennett, Please don't trouble to see us out. Goodbye, sir. Haven't we met somewhere before?" "No. Goodbye." While the well-mannered dialogue drones on, a bomb is touched off.

Scotland Yard, the voice of the master criminal is trapped on a gramophone disc by a bird watcher, the factory containing the matrix is burnt to the ground, an innocent man is sentenced to death, and the public executioner entering the condemned cell finds his own son there. Badly directed, badly acted, it is like one of those plays produced in country towns by stranded actors: it has an old world charm: Scotland Yard is laid up in lavender.

We must retain our sense of proportion. *A Gun For Sale* is better than that! It is also worth noting that Greene was able to admit that *We From Kronstadt* was undoubtedly the best film in London.

Under the suggestive title "Without Beard or Bed" he claims to have uncovered a "beard neurosis" in American films. Perhaps it had something to do with the astrakhan coats film financiers wore: "a kind of whisker weariness."

His characteristic comment on *Parnell* was, "No illegitimate children, no assignations in seaside hotels under assumed names, no furtive vigils at Waterloo station." *Call It A Day* (the adaptation of a Dodie Smith play) is fair game for him: ". . . what agreeable titillations and temptations: what a Dodie dream of a world where all the heavy labour and the missed cues of infidelity are eliminated and the two-backed beast is trotted out quaintly, gaily and whimsically like a character in *Winnie the Pooh*." His dislike of adult innocence and his loathing of concealment are barely under control. Almost weekly he darted out to snarl at the caricatures of men and women behaving like naughty Boy Scouts and sniggering Girl Guides. Reviewing *Saratoga* he mentions a point of documentary interest: "an amusement car in the Racing Special noisy with the innocent songs of men who in this country would be busy in the third-class carriages with packs of cards."

Meanwhile, the campaign against the Monstrous Regiment is gathering force. Jean Harlow's technique was the gangster's: "she toted a breast like a man totes a gun," he wrote wittily and salaciously. But of Irene Dunne singing beside a farm horse he is merely crude: "Miss Dunne is the one without the white patch on the forehead." Next it was the turn of Grace Moore, who "would be more at home among blackboards and the smell of chalk and dusters and the dear children" than singing "Minnie the Moocher," in trousers. "If you want to escape from a cinema where Miss Moore is playing—I always do—before the end, you feel impelled to raise a hand and wait for permission to leave the room." Even Bette Davis comes under the ban, though he had once considered her potentially a great actress, but "now she plugs the emotions with dreadful abandonment." Of one film he complains that despite a hint of adultery the characters have little more sex-life than amoebas; of another he is stimulated to proclaim that "every

close-up of Miss Linden Travers drives the sexuality home:
a leg in the library, buttocks over the billiard table." He
even discovers that Marlene Dietrich cannot act. "She
lends her too beautiful body; she consents to pose," but
acting she leaves to her servants. It is not surprising that,
as a change from films, he was given *Eve in the Sunlight*
to review, and that his notice appeared under the title, "The
Nudest Book of the Week." How he loved to debunk the
classical attitude towards the human form! His desire and
his contempt coalesced to produce a frontal attack on "these
plump slipshod haunches posed among the wild flowers,
these body arms thrown up in suburban ecstasy towards the
sky, these Leighton limbs grouped coyly round a rubber
ball on a beach. . . ." He quotes a caption: 'Nature's supreme
achievement,' and comments: "there the achievement ends:
a toothy smile, knees coyly crossed, one hand on a silver
birch, rather thick ankles hidden in lush grass." His critical
sense, apparently uppermost, is in fact annihilated, else
how could he call invisible ankles "thick"?

The Road Back, based on Remarque's novel, gave him
the opportunity for a full-blooded assault on the Americans.

It might be funny if it weren't horrifying. This is America seeing
the world in its own image. There is a scene in which the
returned soldiers all go back to their school. Sitting in uniform
on the benches they are addressed by the headmaster; they start
their lessons again where they left off—it may be meant as irony
(I'm not sure), but what it really emphasizes is the eternal
adolescence of the American mind, to which literature means
the poetry of Longfellow and morality means keeping Mothers'
Day and looking after the kid sister's purity. One came daunted
out of the cinema and there, strolling up the Haymarket, dressed
up in blue uniforms with little forage caps and medals clinking,
were the American legionaries, arm in arm with women dressed
just the same—all guide books, glasses, and military salutes: caps
marked Santa Anna and Minnesota: hair—what there was of it
—grey, but the same adolescent features, plump, smug, sentimental, ready for the easy tear and the hearty laugh and the

fraternity yell. What use in pretending that with these allies it was ever possible to fight for civilization? For Mothers' Day's, yes, for antivivisection and humanitarianism, the pet dog and the home fire, for the co-ed college and the campus. Civilization would shock them: eyes on the guide book for safety, they pass it quickly as if it were a nude in a national collection.

The Hollywood film moguls could not have enjoyed all this. They resent adult criticism at the best of times, but the combination of ferocity and malice that Greene managed to pack into his notices must have made them writhe. In a sketch entitled "Film Lunch" Greene had even mocked Mr. Louis B. Mayer, one of the Great. It seems probable that they came to a collective if informal decision that Greene must be stopped. One false step, and they would move heaven, earth, and Hollywood to put an end to it. After his onslaught on Americans (quoted above) they passed by some questionable comments on Magda Schreider: "deep-sunk eyes and porcine coquetry . . . trim buttocks and battered girlishness . . . mouth wide open—rather too much gum like a set of false teeth hung up outside a cheap dentist's." It was obvious that they could bide their time—he seemed to be in such a state of frenzy against the whole tribe of actresses, whose photographed charms mocked his insistent carnality, that he would certainly go too far, if not next week, then the week after. And he did. On 28th November, 1937, he reviewed *Wee Willie Winkie,* starring the child actress, Shirley Temple. It would probably be unwise of me to quote, for Miss Temple's solicitors may still be anxious to protect their client against insinuations made twenty years ago, although in a much earlier review Greene had already noted that some of Shirley Temple's popularity "seems to rest on a coquetry quite as mature as Miss Colbert's and on an oddly precocious body as voluptuous in grey flannel trousers as Miss Dietrich's." Briefly, Greene stated that Miss Temple's audience was elderly and its admiration not entirely centred on her acting ability. In the ensuing lawsuit Miss Temple and her studio were awarded $9,800 and *Night and Day*, which was already in difficulties, ceased publication. Just before the end Greene got in a parting shot. *Marie Walewska* "has its moments when the Frenchman Boyer and the Swede Garbo are together alone, but the awful ocean of American vulgarity and good taste (they are the same thing) laps them round —soon Marie's brother will bounce in like a great Buchmanite Blue troubled about sex, or her husband will slip through the lath and plaster, honeyed and Harvard and humane, behaving as America thinks the Polish aristocracy behaved—with new-world courtesy."

Jacob H. Adler

GRAHAM GREENE'S PLAYS:
TECHNIQUE VERSUS VALUE

GREENE'S PLAYS are usually examined in connection with his novels or his philosophy or both. I should like to approach them from the point of view of a playgoer who knows nothing of Greene the novelist or Greene the Catholic (or even Greene the movie scriptwriter) and who will evaluate the plays as plays. This playgoer may miss things that the complete Greene expert would see, and he may make mistakes; but he will, I think, also see important things that any other approach to Greene's plays would miss. There is a sense in which an artist must be granted his material. But when the public finds the material controversial, as it did Ibsen's and as it does Greene's, then the "granting" of it is not easy. Ibsen insisted indignantly that he was not a reformer but a playwright. I should like to take it as a reasonable premise that Greene is trying to be a playwright too.

What, then, are these plays that Greene has given us? The mention of Ibsen strikes an appropriate note, for Greene's second and best-known play is an end play, in which the revelation of the past has a powerful effect upon the present. Indeed *The Potting Shed* is Ibsenian in a number of ways—closer to the master in spirit than most of the "problem plays" which have been parading these many years under his banner. *The Potting Shed* is a play which might have grown directly out of the conclusion of *The Wild Duck*. In that play, the daughter of the household, a girl just reaching adolescence, has committed suicide because she has been suddenly and violently disillusioned by her father. Everything we know of the characters surrounding the father suggests that he will be protected from the remorse that would normally be consequent upon his act. And his principal protectors will be his wife and a doctor friend who sees completely through the father's inadequacies but who knows that he needs to be preserved in his illusions if he is to survive. The doctor foretells the future: "We will talk of this again when the grass has first withered on her grave . . . then you'll see him steep himself in a syrup of sentiment and self-admiration and self-pity. Just you wait!"

In *The Potting Shed*, in the distant past before the play opens, a boy just reaching adolescence has committed suicide because his father has severely disillusioned him; but he is revived by a miracle which (as it happens) is even more embarrassing to his father than his death would have been. The father is protected by his wife and his doctor friend from the consequences otherwise to be expected; but the wife and the doctor have reversed roles, and in *The Potting Shed* it is the wife who is aware that her husband exists for the admiration that has always been granted him; that he is a fake (her own word); that if he is to survive he must be preserved in his "life illusion": almost a statement of the theme of the Ibsen play.

So *The Potting Shed* takes up where *The Wild Duck* left off—a method used by Ibsen himself, who showed in *Ghosts* the consequences of what the public had wanted

the wife to do in *A Doll's House*. In *The Potting Shed*
illusion is preserved in the husband to his very death, at
frightful cost to his wife and at the expense of the complete
ostracization of his son. The son is not one of those who
can live by illusion; he must seek out the past (lost to him
as an amnesiac) so that he can survive. For just as Hedwig
in *The Wild Duck* would have been blind had she lived, so
James Callifer in *The Potting Shed* is blind, to his past and
to love, for half his life. And Ibsenian characters and situations are everywhere in *The Potting Shed*. Mrs. Callifer,
protecting her husband at the expense of her son, is another
Mrs. Alving who has likewise been brought up in a false
system of beliefs, and who is likewise to see the last of her
illusions destroyed. The doctor is the fatuous idealist out
of any number of Ibsen plays; and there is even a second
doctor (consulted by James) who is the clear-sighted but
imperfect spokesman of a "healthy" point of view, like the
doctors in *The Wild Duck* and *An Enemy of the People*.
A girl behaves unexpectedly, as in *The Master Builder,* and
she tries to get at the truth and "save" the hero, as in that
play. The hero is psychologically bound by the past, and
hence incapable of love, like the heroine of *The Lady from
the Sea;* and both plays concern the process of being released from that bondage.

Greene also uses props to make his plot go, in an old-
fashioned way which once seemed realistic and now seems
mechanical, and which we are likely, perhaps not quite
fairly, to associate with Ibsen. In this play there are three
telegrams, an offstage dog (who "gets lost" when he is no
longer needed), a bowl of water for the dog, a stolen bottle
of pills, a toy pistol, a whiskey bottle, a picture of the
Sacred Heart, some holly, the letters and memorabilia
of a dead man, and more. In *The Wild Duck*—but it is only
an example—there are a bottle of brandy, a jug of hot water,
various articles of foodstuff, a photograph and retouching

equipment, a camera, the offstage wild duck, a rabbit skin, a pistol, a letter containing a "deed of gift," a flute, a lampshade, a brush and duster, scissors and paste, and more. Both plays use objects and events as fairly obvious and clear-cut casual symbols—in Ibsen, a game of blindman's buff, a smoking stove; in Greene, the toy pistol, a dream of a lion. Both plays use the titular object—wild duck; potting shed—as a complex overall symbol. Indeed both plays (like many other plays in the Ibsen tradition, such as Chekhov's *Sea Gull*) treat the overall symbols more prominently than any objective explanation seems to justify.

Now there is of course no reason why symbols should be precise, and perhaps considerable reason why they should not be; they are to provide a dimension and a meaning which can be perceived, so to speak, only if one does not look at them. Ibsen's wild duck succeeds greatly here in providing multiple interpretations and a feeling of mood and mystery which *work* in extending the meaning of the play beyond the realistic observation of a handful of people in a small room. In drama, however, such a method is open to three dangers: first, the symbols may obscure the visible action, as in Ibsen's *Master Builder;* second, they may be a coverup for vagueness of meaning; third, they may provide a portentousness which the play does not deserve. *The Potting Shed* is clear enough in structure, so there is no problem there; but one may combine the second and third dangers to wonder whether the potting shed (and even *The Potting Shed*) is worth the attention devoted to it. The one thing James Callifer succeeds in remembering before his great awakening is a toy spade; the potting shed is the scene of the suicide, and it has, for him and even for his mother, an aura of terror about it; the gardener's name was Potter; the title of the play is *The Potting Shed.* Now Potter, of course, brings the *Rubaiyat* to the mind of any literate Englishman. And in this play God, the Potter, does

miraculous things to His vessel in the potting shed. At the
conclusion of the play, moreover, we are told that places
where miracles occur are everyday places, to be contemplated with neither awe nor fear. But the Potter-miracle
explanation is too neat, too mathematically equivalent; it
reduces the voltage of the symbol. And it makes the boy's
fondness for his toy spade, and his choice of the potting
shed as the place to hang himself, merely pumps to inflate
the symbol. It may be that it is impossible for an American to judge adequately of a symbol expressed in strictly
English idiom. But translate *potting shed* to *toolshed* or
greenhouse and the problem remains the same; indeed it
may be rendered easier to work with, since the "potter" pun
evaporates, and hence any other value should make itself
felt. I must confess I find no other value. For a boy to
hang himself in a greenhouse seems no better and no worse,
no more terrible and no less portentous, than to hang himself in an attic or a kitchen or a field. And I can accept
the position that miracles can occur anywhere without the
need for such an elaborate demonstration. Greene's overall
symbol does not work as well as Ibsen's; the insistence upon
it, beyond the plausible fact that James Callifer fears the
place without knowing why, results not in enlargement but
in inflation. One may wonder indeed whether Greene's
choice of a location does not go back to *The Wild Duck;*
for Hedwig's suicide also takes place in a sort of garden-
room where there is an object she loved (as James Callifer
kept his toy spade in the potting shed); the garret was
supposed to be the place where Hedwig was to "sacrifice
. . . for his sake . . . the dearest treasure you have in the
world," just as in the potting shed Father William Callifer
prays to God to "take away what I love most . . . take away
my faith but let him live;" and the wild duck's garret is
built up as a place of mystery, much as the potting shed is.
    But as in most of Ibsen's plays the revelations in *The*

Wild Duck lead to catastrophe. One reason that they do
not in *The Potting Shed* is that the one man to whom the
revelations would have been catastrophic (the father, Henry
Callifer) is dead; and it is an Ibsenian credo that those who
are ready to hear the truth, as James Callifer is, are better
off by far if they hear it. Not only James, but everyone in
The Potting Shed except the fatuous idealist Dr. Baston
and perhaps James's insensitive brother John, is better for
the cleared air. Equilibrium has been restored and life
can be normal once more. But while this is a perfectly
logical result in *The Potting Shed,* it once more reduces the
voltage. The end play may be a real comedy—*The Circle* is
a prime example—but if it is to take itself seriously, it seems
psychologically and dramatically more natural for it to end
in catastrophe. *Oedipus Rex* and *Hamlet* are the two great
exemplars—both plays, incidentally, in which a man seeks
out revelations which will, in a sense, define himself. It is
not for nothing that, of the only two Ibsen end plays which
conclude happily, one, *Pillars of Society,* is considered contrived, and the other, *The Lady from the Sea,* is minor. A
suicide, a miracle, the bitter wasting of large parts of several lives: these are not the materials for an ending which
says, "And they got married and lived happily ever after."
And yet Greene seems to approve philosophically of his
own ending:

> MRS. CALLIFER: What will you do, James?
> JAMES: Marry Sara, I hope.
> MRS. CALLIFER: That's a very simple aim.
> JAMES: I've lived with the complex long enough.

T. S. Eliot may be as wrong as Greene in making *The Cock-
tail Party* a comedy and bringing in a tragic note (the young
woman crucified very near an anthill) only by the way.
But at least Eliot attaches his miracle (of spiritual rebirth)
to the doomed woman, and not to the married couple, whose

lives become happier, to be sure, but whose still comparatively low-voltage living seems not only philosophically but dramatically more apropos.

Greene's play also suffers from a third act full of talk following the successive climactic revelations of Act Two. This is the "discussion" which Shaw found to be the essential new element in Ibsen's plays: but even Shaw, master that he was of discussion, rarely allowed a whole long act of discussion to follow his climaxes; perhaps *Mrs. Warren's Profession* is the only important example. Ibsen himself provides no example at all. Greene's characters are fun to be with, and it is therefore easy to forgive his keeping us with them longer; but one cannot help feeling that the third act exists for the sake of providing an explicit happy ending, which can be achieved only at some length, and for the sake of expounding a philosophy which the effect of the revelation of the miracle demonstrates. In the third act Mrs. Callifer's continuing stubborn silence and final readiness, even eagerness, to talk, are alike rather forced. The entrances and exits are entirely too frequent, and the pricking of Dr. Baston's pretensions is a needless breaking of a butterfly. Anne's dream of the lion which closes the play is charming and "right," but it does not deserve a whole act to lead up to it.

In short, a person coming to *The Potting Shed* with no previous knowledge of Greene would probably feel that here is a disciple of Ibsen who is rather better than most; a creator of characters who are fascinating to watch, though not greatly memorable, and of intelligent dialogue which is fun to hear; a master of suspense and of revelation; but also a man who expects his audience to respond more than most audiences can to *what* he reveals, and to the loving attention he devotes to the effects of the revelations. *The Potting Shed* is an interesting, civilized, literate play; but it is minor where it behaves as though it is major.

The Living Room comes obviously from the same pen as *The Potting Shed* (and came from it, of course, earlier), but it is a different kind of a play. The clear-cut resemblances in detail, though rather numerous, are superficial. Both plays contain a priest; both priests have been ineffectual for many years; both plays contain a man trained in psychology; both plays have symbolic titles; both plays pit the comparatively young against the comparatively old; both plays involve a suicide.

But technically the differences between the plays are greater and more basic than the similarities. *The Living Room* is not in any significant sense an end play. Its attempt at mystification (why are so many rooms shut up?) is rather shallow and soon solved. It does not depend on tremendously dramatic revelations. But the most significant, fundamental difference is probably in the treatment of the titular symbol. The potting shed, as I have shown, functions quite well as a part of the plot, but as a symbol it is not well integrated. In *The Living Room,* the situation is reversed. The fear of death which has led the old women in the play to close up any room in which someone has died, and hence to use a very inappropriate room as a living room, has nothing to do with the plot; and plotwise the attention devoted to these things is an excrescence and an annoyance. But regarded symbolically they give the play a genuine additional depth and significance. The ironic complexities —it is not, for example, a living room but a room for the living dead; the living dead fear death, but the one person in the play who is young and who could love life and give life, deliberately dies in the living room—the ironic complexities ring on and on. When Greene turned to the drama, he clearly knew a great deal about symbol, but had much to learn about the techniques of writing plays.

Compared to *The Potting Shed, The Living Room* lacks focus. It gives the effect of an early draft for a novel. Some materials seem unused and unrealized, few of the characters are sharply developed, the dialogue is not crisp, and the play seems to exist in a vacuum cut off from life. Even the most genuinely dramatic moments in the play are transformed and used more successfully (which is to say more dramatically) elsewhere. The priest in a moment of spiritual crisis is infinitely better realized in *The Potting Shed*, as is the use of the bottle of pills intended for suicide. The sisters reverting to their childhood relationships, which is the effective enough conclusion of *The Living Room*, seems the raw material for the much more effective temporary reversion of the Callifer mother and son to an earlier relationship in midplay. Even the drawing together of man and wife against the lover of one of them, which is subtle and dramatic and more than anything else drives Rose to suicide in *The Living Room*, is more effectively and ironically handled in *The Complaisant Lover*.

Yet *The Living Room*, for all its amateurishness and lack of focus and economy, has a depth which not even *The Potting Shed* can claim, and certainly not *The Complaisant Lover*. *The Potting Shed* is a little bit slick, a little bit tricky. It articulates too neatly, and with insufficient irony for so much precision. It may be significant that while *The Potting Shed* is easily related to Ibsen (and the antecedents of *The Complaisant Lover* are also, as we shall see, easily suggested), the backgrounds of *The Living Room* are harder to identify. There is something of Strindberg, perhaps, in the neurotic domination achieved by two women (Helen Browne and Marion Dennis). The atmosphere of the play, the way its world is cut off from the real world, brings Barrie's *Mary Rose* to mind, and Ibsen's *John Gabriel Borkman*. The neurotic isolation in a residence, and the thwarting of love, may recall *The Three Sisters* or *Uncle Vanya*. The resemblance to a novel, and even some of the material, point toward *Strange Interlude*. And almost all

of these things call up Eliot's *Family Reunion,* which has a
similar atmosphere and movement, and which handles similar problems of love, sin, guilt, and redemption. But most
of this list seems like the merest source-hunting, performed
not because the sources are illuminating, but for their own
sake. The source of this play of Greene's is primarily
Greene. And one may venture the guess that Greene's
awareness of this play's inadequate dramaturgy led him
to adopt established dramatic techniques in his two later
plays.

Yet the greatest depth is in *The Living Room* because
the play is tragic in its implications, and its symbols function well in terms of tragedy. The vision is artistically valid,
as it is not in *The Potting Shed.* More narrative than dramatic in feeling, *The Living Room* has the thickness, if not
the bulk, of a novel. At the explicit level, it is less than
successful; it is indeed less memorable for what it says than
for what it does not say. But in one's first play it is, of
course, an achievement to be memorable at all.

Greene's third play, *The Complaisant Lover,* is an unexpected departure. Not an end play, not a play with a heavy
philosophical or symbolic underlay, it is a bittersweet
middle-class comedy-triangle, told competently and straight-
forwardly, which might almost have come from the pen of
Noel Coward or Somerset Maugham, whose *Constant Wife*
has, in fact, many points of similarity; a look at the title of
both these plays—compare *The Careless Husband, The
Conscious Lovers, The Provoked Wife*—and their un-Puritan
but slightly sentimental attitudes toward sexual love suggest connections with the early 18th century. Perhaps the
most astonishing thing is the complete lack of the special
sort of suspense which even one who had seen only Greene's
other two plays might assume, correctly, to be a Greene
hallmark. Here the only important element of suspense is

the traditional one of When will the husband discover that his wife has a lover, and what will he do when he does?—and even that is not made very suspenseful. On the other hand, the structure of the play is Greene's firmest, since it depends on no miracles or psychoses or violence, and though it continues to rely considerably on props, they are at any rate used with increased integration and skill. And Greene does bring his triangle to a wry sort of conclusion which might have seemed impossible to achieve credibly until he achieved it. But beyond this there seems little or nothing to separate this play from dozens of others of the same type, with equally logical structure, well-drawn characters, and urbane dialogue. Like all Greene's work, it holds one's interest; but *The Living Room* and *The Potting Shed* have the significant virtues of being hard to forget, and *The Complaisant Lover* does not.

To turn for a moment to Greene's subject matter apart from his technique, it is a surprise to discover that beyond his obvious concern with Roman Catholicism in the first two plays, all three plays have their primary subject matter in common: the conflict between love and fear and between different kinds of love. In *The Living Room*, it is love of God *versus* fear of death, sexual love *versus* love of God, love of spouse surviving out of long familiarity, and out of fear of loneliness, *versus* love of mistress grown out of fear of middle age—and so on. In *The Potting Shed*, it is love of husband *versus* love of son, inability to love as a result of disillusionment, the deliberate sacrifice of the ability to love God—and so on. In *The Complaisant Lover*, it is a detailed analysis of a wife's genuine affection for her husband *versus* her genuine sexual love for another man, plus various minor instances. And here again the same sort of development is seen from play to play; from extremely complex cases, each of important weight and all a little too hysterical, to an increasing concentration on fewer and crisper examples: from murky depth to diamond-clear surfaces.

And so the conclusion to be drawn from a study of Greene's plays to date is that here is a competent and profound artist who is, after all, not yet a playwright, but a novelist writing plays: for up to now his increasing competence in dramatic technique has meant decreasing profundity; only in comparatively light comedy has his technique been adequate to his idea. Nevertheless his second and third plays have been highly enjoyable, and when an intelligent and uncompromising artist turns to drama, the fact itself is cause for rejoicing. It takes only the mildest sense of prophecy to predict that there will be far greater cause for rejoicing before Greene's career in the drama is over.

Carolyn D. Scott

THE WITCH AT THE CORNER:
NOTES ON GRAHAM GREENE'S
MYTHOLOGY

IN THE SHORT STORY often lies the microcosm of an author's total vision, and for Graham Greene that medium has provided the emblem for both "the power and the glory" of his longer works. Indeed, the volume *Nineteen Stories* (1949),[1] the best but by no means the only collection of Greene's shorter fiction, contains more than a "hint of an explanation" toward a fuller realization of his world view. Few critics, however, have perceived the significance of the short stories to the whole of Greene's work. Furthermore, those who discuss the short fiction often err in not recognizing the thick web of consciousness surrounding the hero's actions and read them as if they expressed only the conventional Christian dichotomy between good and evil. George Silveira's "Greene's 'The Basement Room,' "[2] for example, searches the *Catholic Encyclopedia* to discover the relation between the Church's designation of man's seventh year for attaining the age of reason and the age of Philip when he rejects responsibility in the world. Vernon Young's review of the whole volume[3] practically diagnoses a sort of Augus-

tinian neurosis as the core of Greene's creation. "His flights
across the threshold of the occult, of the theological," writes
Young, "are impelled by fear of physical being rather than
by visions of the power and the glory."[4] And Sean O'Faolain
in *The Vanishing Hero* strongly allies Greene with "anti-
humanists" like Mauriac and Bernanos who encourage a
return to a medieval world.[5] In fact, nearly all Greene's
works have at one time or another been considered as Christian allegories, dialogues between the body and soul, and
even as Manichean tracts. But surely a man of Greene's
stature, a man who most unquestionably belongs to the
20th century and not the Middle Ages, cannot wholly depend on the Baltimore Catechism for thematic structure.
Like Yeats, Pound, Eliot, Faulkner, Tolkien, and even his
personal favorites, Saki and de la Mare, Greene has created
his own myth, one that reconstructs tradition and ritual yet
speaks with the immediacy of the modern dilemma. Explicitly, Greene's central symbol is the heart of Africa, seat
of our fall, and the whole myth first takes shape in his
autobiographical travelogue, *Journey Without Maps*. It is
continued and brought to fruition within the short stories.

Just as Henry James found in Europe the "thickness"
and "roundness," the "fairy-tale side of life," so Greene
found in Africa a myth of lost childhood, or "Pendélé,"
as he calls it in his latest work, *A Burnt-out Case*. He wishes
to find, by simply penetrating into the African heart, at what
point we went astray—where man fell. No critic can escape
the childhood theme in Greene, for it is the one obsession
out of which his tragedies grow. But, as in Catharine
Hughes' discussion of this matter, Greene's view of childhood has been thought to include a Wordsworthian innocence.[6] This is too simple. It cannot explain the knowledge of death that Francis Morton in "The End of the
Party" possesses, nor Pinkie's early instinctive distaste for his
parents' tawdry Saturday nights in *Brighton Rock*. These
distinctly unromantic elements, however, are placed in per-

spective by "The Lost Childhood," an essay in which Greene both celebrates and laments his discovery of the creative endeavor in Marjorie Bowen's *The Viper of Milan*.[7] Before this intellectual awakening, says Greene, he had lived his first fourteen years in a "wild country without a map" where his only recognition was the ancient witch Gagool of *King Solomon's Mines* whose power haunted his nursery dreams, as we shall see. But inevitably the hand must move along the bookshelf, one must grow up to the moral world, selecting a job, a taste, a death, as surely as Eve's hand moves toward the apple or Oedipus guesses the sphinx's riddle.

So in the childhood of Africa what Greene found was not a prelapsarian Eden, but Eden at the moment the apple is to be plucked: neither guilty nor innocent of the forces of evil. There the childhood of the race is indeed acquainted intimately with the devil, the witch of our dreams; yet in that intimacy it has still not lost the instinctive, ritualistic terror, the imagination which comprehends the supernatural. Thus, for Greene, our civilization has exchanged "supernatural cruelty" for a secular depravity. We have lost a creative sensitivity to witches and angels, the understanding that permits man to create and build a brave new world out of the ruin he placed on nature at the Fall. Our seedy, chrome civilization has made a Manichean sense of evil unfortunately possible.

In Africa, where there is a potential yet unrealized civilization—"the graves not opened yet for gold, the mine not broken with sledges"[8]—Greene discovered the compelling ritual of the Liberian bush devil.[9] These men of power govern the supernatural and natural activities of the community and with raffia skirts and carved masks, go about the countryside both terrorizing and delighting the folk. In an unconsciously erotic ritual, which Greene likens to Europa and the bull, children dance before them, courting that power who leers beneath the carved mask. These bush devils are the initiators of the young, executors of jus-

tice, and demigod priests all in one; yet in reality they may
be merely the harmless village blacksmith. Greene discovered that their "power" contains that simultaneous
quality of good and evil, the essence of black magic that
has been lost in most of our civilized theology. He writes:

"Devil," of course, is a word used by the English-speaking native
to describe something unknown in *our* theology; it has nothing
to do with evil. One might equally call these big bush devils
angels—for they have the angelic properties of alacrity and in-
visibility—if that word contained no element of "good." In a
Christian land we have grown so accustomed to the idea of
a spiritual war, of God and Satan, that this supernatural world,
which is neither good nor evil but simply Power, is almost
beyond sympathetic comprehension. Not quite: for those witches
which haunted our childhood were neither good nor evil. They
terrified us with their power, but we knew all the time that we
must not escape them. They simply demanded recognition:
flight was a weakness.[10]

Here Greene's myth allies itself with the archetypal
recognition of evil which has absorbed the studies of Freud
and Jung. In Freud this dream of the witch, which haunts
Greene's heroes through several works, is part of the
"archaic heritage which the child brings with him into the
world, before any experience of his own, as a result of the
experience of his ancestors."[11] Indeed Freud is on Greene's
mind as he leaves Africa. "Freud has made us conscious as
we have never been before of those ancestral threads which
still exist in our unconscious minds to lead us back."[12] Unlike those of Freud, though, the ancestral threads which
Greene has come upon are not regarded as sources of neurosis. They are rather a "dread of something outside that
has got to come in."[13] Unlike Marlow's descent into hell
which culminates in "the horror" of primitive barbarism, the
whole journey into the African bush confronts Greene with
a "sense of disappointment with what man had made out
of the primitive, what he had made out of childhood."[14]
But Greene, for all this, does not see in childhood the

"clouds of glory" which surround the child of *The Prelude* who, unappalled by the drowned man's face, innocently recognizes evil from fairy tales he once read. Greene's *"something* in that early terror"[15] is perhaps best described in Jacques Maritain's *Creative Intuition in Art and Poetry* as the "spiritual preconscious" which, unlike the "automatic Freudian unconscious" that merely embodies physical behavior or misbehavior, acknowledges the awareness of the primitive as part of the poetic activity.[16] Thus the "something outside that has got to come in" is for Greene, as it was for James in the dream of the Gallerie d'Apollon, the comprehension, the recognition of appalling power, neither good nor evil, but a haunting, compelling synthesis of both. And thus Greene cannot espouse the conventional Christian view of the dichotomy between good and evil. In his comments on the air of evil in James's *The Turn of the Screw*, Greene says: "That story . . . belongs to the Christian, the orthodox imagination. Mine [the witches and preternatural personae of his dreams] were devils *only* in the African sense of beings who controlled power."[17]

The Christian mythos cannot be fully adequate for Greene's highly particular spiritual experience. The comment that Greene "believes in God because he believes in Satan"[18] can only ride on the surface of his works. And so his concern, his obsessions, which, in his own words, makes "every creative writer worth our consideration,"[19] is to pursue those symbols which haunted his and all our nursery dreams: the Princess of Time, the poisoned flowers, an old Arab, Tibetan warriors, and the inevitable witch. They pursue, they persist; and his body struggles only to find they survive, not only in his own childish dreams, but also the dreams of a wailing child who cries for the dance of the bush devil. To triumph we need only to find and recognize this power; flight is weakness. This choice of triumph or weakness is the dilemma of Greene's heroes.

The struggle for and recognition of power is the theme

of several of Greene's more significant short stories. After the African experience, his first descent into the spiritual underworld was "The Basement Room," written in 1936 on the boat back from West Africa. In this work, a power—which is only amoral, not immoral, in fact that power which is associated with the ritual of initiation before the African bush devil—operates in child Philip's dream world to confront him with the moment of choice in what will become a moral situation. Left by his parents with the butler and housekeeper, Mr. and Mrs. Baines, Philip must choose, at the early age of seven, between the nursery and the cellar, between fruition or defeat. But he is determined not to be drawn into the adult world of secrets, love affairs, and jealousy. "For if a grown-up could behave so childishly, you were liable, too, to find yourself in their world. It was enough that it came at you in dreams: the witch at the corner, the man with a knife."[20] However, those powers which work upon us in every situation "demand recognition," and "flight is a weakness," a weakness that Philip does not overcome.

There are two worlds in "The Basement Room," which Philip must recognize and choose between, separated by a green baize door, an image Greene used elsewhere to separate the world of innocence from the world of knowledge, the world of love from the world of hate, the world of the child from the world of the adult. Cross the threshold and you have committed yourself to ruin or triumph. Greene's own fascination with this image appears later in his Mexican adventures, *The Lawless Roads,* when he recalls the baize door between his school and home, between hate and love;[21] and again in *The Ministry of Fear* when Arthur Rowe, beginning to wake up from his dream world and amnesia, passes through the green baize door of the insane asylum to discover the source of evil that has beset him. In his nursery, Philip, burdened with Baine's secret love affair, "strained his ears for Mrs. Baines's coming, for the sound of voices, but the basement held its secrets; the green baize door shut off that world."[22]

Philip's inadequacy also lies in his terror of the dark, of the now unfamiliar rooms of the house where dusters cover the furniture, when nurse and family are away. He too is making a journey without maps. Vivid is the terror he feels for the knock, knock, knock at the door, the bleeding head and glittering eyes of the Siberian wolves, all waiting to be recognized in his dreams. Floating up from that world is the witch, Mrs. Baines, who like the witch with Hansel, plies Philip with jam and pudding, then tricks him into telling the secret. She is like old Gagool, ancient and musty. Her very being is secret as the bush devil; she is "darkness when the night light went out," and is "flowers gone bad."[23] When Philip's eyes open from the dreams, the terror is real, too real for him to face. The witch with her musty hair, her breath hot, leans over his bed in an unexpected visit to ask, "Just tell me where they are." The doors and windows are wrenched open in a breath, and, wretched, he cries out, "Baines, Baines," and the witch falls in a black heap. He cannot escape on a jeweled swan as did the children of Grimm's fairy tale. Philip is not prepared to accept this violent facing of the adult world he cannot understand. He rejects loyalties and unwittingly "tells on" Baines in his reluctance to face that black heap ever again. "He'd spent it all, had been allowed no time to let it grow, no years of gradual hardening; he couldn't even scream."[24]

Philip, in withdrawing from the dream world, surrenders the initiation to life. To use the metaphor of Greene's mythology, the secret school of the bush devil here has failed to prepare Philip for the adult, moral world. For in that primitive kindergarten which Greene once witnessed, the bush children attend lessons given by the devil for two years. They feel terror and awe for this harsh instructor, but knowledge of him prepares them for a rugged life in the

bush. Failure to thrive under his fierce spell may cause
one to end as a lifeless heap of clothes at the parents' door.
It is best to be thrust into the power of the devil and not
resist. This is an African child's baptism and rebirth. "They
brought a screaming child up to the devil," writes Greene,
fascinated, "and thrust him under the devil's muzzle, under
the dusty raffia mane; he stiffened and screamed and
tried to escape and the devil mouthed him."[25] And so it is
with Philip's own initiation under the dusty hair of Mrs.
Baines, only he cannot be reborn because he resists.

The same baptism of terror is performed in "The Hint
of an Explanation" except that here the child survives the
ordeal. Acting in the role of the bush devil, Blacker, the
baker, tempts and ironically instructs for the priesthood,
young David by forcing a moral commitment upon him.
Even though Blacker asks David to commit sacrilege, we
must not interpret this request in any conventionally dia-
bolical sense. Blacker's action betrays much the same
"supernatural cruelty," the fusion of love and hate as is
found in the bush devil's ritual. This reading of young
David's temptation coheres with his own adult observation about the inadequacy of Satan in theology: "The
word Satan is so anthropomorphic."[26] We are instead tried
by a "Thing" or power, says the priestly narrator. He hesi-
tates to say who or what Blacker really serves. Blacker,
whose intense hate becomes permeated with a curiosity
close to love, is viewed by David with the awe of the supernatural similar to that of the villagers of Mosamboluhun
to the local blacksmith-devil. "It is not the mask that is
sacred, nor the blacksmith who is sacred; it is the two in
conjunction . . .," observes Greene.[27] Blacker's appearance
is as terrifying as the devil's mask: one wall-eye, turnip
head, smears of chalk and pastry. His secret knowledge of
bleeding people and opening doors in the night like the
devil who says to the bush child, "I'm going to swallow
you," terrifies the boy into nearly surrendering the Sacred

Host. In the spell of Blacker's professed powers, David fears not to remove the Host from his mouth and place it aside. Like Mrs. Baines, Blacker is the witch who plies his victim with toys to insure his moment of success. Yet, at this moment, the full force of that power shatters into disappointment. Through Blacker's hate for, yet fascination with the Host, that recognition of power which is neither good nor evil intervenes, and the realization of this "Thing's" value for the pulp which is "God there on the chair" saves David and thus prepares him for a new, priestly life. The school of the evil has been his salvation.

This knowledge of a Thing, a power, is almost prophetic in "The End of the Party" when Francis Morton's dream of death comes like a big bird swooping in the darkened house. Francis has dreams which reveal to him that darkness and death are real, dreams that hold secret knowledge to which the adults are cold. These unfeeling adults, Mabel Warren and Mrs. Henne-Falcon, flutter like hens and chickens about the darkening rooms enjoying the hide-and-seek game that is a real and present terror to Francis. Like the bush villagers, the ancient joke of "frightening the child with what had frightened them" governs their unconscious actions.[28] The spiritual terror that leads to death and a powerful realization of the essence of death are but impersonal games to the grownup, civilized world, as impersonal as the nurse's cold torch making a beam through the darkness towards Francis's death. But after death, the power of his terror, conveyed like an electric impulse to his elder twin's hand, overcomes all seedy civilization, all set programs at the birthday party. One is reminded of the significance of this in the later work, *England Made Me,* where twins also have the power of conveying their awe for death. Kate contemplating her quarrel with Tony, who unknown to her has just been killed, compares it to childhood disputes. "In childhood one had been more careful, death was closer; one hadn't this hard grip on life."[29] Even before the African venture then, Greene in these two stories had decided that the racial childhood held understanding of the darkness of man's heart, of the surety in death. He later confirms:

Oh, one wanted to protest, one doesn't believe, of course, in the "visionary gleam," in the trailing glory, but there was something in that early terror and the bareness of one's needs, a harp strumming behind a hut, a witch on the nursery landing, a handful of kola nuts, a masked dancer, the poisoned flowers.[30]

In lesser works, "I Spy," and "A Drive in the Country," the adolescent, too, comes in contact with this power. For example, Charlie Stowe, reversing the Wordsworthian theme, finds the father "doing things in the dark which frightened him."[31] In the second story, the young girl, disillusioned with her father's meticulous dullness, runs off in a wild ride to the dark woods with reckless Fred. In this action she is like the child swaying in the erotic dance before the old bush devil. In her childish dream, she is courting an adult action. In the cold woodsy fog the British girl finds she must flee back to her father's cheap bolted door in terror from a suicide pact that would implicate her with a man who is damning himself. She has awakened from the dreamy dance with the devil to find the leering eyes of an adult blacksmith beneath the painted mask. And too, the man in "The Innocent" discovers an obscenity he drew as a child in painful, intense desire, hidden, waiting for him in a hollow tree. It reveals the loss of that finer taste, keener pleasure, and deeper terror that must inevitably end in seedy civilization, typified by his slatternly friend, Lola.

So Evil creeps into the later dreams: "The man with the gold teeth and rubber surgical gloves; the old woman with ringworm; the man with his throat cut dragging himself across the carpet to the bed."[32] Greene's adult heroes are struggling with the body as is Craven in "A Little Place off the Edgware Road," who is reminded by a religious placard of a dream he had in which there are no worms and dissolution, the body does not decay. His only waking comfort is that it was just a nightmare. Then evil creeps in, dropping upon him the fine bloody spray from the living corpse of the "man with his throat cut" who haunted the author's own dreams. But in "Proof Positive" Greene reaffirms the power in the unity of the body and spirit and the rottenness in their separation when the dominant spirit, robbed of its bodily connection, "decays into whispered nonsense."[33] Metallic civilization has created this separation of body and soul. Adult life directs what childhood instinctively knew. Religious signs are not enough. The sound of music and the drum are silent. We must go to Africa again to embrace the leper who alone can tell us of Pendélé.

Pendélé is that mysterious land of childhood which Querry, in Greene's newest work, A Burnt-out Case, came to Africa to seek, where in his dreams he wishes to go after death. The tawdry, seedy level of the secular, adult world has betrayed him as it betrayed Philip in "The Basement Room." He cannot build and create any more. His architectural skill, like Philip's Meccano set, has been stowed away somewhere. Querry goes to Africa to seek a word that falls from the lips of Deo Gratias, the leper, who whispers the secret of "Pendélé" in the darkness of the bush, very like the forest Greene stumbled through in Liberia many years before.[34] Pendélé, a childhood place of dancing and singing, becomes the central obsession in Querry's view of his new life. Like the bush devils who speak in foreign dialects, Deo Gratias (indeed the name parody cannot be ignored) mutters all night in unintelligible mixtures of French and bush language, except for one word, "Pendélé." Dr. Colin's answer to Querry's inquiry into the meaning is a facile, unimaginative translation—"pride." This is the sort of impersonal judgment about the world which Querry has been fleeing from all his life. He insists, rather, it is this place of our childhood, where there is singing and dancing and games; where we can sleep in a single bed without the responsibilities of adults. Our mortal sins do not explain our hunger, our flight through labyrinthine ways, our exposure to evil and death.

When Querry elaborates this meaning of the word to the Superior of the hospital force, the father answers, "People have to grow up. We are called to more complicated things than that."[35] Querry recalls the ancient initiation, ". . . surely there's something also about having to be as little children if we are to inherit . . . . We've grown-up rather badly. The complications have become too complex."[36] For belief also belongs to the cave man; Christians do not have the corner on faith. What Querry really is looking for is at what point in our childhood we went astray; the Eden Deo Gratias cannot and will not reveal.

So intense is the impact of the metaphor about the lost childhood that later Querry, figuratively, translates his questioning life into a fairy tale about a country boy and a king. Mme. Rycker, his listener, says in disbelief, "You and I are much too old for fairy-stories." "Yes. That in a way *is* the story, as you'll see,"[37] Querry returns. Both have lost the way to Pendélé. The meaning to Querry's little story may be found, I think, in the lines from A. E.'s poem, "Germinal," often quoted by Greene: "In the lost childhood of Judas, Christ was betrayed." The little unformed face of Philip hardens, as does Querry's heart for the world.

Querry's fairy tale is not even a very good story, not so thrilling as Grimm, nor so penetrating as Perrault, but it represents Querry's coming to grips with what was missing in the civilized world, why he came down the river to the leper colony. He is too old for fairy tales, for believing that the King, or God, has sent "a bull, a shower of gold, a son."[38] In a tawdry world where cheap statues and neo-Gothic churches abound, he can no longer cherish the ancient symbols of creativity; he can only recall and be troubled by the memory of them. He envies the unconscious devotions of his parents to the King much in the

same way Greene envies the child swaying before the devil
—Europa swaying before the bull, unaware of the leering
adult beneath who knows of the fall, the forgetfulness.

And Querry, as he steps into the dawn, reflects on the
epigram "The King is dead, long live the King." Perhaps in
the new life and new country, away from the seemingly
impersonal rules of the (man-made, after all) Church, he
can find the King of Pendélé, the bush devil who will mouth
him and dance for him.

Unlike Querry, Greene sees in primitive ritual and myth-
making something which can potentially revitalize our own
civilized institutions, most of which have their origins in
ancient rites. Greene's own jungle discovery thus refreshes
and fulfills his long journey as he comes to realize the
relation of the whirling, demanding devil and his own
European religious longing. Suddenly recalling a childhood
experience where he witnessed the ancient Jack-in-the-
Green rites at a quiet crossroads, Greene writes:

It wasn't so alien to us, this masked dance (in England too there
was a time when man dressed as animals and danced), any more
than the cross and the pagan emblems on the grave were alien.
One had the sensation of having come home, for here one was
finding associations with a personal and a racial childhood, one
was being scared by the same old witches.[39]

The search and discovery of myth seems to bring order
from external or internal chaos. The fact that myth fails
to distinguish the everyday act from symbolic performance
encourages the modern hope that a supernatural power can
permeate all things. In this realization Greene hopes for a
coherent ritual not incompatible with modern institutions.

His fascination for the primitive, of course, would not
exclude such an establishment as the Catholic Church. He
finds for himself, as he claims for Henry James, "the treatment of supernatural evil," "the savage elementary belief"
in prowling evil spirits to be adequate vehicles for expressing the "struggle between the beautiful and the treacher-

ous."[40] In its concept of sacrament the Church preserves those precious remnants of our childhood—the supernatural elements by which "human nature is not despicable."[41] The life within the Catholic Church provides a quality of vision truly catholic in its absorption of the pagan and the primitive. It is not reduceable to moral formulas which bind M. Rycker to his sanctimonious practices, Mme. Rycker to her spouse. The struggle for the beautiful and the treacherous in Greene's heroes and heroines requires a judge whose creative, fruitful powers of synthesis can unite the good in evil, the evil in good. Greene's myth provides that judge and judgment, and that power is God, the hound of heaven, the bush devil.

After his childhood discovery of evil, in *The Viper of Milan,* Greene remarks, "Human nature is not black and white but black and grey."[42] It is from this assumption that Greene's mythology can take shape. In Liberia he reaffirms this basic conviction about life as he uncovers the aboriginal terror in the "grey" visage of the bush devil. Such an impact did this revelation have upon Greene that we are forced to qualify any comment we make on the seeming Manichean qualities of his fiction as well as our thinking about his concept of Hell. As R.W.B. Lewis implies, Hell does lie about Pinkie, Philip, Francis, David, and even Querry in their infancy, but the sterile, chrome, unimaginative boredom of that Hell is not found in Liberia. Rather, Hell is the civilized perversion of the primitive. With the comprehension of what the witch at the corner means to the children of Greene's fiction, with the understanding that these children are like the Liberian boy being initiated to the terror of the bush devil, we find Greene's fiction more intelligible, and even more flexible in its concept of the human act. For the myth opens up to Greene a whole spectrum of possibilities between the theological poles of good and evil, and thus it both extends the range of his ethical sympathies and sophisticates his artistic technique.

Neil Brennan

BIBLIOGRAPHY

Works by and about Graham Greene are listed as follows:

I. Books by Greene
II. Books in Part by Greene
III. Periodical Contributions by Greene: A Note
IV. Books and Dissertations on Greene
V. Books and Dissertations in Part on Greene
VI. Periodical Articles on Greene: A Selected List
VII. Dramas and Films by Greene: A Note
VIII. *Modern Fiction Studies: Graham Greene, Special Number*
IX. *Renascence: Graham Greene, Special Number*
X. Bibliographies

The compiler of this bibliography is greatly indebted to a research grant-in-aid from the Graduate School of Auburn University and to the research assistance of Miss Linda Morley provided by Villanova University.

Items marked with an asterisk were not seen by the compiler.

I. BOOKS BY GREENE

Listed below are first editions of works by Greene. No attempt is made to give reprint data; many of his novels have appeared in over a dozen resettings, at least three in braille. (For a partial list of reprintings, see Phylis Hargreaves, "Graham Greene: A Selected Bibliography," *Modern Fiction Studies*, III (Autumn 1957) 269 ff.) Attention should be called to Greene's statement in the Preface to the uniform edition of *The Man Within* (Heinemann, 1952) that only *The Man Within* among the books appearing in the uniform edition is reset without change. No extensive textual study has yet been conducted, but Professor Gordon Ray has called attention to changes in the uniform edition of *It's a Battlefield,* Professor Bruce Harkness to a small but important change in *The Power and the Glory,* and A. R. Redway to deletions from *Journey Without Maps.* Differences, moreover, are to be noted even between first editions of two other books, *The Third Man* and *The Potting Shed.* In both cases the American edition is the earlier, and the English is the edition the author prefers.

English and American editions of *Nineteen Stories* differ in content rather than text, the later American edition printing "The Hint of an Explanation" in place of "The Lottery Ticket." *Twenty-One Stories* is treated here as a reissue of *Nineteen Stories,* for it is so designated in the uniform edition. It contains three additional stories, however: "The Blue Film," "The Destructors," and "Special Duties," and omits the fragment of an unfinished novel entitled "The Other Side of the Border."

One book by Greene has been omitted from this list because not even its exact title could be determined. Greene has described it as "my rarest first edition: a Who's Who, with introductory essays, to the Azores." It was "published" in an edition limited to twelve copies by the British Foreign Office, presumably in 1942 or 1943. (See *Sunday Times* (14 July 1963) 10.)

Translations are given only when they rank as first editions. Over thirty of Greene's works have been translated, a few into as many as thirty languages.

Data on reviews is restricted for sake of uniformity to those which appear in the London *Times Literary Supplement* and the *New York Times Book Review.* Absence of notation indicates that no review was found there, not that no review exists. Books and monographs on separate works are listed insofar as known, except that school texts—American, British, Dutch, French, German, and Japanese— which discuss or furnish guide questions to stories and essays by Greene are omitted. (For a partial listing of these, see Maurice Beebe, "Criticism of Graham Greene: A Selected Checklist with an Index to Studies of Separate Works," *Modern Fiction Studies,* III (Autumn 1957) 281 ff.) Likewise omitted are the many introductions to the novels in translation.

1   *BABBLING APRIL.*
      Oxford, Blackwell, 1925.
      REVIEW:
      TLS (21 May 1925) 355.
      ARTICLE:
      Snow, Royall, "Oxford: Thin Smoke and Thin Fire," *Poetry* (Chicago), XXVIII (May 1926) 112-14.

2 *THE MAN WITHIN.*
   London, Heinemann, 1929.
   Garden City, N. Y., Doubleday Doran, 1929.
   REVIEWS:
     TLS (20 June 1929) 492.
     NYT (27 Oct. 1929) 6.

3 *THE NAME OF ACTION.*
   London, Heinemann, 1930.
   Garden City, N. Y., Doubleday, 1931.
   REVIEWS:
     TLS (9 Oct. 1930) 804.
     NYT (8 March 1931) 7.

4 *RUMOUR AT NIGHTFALL.*
   London, Heinemann, 1931.
   Garden City, N. Y., Doubleday, 1932.
   REVIEW:
     TLS (3 Dec. 1931) 978.

5 *STAMBOUL TRAIN.*
   London, Heinemann, 1932.
   Garden City, N. Y., Doubleday, 1933, under the title *Orient
     Express.*
   REVIEWS:
     TLS (15 Dec. 1932) 960.
     NYT (12 March 1933) 21.

6 *IT'S A BATTLEFIELD.*
   London, Heinemann, 1934.
   Garden City, N. Y., Doubleday, 1934.
   REVIEWS:
     TLS (8 Feb. 1934) 90.
     NYT (8 April 1934) 7.
   London, Grayson, 1935 (Limited Edition).

7 *THE BEAR FELL FREE.*

8 *ENGLAND MADE ME.*
   London, Heinemann, 1935.
   Garden City, N. Y., Doubleday, 1935.
     Reissued by the Viking Press in 1953 as *The Shipwrecked.*
   REVIEWS:
     TLS (4 July 1935) 430.
     NYT (8 Sept. 1935) 6.

9 *THE BASEMENT ROOM AND OTHER STORIES.*
   London, Cresset, 1935.

REVIEW:
TLS (23 Nov. 1935) 767.
ARTICLE:
Silveira, Gerald E., "Graham Greene's 'The Basement Room,'"
Explicator, XV (Dec. 1956) 13.

10 *JOURNEY WITHOUT MAPS: A Travel Book.*
London, Heinemann, 1936.
Garden City, N. Y., Doubleday, 1936.
REVIEWS:
TLS (23 May 1936) 439.
NYT (8 Nov. 1936) 14.
ARTICLE:
Baker, Denys Val, "My Favorite Forgotten Book," *Tomorrow*,
VII (July 1948) 63-64.

11 *A GUN FOR SALE.*
Garden City, N.Y., Doubleday, 1936, under the title *This Gun for Hire.*
London, Heinemann, 1936.
REVIEWS:
NYT (21 June 1936) 17.
TLS (11 July 1936) 579.

12 *BRIGHTON ROCK.*
New York, Viking, 1938.
London, Heinemann, 1938.
REVIEWS:
NYT (26 June 1938) 6.
TLS (16 July 1938) 447.
ARTICLES:
Cayrol, Jean, "Autour de l'oeuvre de Graham Greene," *Revue de la Pensée Française*, X (April 1951) 68-72.
Consolo, Dominick P., "Music as Motif: The Unity of *Brighton Rock*," *Renascence*, XV (Fall 1962) 12-20.
DeVitis, A. A., "Allegory in *Brighton Rock*," *Modern Fiction Studies*, III (Autumn 1957) 216-24.
Duché, Jean, "Du Rocher de Sysyphe au Rocher de Brighton," *Table Ronde*, no. 2 (Feb. 1948) 306-309.
McGowan, F. A., "Symbolism in *Brighton Rock*," *Renascence*, VIII (Autumn 1955) 25-35.
*Magny, Claude Edmonde, "De Benito Cereno au Rocher de Brighton," *Guilde du Livre*, XVI (July 1951) 150-53.
Powell, Dilys, "A Trio of Thrillers," *Britain To-Day*, no. 178 (Feb. 1951) 36.

13 *THE LAWLESS ROADS.*
London, Longmans Green, 1939.

New York, Viking, 1939, under the title *Another Mexico.*
REVIEWS:
TLS (11 March 1939) 146.
NYT (11 June 1939) 10.
ARTICLE:
Escarpit, Robert, "L'Arriére-plan mexicain dans Lawrence et dans Greene," *Langues Modernes,* XLV (Jan.-Feb. 1951) 44-46.

14 *THE CONFIDENTIAL AGENT.*
London, Heinemann, 1939.
New York, Viking, 1939.
REVIEWS:
TLS (23 Sept. 1939) 553.
NYT (1 Oct. 1939) 20.

15 *THE POWER AND THE GLORY.*
London, Heinemann, 1940.
New York, Viking, 1940, under the title *The Labyrinthine Ways.*
REVIEWS:
TLS (9 March 1940) 121.
NYT (17 March 1940) 6.
BOOKS AND MONOGRAPHS:
Allen, Walter, "Six Novels Discussed. 1. *The Power and the Glory,* by Graham Greene," *Reading a Novel* (London, Phoenix House, 1949) 34-39. Revised ed. (1956) 37-42.
Davies, Horton, "The Confessional and the Altar," *A Mirror of the Ministry in the Modern Novels* (New York, Oxford University Press, 1960) 81-110.
Rillo, Lila E., *The Power and the Glory: A Novel by Graham Greene.* Buenos Aires, The Argentine Association of English Culture, 1946. 11 p. Contains a Foreword by Patrick Orpan Dudgeon, pp. 1-2.
ARTICLES:
Beary, Thomas John, "Religion and the Modern Novel," *Catholic World,* CLXVI (Dec. 1947) 203-11.
Becker, Hubert, "Priestergestalten in der Romanliteratur der Gegenwart," *Stimmen der Zeit,* CLIII (1953) 345-55.
*DeVitis, A. A., "Notes on *The Power and the Glory,*" *The Annotator,* no. 5 (May 1955) 7-10.
Gardiner, Harold C., "Taste and Worth," *America,* LXXV (20 April 1946) 53.
Hillig, Franz, S.J., "Die Kraft und die Herrlichkeit," *Stimmen der Zeit,* CXLIII (Feb. 1949) 354-66.
Hoggart, Richard, "The Art of Caricature: Aspects of the Art of Graham Greene, with Particular Reference to *The Power*

and the Glory," *Essays in Criticism*, III (Oct. 1953) 447-62.

*Ihlenfeld, Kurt, "Kann ein Sünder ein Heiliger Sein?" *Welt*, III (1947 636-37.

Kevin, Neil, "Fiction Priests," *Irish Ecclesiastical Record*, LX (Oct. 1940) 253-57.

Mauriac, François, "La Puissance et la Gloire," *Figaro Littéraire* (30 Oct. 1948) 1, 3. Also in *Renascence*, I (Spring 1949) 25-27.

Parc, Robert du, "Saint ou Maudit, Le prêtre dans 'La Puissance et la Gloire,'" *Études*, no. 260 (March 1949) 366-81.

Patten, Karl, "The Structure of *The Power and the Glory*," *Modern Fiction Studies*, III (Autumn 1957) 225-34.

Pfleger, Karl, "Religiöse Wirklichkeit . . .," *Wort und Wahrheit*, IV (June 1949) 473-78.

Woodcock, George, "Mexico and the English Novelist," *Western Review*, XXI (Autumn 1956) 21-32.

16 *BRITISH DRAMATISTS.*
London, William Collins, 1942.

17 *THE MINISTRY OF FEAR.*
London, Heinemann, 1943.
New York, Viking, 1943.
REVIEWS:
NYT (23 May 1943) 3.
TLS (29 May 1943) 257.
ARTICLE:
Auden, W. H., "The Heresy of Our Time," *Renascence*, I (Spring 1949) 23-24. Also in *The Wind and the Rain*, VI (Summer 1949) 53-54.

18 *THE LITTLE TRAIN.*
London, Eyre and Spottiswoode, 1946.
First published as "Story and Pictures by Dorothy Craigie." Reissued under Greene's name and as "Illustrated by Dorothy Craigie":
London, Max Parrish, 1957.
New York, Lothrop, Lee and Shepard, 1958.

19 *NINETEEN STORIES.*
London, Heinemann, 1947.
New York, Viking, 1949.
Reset and retitled *TWENTY-ONE STORIES*:
London, Heinemann, 1954.
REVIEWS:
TLS (26 July 1947) 377.
NYT (13 Feb. 1949) 3, 28-29.

ARTICLE:
Joseph, Brother, F.S.C., "Greene's 'The Hint of an Explanation,'" *Explicator*, XIX (Jan. 1961) Item 21.

20 *THE HEART OF THE MATTER.*
London, Heinemann, 1948.
New York, Viking, 1948.
REVIEWS:
TLS (29 May 1948) 302.
NYT (11 July 1948) 5.
BOOKS AND MONOGRAPHS:
*Dellevaux, Raymond, *Graham Greene et "Le Fond du Problème."* Brussels, Éditions "La Lecture au Foyer," [1951].
Fournier, Gaston, S.J., *Scobie, ou l'homme victime de sa pitié: "Le Fond du Problème" de Graham Greene.* Toulouse, Imprimerie Parisienne, 1953. 36 p.
Mueller, William Randolph, "Theme of Love: Graham Greene's *The Heart of the Matter," Prophetic Voice in Modern Fiction* (New York, Association Press, 1959) 136-67.
ARTICLES:
Connolly, Frances X., "The Heart of the Matter," *Newsletter: Catholic Book Club*, XL (Midsummer 1948) 1-2.
DeVitis, A. A., "The Church and Major Scobie," *Renascence*, X (Spring 1958) 115-20.
Horst, Karl August, "Argernis der Schöpfung, zur Theologie Graham Greenes," *Merkur*, V (Feb. 1951) 184-87.
Howes, Jane, "Out of the Pit," *Catholic World*, CLXXI (April 1950) 36-40.
Jefferson, Mary Evelyn, "The Heart of the Matter: The Responsible Man," *Carolina Quarterly*, IX (Summer 1957) 23-31.
Jouve, Raymond, "La Damnation de Scobie?" *Études*, no. 263 (Nov. 1949) 164-77.
Montesi, Gotthard, "Tragödie der Nächstenliebe," *Wort und Wahrheit*, III (Aug. 1948) 610-15.
Moré, Marcel, "Les Deux Holocaustes de Scobie," *Dieu Vivant*, no. 16 (1950) 77-105. Also as "The Two Holocausts of Scobie," *Cross Currents*, II (Winter 1951) 44-63. Translated by Erwin W. Geissman.
Rodriguez Monegal, Emir, "'El Revés de la Trama' o la Màscara del Realismo," *Sur*, no. 183 (Jan. 1950) 57-60.
Wall, Barbara, "London Letter," *America*, LXXIX (28 Aug. 1948) 470-71.
Waugh, Evelyn, "Felix Culpa?" *Tablet*, CXCI (5 June 1948) 352-54 and *Commonweal*, XLVIII (16 July 1948) 322-25.

21 *°AFTER TWO YEARS.*
    A collection of verse. Privately printed, 1949.

22 *THE THIRD MAN.*
    New York, Viking, 1950.
    London, Heinemann, 1950. *The Third Man and the Fallen
    Idol.* Approved text. This edition also contains two prefaces
    by Greene, the second to "The Basement Room," under its
    film title *The Fallen Idol.*
    (See also II. 19)
    REVIEW:
    TLS (4 August 1950) 481.
    ARTICLE:
    Alloway, Lawrence, "Symbolism in *The Third Man,*" *World
    Review,* new series no. 13 (March 1950) 57-60.

23 *THE LITTLE FIRE ENGINE.*
    London, Max Parrish, 1950.
    New York, Lothrop, Lee and Shepard, 1953, under the title
    The Little Red Fire Engine.
    REVIEWS:
    TLS (17 Nov. 1950) CBS iv.
    NYT (22 Feb. 1953) 28.

24 *THE LOST CHILDHOOD AND OTHER ESSAYS.*
    London, Eyre and Spottiswoode, 1951.
    New York, Viking, 1952.
    REVIEWS:
    TLS (6 April 1951) 208.
    NYT (17 Feb. 1952) 1, 31.
    ARTICLES:
    Braybrooke, Neville, "Graham Greene as Critic," *Commonweal,*
        LIV (6 July 1951) 312-14. Also in the *New Adelphi,*
        XXVIII (Fourth Quarter 1951) 425-30, and *Irish Monthly,*
        LXXXI (Oct. 1953) 383-88.
    Pritchett, V. S., "A Literary Letter from London," *New York
        Times Book Review* (4 Nov. 1951) 41.
    Turnell, Martin, "Baroque Art and Poetry," *Commonweal,* LV
        (26 Oct. 1951) 55-57.
    Vallette, Jacques, "La Jeunesse de Graham Greene," *Mercure
        de France,* no. 1058 (Oct. 1951) 326-27.

25 *THE END OF THE AFFAIR.*
    London, Heinemann, 1951.
    New York, Viking, 1951.
    REVIEWS:
    TLS (7 Sept. 1951) 561.
    NYT (28 Oct. 1951) 5.

Books:

Fournier, R. P. Gaston, S.J., *Le Tourment de Dieu Chez les Amants de Graham Greene.* Toulouse, Imprimerie Parisienne, [1953]. 34 p.

Gardiner, Harold C., S.J., "Mr. Greene Does It Again" and "Second Thoughts on Greene's Latest," *In All Conscience* (New York, Hanover House, 1959) 96-102.

Gregor, Ian, and Brian Nicholas, "Grace and Morality . . . ," *The Moral and the Story* (London, Faber and Faber, 1962) 185-216.

West, Anthony, "Graham Greene," *Principles and Persuasions* (New York, Harcourt Brace, 1957) 195-200.

Articles:

"Novelist Graham Greene: Adultery Can Lead to Sainthood," *Time,* LVIII (29 Oct. 1951) 98-104.

Braybrooke, Neville, "Graham Greene and the Double Man: An Approach to *The End of the Affair," Dublin Review,* CCXXVI (First Quarter 1952) 61-73.

Downing, Francis, "The Art of Fiction," *Commonweal,* LV (28 Dec. 1951) 297-98.

Lodge, David, "Use of Key Words in the Novels of Graham Greene: Love, Hate, and *The End of the Affair," Blackfriars,* XLII (Nov. 1961) 468-74.

Spier, Ursula, "Melodrama in Graham Greene's *The End of the Affair," Modern Fiction Studies,* III (Autumn 1957) 235-40.

Waugh, Evelyn, "Heart's Own Reasons," *Commonweal,* LIV (17 Aug. 1951) 458-59 and *Month,* VI (Sept. 1951) 174-76.

26   *FOR CHRISTMAS.

A collection of verse. Privately printed, 1951.

27   ESSAIS CATHOLIQUES.

Paris, Éditions de Seuill, 1953.

Six essays translated from English by Marcelle Sibon. Three of the essays had not appeared in English: "Message aux catholiques français," "La civilisation chrétienne est-il en péril?" and "Les paradoxes du Christianisme." All three had appeared in French books or periodicals, in 1948-1951, but as of June 1963 still had not appeared in English. Two others—"Le paradoxe du pape" and "Notre Dame et son assumption"—had earlier appeared in English (in *Life,* 1950-1951), in French, and in German, but only one, "L'Aspect religieux de Henry James," had been collected by Greene (in *The Lost Childhood,* 1951).

German translation by Elisabeth Schnack, with an introduction by Gertrud von le Fort, *VOM PARADOX DES CHRIS-*

TENTUMS. Zurich, Verlag der Arche, 1953. Eight items. This adds to the essays in the French edition "Warum Ich Schreibe" (two letters by Greene from *Why Do I Write?*), "Tischgesprach mit Graham Greene" (see Moré, VI. 76), and "Brief an Marcel Moré" (a letter from Greene concerning Scobie's last words, also published earlier only in French, in *Dieu Vivant*). On the other hand, the German edition omits the essay "The Religious Sense of Henry James" which was appearing about this time in the German translation of *The Lost Childhood, Die Verlorene Kindheit und Andere Essays,* 1953.

* Dutch-Flemish translation by A. Noorbeek, *DE PARADOX VAN HET CHRISTENDOM.* Amsterdam, Voorhout, 1953. With an additional preface by Anton van Duinkerken. Contents otherwise the same.

* Spanish translation by Maria Luisa del Carril, *ENSAYOS CATOLICOS.* Buenos Aires, Sur, 1955. [No list of contents seen.]

* Italian translation, from the French by Piero Jahier, and from the German by Italo Alighiero Chivsano, *SAGGI CATTOLICI.* Milan, Mondadori, 1958. Nine items. Said to contain the items in the German edition, plus the essay on Henry James and an additional preface by David Maria Turoldo.

* Portuguese translation by Joao Albuquerque, *ENSAIOS CA-THOLICOS.* Lisbon, Atica, 1958. [No list of contents seen.]

28 *THE LIVING ROOM.*
Stockholm, Norstedt, 1952. *I Sista Rummet,* trans. from MS by Jane Lundblad.
London, Heinemann, 1953.
New York, Viking, 1954.
REVIEW:
TLS (10 July 1953) 450. Note only.
BOOKS:
Bentley, Eric, "A Real Writer," *What Is Theatre?* (New York, Horizon Press, 1956) 25-29.
Kerr, Walter, "Playwrights," *Pieces at Eight* (New York, Simon and Schuster, 1957) 143-49.
Tynan, Kenneth, *"The Living Room,* by Graham Greene, at Wyndham's," *Curtains* (New York, Atheneum, 1961) 47-49.
ARTICLES:
Brown, John Mason, "Parish Greene," *Saturday Review,* XXXVII (18 Dec. 1954) 24-25.
Cronin, Vincent, "Graham Greene's First Play," *Catholic World,* CLXXVII (Sept. 1953) 406-10.

Findlater, Richard, "Graham Greene as Dramatist," *Twentieth Century*, CLIII (June 1953) 471-73.

Gregor, Ian, "The New Romanticism: A Comment on *The Living Room*," *Blackfriars*, XXXIV (Sept. 1953) 403-406.

Guerrero Zamora, Juan, "Graham Green su cuarto de estar contra la muerte," *Indice*, VIII (30 Sept. 1953) 24.

Hynes, Sam, "Religion in the West End," *Commonweal*, LIX (12 Feb. 1954) 475-78.

Klein, Luce A., "La Première Pièce de Graham Greene Sera Jouée à Paris," *Arts*, no. 388 (5 Dec. 1952) 3.

Koster, Wilhelm, "Dennoch nicht," *Frankfurter Hefte*, VIII (April 1953) 314-15.

Lewis, Theophilus, "Post Mortem Report," *America*, XCII (8 Jan. 1955) 386-87.

Madaule, Jacques, "El misterio del amor en la obra de Graham Greene," *Sur*, no. 226 (Jan.-Feb. 1954) 48-65.

Madden, Joan, "With Crooked Lines: Greene's *The Living Room*," *America*, XC (6 March 1954) 600-602.

Maguire, Mother C.E., "Grace and the Play," *America*, XCIII (30 July 1955) 433-35.

Maudit, Jean, " 'Le Living-Room' de Graham Greene," *Etudes*, no. 283 (Nov. 1954) 365-71.

Mondrone, Domenico, S.J., "Uno sguardo su Graham Greene da 'L'Ultima stanza,' " *Civiltà Cattolica*, CVIII (May 1957) 279-93.

Stanley, John, "Life in the Living Room," *Commonweal*, LXI (31 Dec. 1954) 354-55 and LXXI (30 Oct. 1959) 123-24.

29 *THE LITTLE HORSE BUS.*
London, Max Parrish, 1952.
New York, Lothrop, Lee and Shepard, 1954.
REVIEWS:
TLS (28 Nov. 1952) CBS iv.
NYT (7 March 1954) 22.

30 *THE LITTLE STEAMROLLER: A Story of Mystery and Detection.*
London, Max Parrish, 1953.
New York, Lothrop, Lee and Shepard, 1955.
REVIEWS:
TLS (27 Nov. 1953) CBS vii.
NYT (13 March 1955) 26.

31 *NINO CAFFÈ.*
An appreciation of the Italian painter Nino Caffè. Printed in Italy for the Knoedler Galleries of New York City. Distributed at the exposition which opened in December 1953.
4 p.

32 *LOSER TAKES ALL.*
   London, Heinemann, 1955.
   New York, Viking, 1957.
   REVIEW:
   TLS (18 Feb. 1955) 101.

33 *THE QUIET AMERICAN.*
   Stockholm, Norstedt, 1955. *Den Stillsame Amerikanen*, trans. from MS by Jane Lundblad.
   London, Heinemann, 1955.
   New York, Viking, 1956.
   REVIEWS:
   TLS (9 Dec. 1955) 737.
   NYT (11 March 1956) 1, 32.
   ARTICLES:
   "Américain tranquille," *Nouvelles Littéraires* (8 March 1956) 7.
   Bechner, Hubert, "Der Stille Amerikaner," *Stimmen der Zeit,* CLX (April 1957) 68-72.
   Bouscaren, Anthony T., "France and Graham Greene versus America and Diem," *Catholic World*, CLXXI (Sept. 1955) 414-17.
   Breit, Harvey, "The Quiet Englishman," *New York Times Book Review* (26 Aug. 1956) 8.
   Brennan, Neil, "Coney Island Rock," *Accent,* XVI (Spring 1956) 140-42.
   Cassidy, John, "America and Innocence: Henry James and Graham Greene," *Blackfriars*, XXXVIII (June 1957) 261-67.
   Elistratova, Anna, "Graham Greene and His New Novel," *Soviet Literature*, VIII (1956) 149-55.
   Evans, Robert O., "Existentialism in Greene's *The Quiet American,*" *Modern Fiction Studies*, III (Autumn 1957) 241-48.
   Freedman, Ralph, "Novel of Contention: *The Quiet American,*" *Western Review*, XXI (Autumn 1956) 76-81.
   Hicks, Granville, "In a Novel It's the Life, Not the Politics, That Counts," *New York Times Book Review* (12 Aug. 1956) 5.
   Hinchliffe, Arnold P., "The Good American," *Twentieth Century*, CLXVIII (Dec. 1960) 529-39.
   Hughes, Riley E., "*The Quiet American*: The Case Reopened," *Renascence,* XII (Fall 1959) 41-42, 49.
   Liebling, A. J., "A Talkative Something-or-Other," *New Yorker*, XXXII (7 April 1956) 148-54.
   McCormick, John O., "The Rough and Lurid Vision: Henry James, Graham Greene and the International Theme," *Jahrbuch für Amerikastudien*, IX (1957) 158-67.

Rahv, Philip, "Wicked American Innocence," *Commentary*, XXI (May 1956) 488-90.
*Rudman, Harry W., "Clough and Graham Greene's *The Quiet American*," *Victorian Newsletter*, XIX (1961) 14-15.

34 *THE POTTING SHED.*
New York, Viking, 1957.
London, Heinemann, 1958.
REVIEW:
TLS (21 Feb. 1958) 107. Note only.
BOOKS:
Clurman, Harold, "Graham Greene 1957," *Lies Like Truth* (New York, Macmillan, 1958) 176-78.
Gassner, John, "Religion and Graham Greene's *The Potting Shed*," *Theatre at the Crossroads* (New York, Holt, 1960) 155-57.
Tynan, Kenneth, "*The Potting Shed*, by Graham Greene, at the Globe," *Curtains* (New York, Atheneum, 1961) 207-209.
ARTICLES:
Blajot, J., "La renuncia a la fe de Father William Callifer," *Razon y Fe*, CLX (Dec. 1959) 441-50.
McCarthy, Mary, "Sheep in Wolves' Clothing," *Partisan Review*, XXIV (Spring 1957) 270-74.
McLaughlin, J. J., "Potting Shed and the Potter's Wheel," *America*, XCVII (17 Aug. 1957) 505-506, 508.
Mesnet, Marie-Beatrice, "Le Potting Shed de Graham Greene," *Études*, no. 298 (Sept. 1958) 238-47.
*Murphy, John P., "*The Potting Shed* and Catholic Critics," *Tablet*, CCXI (1 March 1958) 210.
——————, "*The Potting Shed*: Dogmatic and Dramatic Effects," *Renascence*, XII (Fall 1959) 43-49.
Rewak, J., "*The Potting Shed*: Maturation of Graham Greene's Vision," *Catholic World*, CLXXXVI (Dec. 1957) 210-13.
Stratford, Philip, "Unlocking the Potting Shed," *Kenyon Review*, XXIV (Winter 1962) 129-43.
Wyatt, E. van R., "God in a Garden," *Critique*, I (Feb. 1958) 45-48.

35 *OUR MAN IN HAVANA.*
London, Heinemann, 1958.
New York, Viking, 1958.
REVIEWS:
TLS (10 Oct. 1958) 573.
NYT (26 Oct. 1958) 5.
BOOK:
Kazin, Alfred, "Graham Greene and the Age of Absurdity," *Contemporaries* (Boston, Little Brown, 1962) 158-61.

258   *Neil Brennan*

ARTICLES:

"Graham Greene vs. Selwyn Lloyd," *Time and Tide*, XL (17 Jan. 1959) 65.

Kauffman, Stanley, "With Graham Greene in Havana," *New Republic*, CXLII (15 Feb. 1960) 22-23.

Taber, Robert, "Castro's Cuba," *Nation*, CXC (23 Jan. 1960) 63-64.

Tarnawski, Wit, "Przemiany Grahama Greene's," *Kultura*, no. 138 (April 1959) 131-37.

36   *THE COMPLAISANT LOVER.*

London, Heinemann, 1959.

New York, Viking, 1960.

REVIEW:

TLS (31 July 1959) 448.

ARTICLE:

Spinucci, Pietro, "L'Ultimo dramma di Graham Greene," *Humanitas* (Brescia), XV (Nov. 1960) 820-25.

37   *A BURNT-OUT CASE.*

Stockholm, Norstedt, 1960. *Utbrand,* trans. from MS by Torsten Blomkvist.

London, Heinemann, 1961.

New York, Viking, 1961.

REVIEWS:

TLS (20 Jan. 1961) 37.

NYT (19 Feb. 1961) 4.

ARTICLES:

Hess, M. Whitcomb, "Graham Greene's Travesty on *The Ring and the Book*," *Catholic World*, CXCIV (Oct. 1961) 37-42.

Highet, Gilbert, "Our Man in Purgatory," *Horizon*, III (May 1961) 116-17.

Noxon, James, "Kierkegaard's Stages and *A Burnt-Out Case*," *Review of English Literature* (Leeds), III (Jan. 1962) 90-101.

Sackville-West, Edward, "Time-Bomb," *Month*, XXV (March 1961) 175-78.

Servotte, Herman, "Bedenkingen bij *A Burnt-Out Case*, Graham Greene's Jongste Roman," *Dietsche Warande en Belfort*, CVI (June 1961) 371-75.

Weyergans, Franz, "'La Saison des Pluies,' de Graham Greene," *Revue Nouvelle*, XXXIII (April 1961) 417-20.

38   *IN SEARCH OF A CHARACTER: Two African Journals.*

London, Bodley Head, 1961.

New York, Viking, 1962.

REVIEWS:

TLS (27 Oct. 1961) 772.

NYT (7 Jan. 1962) 4.
ARTICLE:
 Engelborghs, Maurits, "Dagboek van een romancier," *Dietsche Warande en Belfort,* CVII (May-June 1962) 372.

39 *IN SEARCH OF REALITY.*
 Contains four stories: "Under the Garden," "Dream of a Strange Land," "A Visit to Morin," and "A Discovery in the Woods."
 London, Bodley Head, 1963.
 New York, Viking, 1963.
REVIEWS:
 TLS (21 June 1963) 457.
 NYT (14 July 1963) 4, 20.
ARTICLE:
 Wassmer, Thomas A., S.J., "Faith and Reason in Graham Greene," *Studies* (Dublin), XLVIII (Summer 1959) 163-67. Reprinted as "Faith and Belief: A Footnote to Greene's 'Visit to Morin,'" *Renascence,* XI (Winter 1959) 84-88. Also as "Reason and Faith as Seen by Graham Greene," *Drama Critique,* II (Nov. 1959) 126-30.

II. BOOKS IN PART BY GREENE

(Books containing stories, essays, or introductions that are readily found in collections by Greene are not listed.)

1 *PUBLIC SCHOOL VERSE: An Anthology,* III, 1921-1922. Edited by Martin Gilkes, Richard Hughes, and P. H. B. Lyon.
 London, Heinemann, 1923.
 Contains Greene's poem "The Gamesters," p. 15.

2 *OXFORD POETRY,* 1923. Edited by David Cleghorn Thompson and F. W. Bateson.
 Oxford, Blackwell, 1923.
 Contains the poems "Stepping Stones" and "Apologia," pp. 27-28.

3 *OXFORD POETRY, 1924.* Edited by Harold Acton and Peter Quennell.
 Oxford, Blackwell, 1924.
 Contains the poems "Paint and Wood" and "Childishness," pp. 16-17.

4 *OXFORD POETRY, 1925.* Edited by Patrick Monkhouse and Charles Plumb.
 Oxford, Blackwell, 1925.

Contains the poems "I Shall Be Happy" and "Sonnet—All These Belong . . . ," pp. 19-20.

5   THE BEST POEMS OF 1925. Edited by L. A. G. Strong.
    Boston, Small Maynard, 1925.
    Contains Greene's poem "A Tramp Finds Himself Inspected by an Owl," p. 112.

6   *SPECTATOR'S GALLERY: Essays, Sketches, Short Stories, and Poems from The Spectator 1932. Edited by Peter Fleming and Derek Verschoyle.
    London, Cape, 1933.
    Contains Greene's review, "Anthony à Wood."

7   THE OLD SCHOOL: Essays by Divers Hands. Edited by Graham Greene.
    London, Cape, 1934.
    Contains the editor's "Preface" and "The Last Word," pp. 7-8, 247-56.

8   THEN AND NOW, 1921-1935: A Selection of Articles, Stories, and Poems taken from the first fifty numbers of Now and Then, 1921-1935.
    London, Cape, 1935.
    Contains Greene's essay, "The Travellers' Library," pp. 153-55.

9   THE BACHELOR OF ARTS. A novel by R. K. Narayan.
    London, Nelson, 1937.
    Contains an "Introduction" by Greene, pp. v-x.

10 FOOTNOTES TO THE FILM. Edited by Charles Davy.
    London, Dickson, 1937.
    Contains Greene's essay, "Subjects and Stories," pp. 57-70.

11 GARBO AND THE NIGHT WATCHMAN: A Selection from the Writings of British and American Film Critics. Assembled and edited by Alistair Cooke.
    London, Cape, 1937.
    Contains reviews of sixteen films (reprinted from the Spectator, 1935-1937), pp. 207-39, 344-46.

12 THE MINT: A Miscellany of Literature, Art and Criticism. Edited by Geoffrey Grigson.
    London, Routledge, 1946.
    Contains Greene's travel-diary selections, "Convoy to West Africa," pp. 40-50.

13 FIRESIDE BOOK OF SUSPENSE. Edited by Alfred Hitchcock.
    New York, Simon and Schuster, 1947.
    Contains Greene's story, "The News in English," pp. 18-27.

14 *THE GREEN CHILD.* A novel by Herbert Read.
London, Eyre and Spottiswoode, 1947.
Contains an "Introduction" by Greene, pp. v-viii.

15 *WHY DO I WRITE? An Exchange of Views between Elizabeth Bowen, Graham Greene, and V. S. Pritchett.*
London, Marshall, 1948.
Contains letters by Greene, pp. 27-33, 46-52. The first of these letters, to Elizabeth Bowen, had appeared a few months earlier in *THE WORLD OF NEIGHBORS,* edited by A. G. Weidenfeld. London, Contact, 1947.
See also *Partisan Review,* XV (Nov. 1948) 1175-89, for a selection from this correspondence.

16 *THE BEST OF SAKI.* Edited by Graham Greene.
London, British Publisher's Guild, 1950.
New York, Viking (Compass), 1961.
Contains an "Introduction" by Greene, pp. vii-xi.

17 *THE LIVING GOD.* By Armand Pierhal. Translated from the French by Wilhemina Guerard.
New York, Harper, 1950.
Contains an "Introduction" by Greene, pp. 7-9. The original publication, *Science sans Conscience,* does not contain this introduction.

18 *THE AUTOBIOGRAPHY OF AN ELIZABETHAN.* By John Gerard. Translated from the Latin by Philip Caraman.
London, Longmans Green, 1951.
Contains an "Introduction" by Greene, pp. vii-xi.

19 *CINEMA 1951.* Edited by Roger Manvell and R. K. Neilson Baxter.
London, Pelican Books, 1952.
Contains an extract from the postproduction script of *The Third Man,* pp. 67-87.

20 *THE FINANCIAL EXPERT.* A novel by R. K. Narayan.
London, Methuen, 1952.
Contains an "Introduction" by Greene, pp. v-vi.

21 *VENUS IN THE KITCHEN: or Love's Cookery Book.* By "Pilaff Bay." Edited by Norman Douglas.
London, Heinemann, 1952.
Contains an "Introduction" by Greene, pp. vii-x.

22 *EIGHT EUROPEAN ARTISTS.* Photographed and edited by Felix H. Man.
London, Heinemann, 1954.

Contains an "Introduction" by Greene, p. [vii]. Translations of the introduction into French and German follow, pp. [viii-ix].

23 *FATHER SIX: Parish Priest and Viceroy.* By Mgr. Armand Olichon. Translated from the French by Barbara Wall.
London, Burns and Oates, 1954.
Contains an "Introduction" by Greene, pp. v-vi. (The original publication, *Le Père Six: Curé de Phatdiem, Vice-Roi en Annam,* does not contain this introduction.)

24 *MEN: A Dialogue between Women.* By Allegra Sander. Translated from the French by Vyvyan Holland.
London, Cresset Press, 1955.
Contains a "Prefatory Letter" by Greene, pp. 5-8. (The original publication, *Les Hommes ces Demi-Dieux,* does not contain this introduction.)

25 *UN HOMME DANS LA RIZIÉRE.* By Colonel Jean Leroy.
Paris, Éditions de Paris, 1955.
Contains a Preface by Greene, translated into French by Marcelle Sibon.

26 *THE MAUGHAM ENIGMA.* Edited by Klaus W. Jonas.
London, Peter Owen, [c.1955].
Contains Greene's review of *Spanish Gold,* "Don Fernando," pp. 194-96.

27 *A SPY'S BEDSIDE BOOK.* Edited by Graham Greene and Hugh Greene.
London, Hart-Davis, 1957.
Contains Greene's "Introduction," pp. 11-13.

28 *INTERNATIONAL FILM ANNUAL NUMBER 2.* Edited by William Whitebait.
London, Calder, 1958.
Contains an article by Greene, "The Novelist and the Cinema —A Personal Experience," pp. 54-56, 61.

29 *THE PICK OF PUNCH.* Edited by Nicholas Bentley.
New York, Dutton, 1958.
Contains Greene's story, "Awful When You Think of It," pp. 72-75.

III. PERIODICAL CONTRIBUTIONS BY GREENE: A NOTE

Graham Greene began publishing stories and poems in *The Berkhamstedian,* the monthly magazine of the public school he attended.

Early in 1921, a London newspaper published his story "The Tick of the Clock, A Legend," and several poems were printed in the national periodical, *The Weekly Westminster*, before he went up to Oxford in 1922. Thereafter, his work appeared in the *Oxford Outlook* (of which he became a coeditor), the *Oxford Chronicle*, the *Cherwell*, the *Isis*, and *The Decachord*. Many of the poems written at this time were collected in *Babbling April* in 1925, but the prose remains scattered.

Greene's work on the editorial staff of the *Nottingham Journal* (1925-1926) and on the *London Times* (1926-1929) does not leave much of a literary trail. However, he also contributed reviews during this time to the *Glasgow Herald* and the *Weekly Westminster*, a serialized detective story to *The Graphic*, and poems and articles to several other periodicals. Early in 1932 Greene began to review books for the *Spectator*. In the decade that followed the *Spectator* published nearly four hundred of his reviews, many of them (after 1935) cinema reviews and some (during the Second World War) drama reviews. The *London Mercury*, the *Fortnightly Review*, the *Observer*, *Time and Tide*, *Now and Then*, *Life and Letters* and (especially in 1936-1938) the *Tablet* also published articles, poems, stories, or reviews by Greene. His association with the *Spectator* was interrupted for six months in 1937 when he became cinema reviewer for *Night and Day*, and again in 1943 when he went to Africa on government business.

In June 1945 he resumed book reviewing, for the *Evening Standard*, and in 1946 shifted to reviewing, though less regularly, for the *New Statesman*. *The Listener* (after 1947), *The Month* (after 1949), the *Sunday Times* (after 1952), *Picture Post* (after 1953), the *London Magazine* (after 1954), and *Punch* (after Malcom Muggeridge became editor in 1954) have all published a number of items by Greene since the war, as have the American magazines *Commonweal*, *Life*, *Harper's*, *The New Yorker*, *Esquire*, and the *New Republic*.

IV. BOOKS AND DISSERTATIONS ON GREENE

1 ALLOTT, Kenneth and Miriam Farris, *The Art of Graham Greene*.
   London, Hamish Hamilton, 1951. 253 p.

2 ATKINS, John, *Graham Greene*.
   London, J. Calder, 1957. 240 p.

3 BEDARD, Bernard John, "The Thriller Pattern in the Major Novels of Graham Greene."
   University of Michigan doctoral dissertation, 1959. 250 p. MS.
   Synopsis in *Dissertation Abstracts*, XX (Nov. 1959) 1779-80.

4 *CONSOLO, Dominick Peter, "The Technique of Graham
Greene: A Stylistic Analysis of Five Novels."
State University of Iowa doctoral dissertation, 1959. 160 p.
MS.
Synopsis in *Dissertation Abstracts*, XX (July 1959) 297.

5 DE PANGE, Victor, *Graham Greene.*
With a preface by François Mauriac, pp. 11-12.
Paris, Éditions Universitaires, 1953. 129 p.
*Spanish translation by Patricia Matthews, Buenos Aires,
Editorial La Mandragora, 1953.

6 *EIGNER, Franz, "Der Symbolcharakter der Landschaftsbildes
in den Werken Graham Greenes."
University of Vienna doctoral dissertation, 1952. 110 p. MS.

7 JONSSON, Thorsten, "Ett Portraatt au Scobie," and Erik
LINDEGREEN, "Graham Greene," *Tva Essayer on Graham
Greene.*
Stockholm, Norstedt, 1950. 16 p.

8 KOHN, Lynette, *Graham Greene: The Major Novels.*
Stanford Honors Essays in Humanities No. 4.
Stanford, Calif., 1961. 54 p.

9 *KREUZER, Wilhelm, "Die Auswirkung der weltanschaulicher
Grundhaltung auf Charackterzeichnung und Stoffgestaltung
in Greenes Werken."
University of Graz doctoral dissertation, 1952.

10 KUNKEL, Francis L., *The Labyrinthine Ways of Graham Greene.*
New York, Sheed and Ward, 1960. 182 p.
Synopsis in *Dissertation Abstracts*, XX (Aug. 1959) 670-71,
under the title "A Critical Study of Graham Greene."

11 MADAULE, Jacques, *Graham Greene.*
Paris, Éditions de Temps Present, 1949. 390 p.
*Spanish translation by Dr. Santiago Cunchilles Manterola,
Buenos Aires, Ediciones Desclée de Brouwer, 1952.

12 MATTHEWS, Ronald, *Mon Ami Graham Greene.*
Paris, Desclée de Brouwer, 1957. 271 p.
*German translation by Walter Puchwein, *Mein Freund
Graham Greene.* Hamburg-Vienna, Zsolnay, 1957. 348 p.
*Dutch-Flemish translation by Valeer van Kerkhove, *Uren
met Graham Greene.* Brussels, Desclée de Brouwer, 1957.
309 p.

13 MESNET, Marie-Béatrice, *Graham Greene and the Heart of the
Matter.*

London, Cresset Press, 1954. 116 p.
*Dutch-Flemish translation by Simone Simons, *De Trilogie van Graham Greene*. Antwerp, 't Groeit, 1957. 179 p.

14 RISCHIK, Josef, *Graham Greene und sein Werk*.
Schweizer Anglistische Arbeiten. Bd. 28.
Bern, A. Francke, 1951. 114 p.

15 ROSTENNE, Paul, *Graham Greene, Témoin des Temps Tragiques*.
With a Prefatory Letter by Greene, pp. 11-12.
Paris, Julliard, 1949. 243 p.

16 SIECKE, Gerda, "Das Romanwerk Graham Greenes in seinem Verhältnis zu den Romanen von Georges Bernanos und François Mauriac."
Friedrich-Alexander University of Erlangen doctoral dissertation, 1955. 141 p. Mimeographed.

17 SLATE, Audrey Nelson, "Technique and Form in the Novels of Graham Greene."
University of Wisconsin doctoral dissertation, 1960. 408 p. MS.
Synopsis in *Dissertation Abstracts*, XXI (Sept. 1960) 629-30.

18 *STURZL, Erwin, *Von Satan zu Gott: Religiöse Probleme bei Graham Greene*.
Vienna, Graph. Lerh. und Versuchs-Anstalt, 1954. 39 p.

19 WYNDHAM, Francis, *Graham Greene*.
London, Longmans Green, 1955. 20 p.

V. BOOKS AND DISSERTATIONS IN PART ON GREENE

(Reference books, literary histories, and general studies of the novel are not included here, nor are those books which treat the subject only discursively.)

1 ALLEN, Walter, "The Novels of Graham Greene," *Writers of Today*, ed. by Denys Val Baker (London, Sedgwick and Jackson, 1946) 15-27. Reprinted from *Penguin New Writing 18*.

2 CALDER-MARSHALL, Arthur, "Graham Greene," *Little Reviews Anthology* (London, Allen and Unwin, 1943) 197-204. Reprinted from *Horizon*, 1940.

3 ——————, "Graham Greene," *Living Writers: Studies Broadcast by the B. B. C. Third Programme*, ed. by Gilbert H. Phelps (London, Sylvan Press, 1947) 39-47.

4 CHAIGNE, Louis, "Graham Greene," *Vies et Oeuvres d'écrivains*, III (Paris, Lanore, 1950) 193-237.

5 °DEVITIS, Angelo, "The Religious Theme in Rex Warner, Evelyn Waugh, and Graham Greene." University of Wisconsin doctoral dissertation, 1953.

6 ENGEL, Claire Elaine, "Graham Greene," *Esquisses Anglaises* (Paris, Éditions "Je Sera," 1949) 57-98.

7 GRAFF, Hilda, "Graham Greene," *Modern Gloom and Christian Hope* (Chicago, Regnery, 1959) 84-97.

8 KARL, Frederick R., "V. Graham Greene's Demonical Heroes," *The Contemporary English Novel* (New York, Farrar Straus, 1962) 85-106.

9 KERMODE, Frank, "Mr. Greene's Eggs and Crosses," *Puzzles and Epiphanies: Essays and Reviews 1958-1961* (London, Routledge and Kegan Paul, 1962) 176-87.

10 KNAAK PEUSER, Angélica, "La Novela de Graham Greene," *El Espiritu y la Carne en las Grandes Creaciones Literarias* (Buenos Aires, Ediciones Peuser, [1952?]) 161-79.

11 LEWIS, R. W. B., "Graham Greene: The Religious Affair," *The Picaresque Saint: Representative Figures in Contemporary Fiction* (New York, Lippincott, 1959) 220-74. Reprinted from *Kenyon Review*, 1957.

12 MAURIAC, François, "Graham Greene," *Mes Grandes Hommes* (Monaco, Éditions de Rocher, 1949). Trans. by Elsie Pell, *Men I Hold Great* (New York, Philosophical Library, 1951) 124-28, and *Great Men* (London, Rockliff, 1952). Also in Mauriac's *Oeuvres Completes* (Paris, Fayard, 1950), VIII, 429-32.

13 MOELLER, Charles, "Graham Greene ou le martyre de l'espérance," *Littérature Du XXᵉ Siècle et Christianisme: I: Silence De Dieu* (Tournai, Belgium, Casterman, 1953) 259-301.

14 O'DONNELL, Donat *pseud.* [Conor Cruise O'Brien], "Graham Greene: The Anatomy of Pity," *Maria Cross: Imaginative Patterns in a Group of Modern Catholic Writers* (New York, Oxford University Press, 1952) 63-94. Adapted from an article in *A.D. 52*.

15 O'FAOLAIN, Sean, "Graham Greene, or 'I suffer, therefore I am,'" *The Vanishing Hero: Studies in Novelists of the Twenties* (London, Eyre and Spottiswoode, 1956) 71-97.

16 SAUER, Josef, "Die Darstellung des Katholischen Menschen bei Archibald Joseph Cronin und Graham Greene." University of Erlangen doctoral dissertation, 1953.

17 *STRASILL, Edmund, "Die Kunst der Personenbeschreibung in Romanen Galsworthys, Maughams und Graham Greenes." University of Graz doctoral dissertation, 1949.

18 *WALTERS, Dorothy Jeanne, "The Theme of Destructive Innocence in the Modern Novel: Greene, James, Cary, Porter." University of Oklahoma doctoral dissertation, 1960. Synopsis in *Dissertation Abstracts*, XXI (Feb. 1961) 2300-301.

19 WOODCOCK, George, "Graham Greene," *The Writer and Politics* (London, Porcupine Press, 1948) 125-53. Reprinted from *Now*, 1946.

20 ZABEL, Morton D., "Graham Greene: The Best and the Worst," *Craft and Character in Modern Fiction: Texts, Method, and Vocation* (New York, Viking, 1957) 276-96.
This essay originally appeared in *The Nation* (3 July 1943) and had been brought up to date for subsequent appearances in *Forms of Modern Fiction: Essays Collected in Honor of Joseph Warren Beach,* ed. by William Van O'Connor (Minneapolis, University of Minnesota Press, 1948) and *Critiques and Essays on Modern Fiction, 1920-1951,* ed. by John W. Aldridge (New York, Ronald Press, 1952).

VI. PERIODICAL ARTICLES ON GREENE: A SELECTED LIST

(General articles which appear in special numbers devoted to Greene are separately listed. See VIII and IX.)

1 AGUIRRE DE CARCER, Nuno, "La novela en la Inglaterra actual: II. Graham Greene," *Arbor*, XIV (Sept.-Oct. 1949) 99-113.

2 ALLEN, W. Gore, "Evelyn Waugh and Graham Greene," *Irish Monthly*, LXXVII (Jan. 1949) 16-22.

3 ———, "The World of Graham Greene," *Irish Ecclesiastical Record*, LXXI (Jan. 1949) 42-49. An excerpt in *Catholic World*, CLXIX (April 1949) 69-70.

4 BARNES, Robert J., "Two Modes of Fiction: Hemingway and Greene," *Renascence*, XIV (Spring 1962) 193-98.

5 BARRA, Giovanni, "La Conversione di Graham Greene," *Vita e Pensiero*, XXXVI (July 1953) 310-15.

6 BATTOCK, Marjorie, "The Novels of Graham Greene," *Norse-man*, XIII (Jan.-Feb. 1955) 45-52.

7 BEDOYERE, Michael de la, "From My Window in Fleet Street," *Catholic World*, CXXIV (Oct. 1951) 56-61.

8 BEIRNAERT, Louis, "Die menschliche Armseligkeit und die Gnade: Zu Graham Greenes Gestalten," *Universitas*, V (Nov. 1950) 395-97. And "Does Sanctification Depend on Psychic Structure?" *Cross Currents*, no. 2 (Winter 1951) 39-43. Trans. by Joseph L. Caulfield.

9 BELTZIKOFF, Boris, "Kaj Munk och Graham Greene: En studie i Kristen Kriminologi," *Ord och Bild*, LXVI (1957) 249-58. See also pp. 331-36.

10 BLANCHET, André, "Un nouveau 'Type' de Prêtre dans le roman contemporain," *Études*, no. 279 (Feb. 1954) 145-64 and no. 280 (March 1954) 303-10.

11 BOWEN, Elizabeth, "Story, Theme, and Situation," *Listener*, LVI (25 Oct. 1956) 651-52.

12 BOYLE, Alexander, "Graham Greene," *Irish Monthly*, LXXVII (Nov. 1949) 319-25.

13 °————, "The Symbolism of Graham Greene," *Irish Monthly*, LXXX (Aug. 1952) 98-102.

14 °BOYLE, Raymond M., "Man of Controversy," *Grail*, XXXV (July 1952) 1-7.

15 BRADY, Charles A., "Melodramatic Cousin of R. L. S.," *America*, LXIV (25 Jan. 1941) 439-40.

16 ————, "Contemporary Catholic Authors: Graham Greene, Novelist of Good and Evil," *Catholic Library World*, XVI (Dec. 1944) 67-74, 89.

17 °BRANDSTRUP, Ole, "Til Helvede med Succesen," *Perspektiv (Det Danske Magasin)*, VIII (1961) 47-50.

18 BRAYBROOKE, Neville, "Graham Greene," *Envoy*, III (Sept. 1950) 10-23. Abridged as "Graham Greene, a Pioneer Novelist," *College English*, XII (Oct. 1950) 1-9 and the *English Journal*, XXXIX (Oct. 1950) 415-23.

19 BRION, Marcel, "Les romans de Graham Greene," *Revue des Deux Mondes*, no. 6 (15 March 1950) 367-75.

20 BRISSAUD, André, C'est un champ de bataille / C'est un

homme traqué / C'est l'univers de Graham Greene," *Arts*, no. 434 (22 Oct. 1953) 5.

21 BROWNE, E. Martin, "Graham Greene: Theatre's Gain," *Theatre Arts*, XLV (Nov. 1961) 20-24.

22 CAYROL, Jean, "Autour de l'oeuvre de Graham Greene," *Revue de la Pensée Française*, X (April 1951) 68-72.

23 CHAVARDES, Maurice, "Graham Greene, ou La Nudité de Dieu," *Vie Intellectuelle*, no. 7 (July 1950) 113-17.

24 CODEY, Regina, "Notes on Graham Greene's Dramatic Technique," *Approach*, XVII (1955) 23-27.

25 CONNELLY, Francis X., "Inside Modern Man: The Spiritual Adventures of Graham Greene," *Renascence*, I (Spring 1949) 16-23.

26 COSMAN, Max, "An Early Chapter in Graham Greene," *Arizona Quarterly*, XI (Summer 1955) 143-47.

27 ————, "Disquieted Graham Greene," *Colorado Quarterly*, VI (Winter 1958) 319-24.

28 COSTELLO, D. P., "Graham Greene and the Catholic Press," *Renascence*, XII (Fall 1959) 3-28.

29 CRUBELLIER, Maurice, "Graham Greene: La Tragédie de la Pitié," *Vie Intellectuelle*, no. 12 (Dec. 1951) 57-78.

30 DE HEGEDUS, Adam, "Graham Greene: The Man and his Work," *World Review*, XV (Aug. 1948) 57-61. Also in *Tomorrow*, VIII (Oct. 1948) 54-56.

31 DELPECH, Jeanine, "Graham Greene à Paris," *Nouvelles Littéraires* (19 Dec. 1946) 1-2.

32 DELTEIL, F., "Romanciers catholiques anglais: II. Graham Greene," *Livres et Lectures*, no. 17 (1948) 433-35.

33 DEVITIS, A. A., "The Entertaining Mr. Greene," *Renascence*, XIV (Fall 1961) 8-24.

34 DINKINS, Paul, "Graham Greene: The Incomplete Version," *Catholic World*, CLXXVI (Nov. 1952) 96-102.

35 DOWNING, Francis, "Graham Greene and the Case for Disloyalty," *Commonweal*, LV (14 March 1952) 564-66.

36 DUCHÉ, Jean, "Je n'écrivai plus de romans policiers, nous dit Graham Greene," *Figaro Littéraire* (20 Dec. 1947) 6.

37 DUESBERG, Jacques, "Un épigone du 'Misérabilisme': Graham Greene," *Synthèses*, no. 69 (Feb. 1952) 348-53.

38 DUFFY, Joseph M., "The Lost World of Graham Greene," *Thought*, XXXIII (Summer 1958) 229-47.

39 ELLIS, William D., Jr., "The Grand Theme of Graham Greene," *Southwest Review*, XLI (Summer 1956) 239-50.

40 ELSEN, Claude, "Graham Greene ou la geste de l'homme traqué," *Table Ronde*, no. 14 (Feb. 1949) 297-301.

41 ENGEL, Claire Elaine, "Einige Englische Romanciers von Heute," *Du*, VIII (Jan. 1948) 28.

42 FOUCHET, Max-Pol, "Graham Greene," *Revue de Paris*, LVII (July 1950) 59-68.

43 °FOWLER, A. D. S., "Novelist of Damnation," *Theology*, LVI (July 1953) 259-64.

44 FYTTON, Francis, "Graham Greene: Catholicism and Controversy," *Catholic World*, CLXXX (Dec. 1954) 172-75.

45 GARDINER, Harold C., "Graham Greene, Catholic Shocker," *Renascence*, I (Spring 1949) 12-15.

46 GLICKSBERG, Charles I., "Graham Greene: Catholicism in Fiction," *Criticism*, I (Fall 1959) 339-53.

47 GRUBBS, Henry A., "Albert Camus and Graham Greene," *Modern Language Quarterly*, X (March 1949) 33-42.

48 °GRUNT, Olav Paus, "Grunntrekk i Graham Greenes Fortellerkunst," *Samtiden*, LXIII (1954) 341-49.

49 HAHN, Karl J., "Graham Greene," *Hochland*, XLI (July 1949) 455-65.

50 HAYES, H. R., "A Defense of the Thriller," *Partisan Review*, XII (Winter 1945) 135-37.

51 HAYMAN, Ronald, "Le Roman Anglais d'Après-Guerre, III," *Revue de lettres modernes*, III (April 1954) 88-93.

52 HERLING, Gustav, "Two Sanctities: Greene and Camus," *Adam International Review*, no. 201 (Dec. 1949) 10-19.

53 HERZOG, Bert, "Welt unter geschlossenem Himmel, zu den Büchern von Graham Greene," *Stimmen der Zeit*, CLI (March 1952) 420-26 and (Oct. 1952) 20-25.

54 HOGGART, Richard, "The Force of Caricature: Aspects of the

Art of Graham Greene, with Particular Reference to *The Power and the Glory,*" *Essays in Criticism,* III (Oct. 1953) 447-62.

55 HUGHES, Catharine, "Innocence Revisited," *Renascence,* XII (Fall 1959) 29-34.

56 °IVASCHOVA, V., "Legende und Wahrheit über Graham Greene," *Zeitschrift für Anglistik und Amerikanistik* (East Berlin), X (1962) 229-58.

57 JANS, Adrien, "Graham Greene, entre le péché et l'amour," *Empreintes,* IV (Feb.-April 1948) 46-49.

58 JERROLD, Douglas, "Graham Greene, Pleasure-Hater," *Picture Post,* LIV (15 March 1952) 51-53 and *Harper's,* CCV (Aug. 1952) 50-52.

59 JOHNSTON, J. L., "Graham Greene—The Unhappy Man," *The Central Literary Magazine* (Birmingham), XXXVIII (July 1954) 43-49.

60 KENNY, Herbert A., "Graham Greene," *Catholic World,* CLXXXV (Aug. 1957) 326-29.

61 KERMODE, Frank, "Mr. Greene's Eggs and Crosses," *Encounter,* XVI (April 1961) 69-75.

62 KUNKEL, Francis L., "The Priest as Scapegoat in the Modern Catholic Novel," *Ramparts,* I (Jan. 1963) 72-78.

63 LAS VERGNAS, Raymond, "A Propos de Graham Greene," *Hommes et Mondes,* IX (May 1949) 147-51.

64 LAURENS, A., "Comment j'ai introduit Graham Greene en France," *France-Asie* (Saigon), III (April 1948) 455-59.

65 LEES, F. N., "Graham Greene: a Comment," *Scrutiny,* XIX (Oct. 1952) 31-42.

66 °LEMAITRE, Henri, "Un romancier chrétien de l'absurde: Graham Greene," *Culture Catholique,* IV (Sept. 1949).

67 LOHF, Kenneth A., "Graham Greene and the Problem of Evil," *Catholic World,* CLXXIII (June 1951) 196-99.

68 McCARTHY, Mary, "Graham Greene and the Intelligentsia," *Partisan Review,* XI (Spring 1944) 228-30.

69 McLAUGHLIN, Richard, "Graham Greene, Saint or Cynic?" *America,* LXXIX (24 July 1948) 370-71.

70 MAGNY, Claude-Edmonde, "Graham Greene," *Poésie 46*, no. 32 (May 1946) 32-37.

71 MARSHALL, Bruce, "Graham Greene and Evelyn Waugh," *Commonweal*, LI (3 March 1950) 551-53.

72 MASON, H. A., "A Note on Contemporary 'Philosophical' Literary Criticism in France," *Scrutiny*, XVI (March 1949) 54-60.

73 MILLER, Bruce, "Graham Greene," *Meanjin*, V (Spring 1946) 193-97.

74 MONROE, N. Elizabeth, "The New Man in Fiction," *Renascence*, VI (Aug. 1953) 9-12.

75 MORÉ, Marcel, "A Propos de Newman," *Dieu Vivant*, no. 15 (1950) 63-81.

76 MORÉ, Marcel, and Père Jouve, "Propos de Table avec Graham Greene," *Dieu Vivant*, no. 16 (1950) 127-37.

77 NICHOLSON, Jenny, "Graham Greene—A Third Man of Real Life," *Picture Post*, LXIV (14 Aug. 1954) 18-19.

78 *O'DONNELL, Donat, "An Epic of the Thirties: Graham Greene," *The Bell*, XIII (Feb. 1947) 7-16. Expanded in *Chimera*, V (Summer 1947) 18-30. See V. 14.

79 O'FAOLAIN, Sean, "The Novels of Graham Greene," *Britain To-Day*, no. 148 (Aug. 1948) 32-36.

80 O'GRADY, Emmett, "Graham Greene, écrivain eschatologique," *Revue de l'Université d'Ottawa*, XXII (April 1952) 156-70.

81 OSTERMANN, Robert, "Interview with Graham Greene," *Catholic World*, CLXX (Feb. 1950) 356-61.

82 PARINAUD, André, "La Leçon de Vengeance de Graham Greene," *Arts*, no. 565 (25 April 1956) 1, 6.

83 PETERS, W., "The Concern of Graham Greene," *Month*, X (Nov. 1953) 281-90.

84 ROLO, Charles J., "The Man and the Message," *Atlantic*, CCVII (May 1961) 60-65.

85 ROSTENNE, Paul, "Introduction à Graham Greene: Romancier Catholique," *Revue Nouvelle*, VI (15 Sept. 1947) 193-204.

86 ROY, Jean-Henri, "L'Oeuvre de Graham Greene, ou Un Chris-

tianisme de la damnation," *Temps Modernes*, V (Feb. 1950) 1513-19.

87 SACKVILLE-WEST, Edward, "The Electric Hare: Some Aspects of Graham Greene," *Month*, VI (Sept. 1951) 141-47.

88 SCHMIDTHÜS, Karlheinz, "Graham Greenes Katholizismus: Die religiöse Erfahrung der Welt in seinem Romanen," *Wort und Wahrheit*, XII (Jan. 1957) 39-51.

89 SEWARD, Barbara, "Graham Greene: A Hint of an Explanation," *Western Review*, XXII (Winter 1958) 83-95.

90 SEWELL, Elizabeth, "Graham Greene," *Dublin Review*, CVIII (First Quarter 1954) 12-21. And as "The Imagination of Graham Greene," *Thought*, XXIX (March 1954) 51-60. Also in *Wort und Wahrheit*, IX (April 1954) 281-88.

91 SHUTTLEWORTH, Martin and Simon Raven, "The Art of Fiction. III. Graham Greene," *Paris Review*, no. 3 (Autumn 1953) 24-41.

92 SILVA DELGADO, Adolfo, "La Carrera literaria de Graham Greene," *Marcha*, XIII (23 Nov. 1951) 14-15, 71.

93 SIMONS, Katherine, "Graham Greene," *Book-of-the-Month-Club News* (June 1948) 6-7.

94 SMITH, A. J. M., "Graham Greene's Theological Thrillers," *Queen's Quarterly*, LXVIII (Spring 1961) 15-33.

95 °SORDET, Etienne, "Signification de Graham Greene," *Cahiers Protestants*, XXXVII (1953) 239-50.

96 STRATFORD, Philip, "Graham Greene, Master of Melodrama," *Tamarack Review*, XIX (Spring 1961) 67-86.

97 ———, "The Uncomplacent Dramatist: Some Aspects of Graham Greene's Theatre," *Wisconsin Studies in Contemporary Literature*, II (Fall 1961) 5-19.

98 SYLVESTER, Harry, "Graham Greene," *Commonweal*, XXXIII (25 Oct. 1940) 11-13.

99 TOYNBEE, Philip, "Literature and Life–2 / Graham Greene on 'The Job of the Writer,'" *Observer* (15 Sept. 1957) 3.

100 TRAVERSI, Derek, "Graham Greene: The Earlier Novels," *Twentieth Century*, CXLIX (March 1951) 231-40 and ". . . The Later Novels," *Twentieth Century*, CXLIX (April 1951) 318-28.

101 TURNELL, Martin, "The Religious Novel," *Commonweal*, LV (26 Oct. 1951) 55-57.

102 TYNAN, Kenneth, "An Inner View of Graham Greene," *Harper's Bazaar*, LXXXVI (Feb. 1953) 128-29, 209-10, 214-15. Abridged in *Persona Grata* (London, Wingate, 1953) 53-56.

103 VIATTE, A., "Graham Greene, romancier de la grâce," *Revue de l'Université Laval*, IV (April 1950) 753-58.

104 °VIEIRA, Manuel, "Notas para um Estudo sobre Graham Greene," *Tempo Presente*, XX (1960) 46-52.

105 VOORHEES, Richard J., "Recent Greene," *South Atlantic Quarterly*, LXII (Spring 1963) 244-55.

106 ———, "The World of Graham Greene," *South Atlantic Quarterly*, L (July 1951) 389-98.

107 WALL, Barbara, "London Letter," *America*, LXXVII (9 Aug. 1947) 521-22.

108 WASSMER, Thomas A., S.J., "Graham Greene: Literary Artist and Philosopher-Theologian," *Homiletic and Pastoral Review*, LVIII (March 1958) 583-89. Also as "Graham Greene: A Look at His Sinners," *Critic*, XVIII (Dec. 1959-Jan. 1960) 16-17, 72-74.

UNSIGNED ARTICLES:

109 "The Angry Man Within [an interview]," *Sunday Times* (12 April 1953) 5.

110 "The Greeneland Aboriginal [a profile]," *New Statesman*, LXI (13 Jan. 1961) 44-45, 139.

111 "Profile—Graham Greene," *Observer* (27 Nov. 1949) 2.

VII. DRAMAS AND FILMS BY GREENE: A NOTE

In addition to the plays Greene has written, at least five of his novels have been dramatized: *Brighton Rock* (Washington, D. C., 1942; and London, 1943), *The Heart of the Matter* (Boston, 1950), *The Power and the Glory* (Mulhouse, etc., 1952), *The Quiet American* (Moscow, 1960), and *Our Man in Havana* (Prague, 1961). *Our Man in Havana* has also been converted into an opera, with libretto by Sydney Gilliat and music by Malcolm Williamson (London, 1963). (A report states that *The End of the Affair* was to be produced in a German dramatization in 1957, but the writer has no confirmation.) Greene has publicly approved of Pierre Bost's dramatization of *The*

Power and the Glory. He has been involved personally in the dramatization only of *The Heart of the Matter,* which was highly praised but closed after a short run.

Films have been made from three of Greene's stories: "The Lieutenant Died Last" (*Went the Day Well,* 1943; retitled *48 Hours* in the United States), "The Basement Room" (*The Fallen Idol,* 1948), and "Across the Bridge" (1957). Twelve of Greene's novels have been filmed, one twice: *Stamboul Train* (*Orient Express,* 1934), *A Gun for Sale* (*This Gun for Hire,* 1942, and *Short-cut to Hell,* 1957), *The Ministry of Fear* (1944), *The Confidential Agent* (1945), *The Man Within* (*The Smugglers,* 1947), *The Power and the Glory* (*The Fugitives,* 1947), *Brighton Rock* (1948; retitled *Young Scarface* in the United States), *The Heart of the Matter* (1953), *Loser Takes All* (1954), *The End of the Affair* (1956), *The Quiet American* (1958), and *Our Man in Havana* (1960). Greene took a major hand in the film scripts of only four of these: *The Fallen Idol, Brighton Rock, Loser Takes All,* and *Our Man in Havana.* For none of the other films does he hold himself at all responsible. He has, however, written scripts for at least four other films—*The Future's in the Air* (1937), *The Third Man* (1949), *The Stranger's Hand* (1952) and *St. Joan* (1957)—the last an adaptation of Shaw's play—and he has been involved in the production of at least two other filmscripts, those for *Twenty-One Days Together* (1938) and *The Green Cockatoo* (1940).

All film plans have not materialized. Nancy Cunard reports that Greene at one time planned to film Norman Douglas's novel *South Wind* (see *Grand Man*). Other comments of interest on Greene's career in the cinematic world are to be found in *A Film Star in Belgrave Square,* by Bobby Henrey (London, Davies, 1954); in Vernon Young's article "Hollywood: Lost Moments," *Accent,* IX (Winter 1949) 120-28; and in R. E. Ginna's photographic article, "Carol Reed Directs 'Our Man in Havana,'" *Horizon,* II (Nov. 1959) 26-31, 122-26.

VIII. *MODERN FICTION STUDIES: Graham Greene, Special Number,* III (Autumn 1957):

Beebe, Maurice, "Criticism of Graham Greene: A Selected Checklist with an Index to Studies of Separate Works."

Cottrell, Beekman W., "Second Time Charm: The Theatre of Graham Greene."

DeVitis, A. A., "Allegory in *Brighton Rock.*"

Evans, Robert O., "Existentialism in Greene's *The Quiet American.*"

Haber, Herbert R., "Two Worlds of Graham Greene."

Hargreaves, Phylis, "Graham Greene: A Selected Bibliography."

Lewis, R. W. B., "The 'Trilogy' of Graham Greene."

Patten, Karl, "The Structure of *The Power and the Glory.*"

Spier, Ursula, "Melodrama in Graham Greene's *The End of the Affair.*"

IX. *RENASCENCE: Graham Greene, Special Number,* XII (Fall 1959):

Costello, Donald P., "Graham Greene and the Catholic Press."

————, "The Latest in Greene Criticism."

Hughes, Catharine, "Innocence Revisited."

Hughes, Riley E., "*The Quiet American*: the Case Reopened."

Murphy, John P., "*The Potting Shed*: Dogmatic and Dramatic Effects."

Puentevella, Renato, S.J., "Ambiguity in Greene."

X. BIBLIOGRAPHIES

(This bibliography must acknowledge many debts to the bibliographies listed below. All contain useful data of one kind or another not included here.)

1   "A Bibliography of Graham Greene," *Marginalia,* II (April 1951) 16-19. A mimeographed bulletin of the Manuscript Club of Northwestern University, Evanston, Illinois.

2   BEEBE, Maurice, "Criticism of Graham Greene: A Selected Checklist with an Index to Studies of Separate Works," *Modern Fiction Studies,* III (Autumn 1957) 281-88.

3   BIRMINGHAM, William, "Graham Greene Criticism: A Bibliographical Study," *Thought,* XXVII (Spring 1952) 72-100.

4   HARGREAVES, Phylis, "Graham Greene: A Selected Bibliography," *Bulletin of Bibliography,* XXII (Jan.-April 1957) 45-48. Expanded in *Modern Fiction Studies,* III (Autumn 1957) 269-80.

5   REMORDS, G., "Graham Greene: Notes Biographiques et Bibliographiques," *Bulletin de la Faculté des Lettres de Strasbourg,* XXIX (May-June 1951) 393-99.

NOTES

THE WORLD OF GRAHAM GREENE

[1] The essay was completed before the appearance of Greene's two latest books, *A Burnt-out Case* and *A Sense of Reality;* it has, however, been revised to take note of them but does not pretend to treat them fully (Ed.).

[2] The situation, not perhaps so unusual as Greene's portrayal of it suggests, has a rough parallel in Evelyn Waugh's *Brideshead Revisited, q.v.* (Ed.).

CHRISTIAN TRAGEDIAN

[1] Professor Scott's article is a revised version of one that appeared first in *The Volusia Review,* I, No. 1 (1954), 29-42, and is used with permission. The reader should remember that the essay deals with Greene's work only to 1954.

[2] W. H. Auden, "Petition," *The Collected Poetry* (New York, 1945), p. 110.

[3] The exceptions are *It's a Battlefield* (1934), *The Heart of the Matter* (1948), and *The End of the Affair* (1951).

[4] Donat O'Donnell, "Graham Greene," *Chimera,* V (Summer 1947), 30.

[5] Greene has designated certain of his novels as "entertainments" *(Stamboul Train, A Gun for Sale, The Confidential Agent,* and *The Ministry of Fear),* by which, presumably, he intends to suggest some relaxation of serious purpose. But, as Walter Allen has reminded us in an essay subsequently to be cited, "just as the little girl wrote of Shakespeare that his comedies were as good as tragedies by anybody else, so Greene's 'entertainments' are at least as good as most people's novels."

[6] Walter Allen, "Graham Greene," in *Writers of Today*, ed. Denys Val Baker (London, 1946), pp. 22-23.

[7] It may well be the prominence of violent lawlessness in many of Greene's early novels which has led certain French critics to insist upon the affinity between him and those existentialist writers who regard the *acte gratuite* as the means whereby one's moral identity is discoverable.

[8] Allen, p. 23.

[9] T. S. Eliot, "Baudelaire," *Selected Essays: 1917-1932* (New York, 1932), p. 344.

[10] Preston Roberts, "A Christian Theory of Dramatic Tragedy," *The Journal of Religion*, XXXI (January 1951), 7.

[11] *Ibid.*

[12] *Ibid.*

[13] *Ibid.*, p. 8.

[14] T. S. Eliot, *Murder in the Cathedral* (New York, 1935), p. 69.

[15] T. S. Eliot, "East Coker," *Four Quartets* (New York, 1943), p. 17.

[16] Morton Dauwen Zabel, "Graham Greene," in *Forms of Modern Fiction*, ed. William Van O'Connor (Minneapolis, 1948), p. 293.

[17] F. R. Leavis, *The Great Tradition* (London, 1948), p. 16.

THE THEME OF SIN AND GRACE

[1] This essay appeared in substantially the same form under the title of "Greene's Catholic Themes" in Francis L. Kunkel's book, *The Labyrinthine Ways of Graham Greene* (New York, 1960).

[2] "A Visit to Morin," *Harper's Bazaar*, January 1957, p. 95.

[3] Paul Rostenne, *Graham Greene: témoin des temps tragiques* (Paris, 1959), pp. 11-12.

[4] Wallace Fowlie, *"The Lost Childhood and Other Essays"* (review), New York *Times Book Review*, February 17, 1952, p. 31.

[5] Blaise Pascal, *Pensées* (New York, 1941), p. 139.

[6] "The Spiritual Adventures of Graham Greene," *Renascence*, I (Spring 1949), 20.

[7] "Francois Mauriac: A Woman of the Pharisees," *Penguin New Writing*, XXXI (1947), 102.

[8] *Catholic Encyclopedia* (New York, 1936), VIII, 285-94.

[9] Pascal, p. 65.

[10] *The Ministry of Fear*, p. 145.

[11] *The Lost Childhood and Other Essays*, p. 16.

[12] *The Vanishing Hero* (Boston, 1957), p. 47.

[13] *The Lost Childhood . . .*, p. 16.

[14] *The Heart of the Matter*, p. 298.

[15] *Brighton Rock*, p. 347.

[16] *The Heart of the Matter*, p. 264.
[17] *Brideshead Revisited* (New York, 1946), p. 288.
[18] *Brighton Rock*, p. 205.
[19] *Ibid.*, p. 93.
[20] *Another Mexico*, p. 5; *Brighton Rock*, p. 240.
[21] *Brighton Rock*, p. 48.
[22] *Journey Without Maps*, p. 32.
[23] *The Lost Childhood* . . . , p. 17.
[24] *The Enemy* (New York, 1949), p. 279.
[25] "A Visit to Morin," p. 95.
[26] "The Sanctified Sinner," *New Yorker*, XXIV (July 17, 1948), 61.
[27] "An Inner View of Graham Greene," *Harper's Bazaar*, February 1953, p. 128.
[28] "Sin mysticism" is a trend associated with what, in Roman Catholic circles, is called la nouvelle théologie. In an allocution to the Fédération Mondiale des Jeunesses Feminines Catholiques, His late Holiness Pope Pius XII condemned it.
[29] "The Two Worlds of Graham Greene," *Modern Fiction Studies*, III (Autumn 1957), 266.
[30] Greene quotes Péguy in the epigraph to *The Heart of the Matter:* "Le pécheur est au coeur même de chretiéne. . . . Nul n'est aussi compétent que le pécheur en matière de chrétienté. Nul, si ce n'est le saint."
[31] Tynan, p. 128.
[32] *Summa Theologica* (London, 1922), II-II, q. 162, a. 7.
[33] "The Symbolism of Graham Greene," *Irish Monthly*, LXXX (March 1952), 102.
[34] "The Imagination of Graham Greene," *Thought*, XXIX (Spring 1954), 56.
[35] *True Morality and Its Counterfeits* (New York, 1955), p. 3.
[36] *The Power and the Glory*, p. 273.
[37] *The Heart of the Matter*, p. 17.
[38] *Ibid.*, p. 174.
[39] *The Power and the Glory*, p. 129.
[40] *The End of the Affair*, p. 136.
[41] *Ibid.*, p. 134.
[42] See, for example, Elizabeth Sewell, "The Imagination of Graham Greene," *Thought*, XXIX (Spring 1954), 55; William Birmingham, "Graham Greene Criticism: A Bibliographical Study," *Thought*, XXVII (Spring 1952), 87-88; Tynan, p. 128.
[43] *The Living Thoughts of Pascal*, Foreword by François Mauriac (New York, 1940), p. 6.
[44] *La Vie de Jean Racine* (Paris, 1928), p. 47.
[45] *Woman of the Pharisees* (New York, 1946), p. 140.
[46] *The Confidential Agent*, p. 114.

STYLE AND STYLISTICS IN FIVE NOVELS

[1] All quotations are from the American editions published by the Viking Press.

[2] Mark Schorer, "Technique as Discovery," in *Essays in Modern Literary Criticism*, ed. Ray B. West, Jr. (New York, 1952), p. 191.

[3] J. Middleton Murry, *The Problem of Style* (London, 1922), p. 15.

[4] Schorer, p. 191.

[5] Evelyn Waugh, "Felix Culpa?" *The Commonweal*, XLVIII (July 16, 1948), 323.

[6] Walter Allen, "Graham Greene," *Writers of Today*, ed. Denys Val Baker (London, 1946), p. 22.

[7] Neville Braybrooke, "Graham Greene," *Envoy*, III (Sept. 1950), 18.

[8] Arthur Calder-Marshall, "The Works of Graham Greene," *Horizon*, I (May 1940), 374.

[9] Arthur Calder-Marshall, "Graham Greene," in *Living Writers*, ed. Gilbert Phelps (London, 1947), p. 41.

[10] "François Mauriac," *The Lost Childhood and Other Essays* (London, 1951), p. 70.

[11] *Ibid.*, p. 71.

[12] Graham Greene, "An Exchange of Letters," *Partisan Review*, XV (Nov. 1948), 1188.

[13] Morton D. Zabel, *Craft and Character in Modern Fiction* (New York, 1957), p. 280.

[14] Mary McCarthy, "Graham Greene and the Intelligentsia," *Partisan Review*, XI (Spring 1944), 230.

[15] Zabel, p. 294.

[16] Percy Lubbock, *The Craft of Fiction* (New York, 1921), pp. 1, 3.

AMBIGUITY IN THE "CATHOLIC NOVELS"

[1] The essay was completed before the publication of *A Burnt-out Case* (Ed.).

[2] For extensive description of Gnostic theology, see, e.g., Rudolph Bultmann, *Primitive Christianity in Its Contemporary Setting* (New York, 1956) and Henri-Charles Puech, "Gnosis and Time," in *Man and Time*, ed. Joseph Campbell (New York, 1957).

THE END OF THE CATHOLIC CYCLE

[1] "The Lesson of the Master," *The Lost Childhood and Other Essays* (New York, 1952), p. 50.

² All quotes from the novel are from the English edition (London, 1957).

³ Written before *A Burnt-out Case*, which may be thought to take up where the 'cycle' left off.

⁴ *Why Do I Write?* An exchange of views between Elizabeth Bowen, Graham Greene, V. S. Pritchett (London, 1948), p. 48.

⁵ *The Lost Childhood* . . ., p. 50.

⁶ The psychological dynamics of Bendrix's situation are most strikingly anticipated in Kierkegaard's *Fear and Trembling*, especially where the writer discusses what he calls the "paradoxical." I am grateful to Professor Geoffrey Clive, a friend and colleague, for some all too brief talks about Kierkegaard. Professor Clive's *The Romantic Enlightenment* (New York, 1960) demonstrates that he is only too aware of the relevance of the Kierkegaardian categories to modern literature, and I have here borrowed his term "dehumanization" which he finds to be synonymous with Kierkegaard's "aesthetic mode of existence".

⁷ "Man has places in his heart which do not yet exist, and into them enters suffering that they may have existence." For this novel Greene might equally well have chosen that remark of Bernanos to qualify the epilogue from Bloy: "The scandal of the universe isn't suffering but freedom." *The Last Essays of Georges Bernanos*, trans. Joan and Barry Ulanov (Chicago, 1955), p. 235.

⁸ As quoted in Jacques Maritain's *The Responsibility of the Artist* (New York, 1960), p. 115.

⁹ Bendrix received the scar in the selfless act of attempting to save a man's life during an air raid.

¹⁰ "The novel by its nature is dramatic, but it need not be melodramatic, and James's problem was to admit violence without becoming violent. He musn't let violence lend the tone (that is melodrama): violence must draw its tone from the rest of life; it must be subdued, and it must not, above all, be sudden and inexplicable. The violence he worked with was not accidental; it was corrupt; it came from the Pit, and therefore it had to be fully understood. Otherwise, the moral background would be lost. This, too, helped to determine his method, for fully to understand, unless the author indulged in tiresome explanation, in the 'platitude of statement' you have to be yourself inside the story, within a consciousness of unusual intelligence." *The Lost Childhood*, p. 49. This method of James's, or what Greene has taken to be one of James's methods and in part conformed to himself, is one that Bendrix lacks that "unusual intelligence to pursue." He is, so to speak, too far "inside the story," nor can he, in his own words, "disinter the human character from the heavy scene—the daily newspaper, the daily meal, the traffic grinding towards Battersea, the gulls coming up from the Thames looking for bread, and the early

summer of 1939 glinting on the park where the children sailed their boats—one of those bright condemned pre-war summers" (p. 24).

[11] "Francois Mauriac and Freedom," *Literary Essays* (New York, 1957), pp. 19-20.

[12] *Basic Writings of Saint Augustine* (New York, 1948), p. 195.

[13] "The Fiction of Graham Greene: Between the Horror and the Glory," *The Kenyon Review,* XIX (Winter 1957), 69.

[14] Bendrix's envisioning of the saints here recalls their more lyrical description by Georges Bernanos: "those richly destined souls, more than all others, escape every kind of determinism; they radiate, they shine with a dazzling freedom." *The Last Essays of Georges Bernanos,* p. 219.

[15] Answering Robert Gorham Davis's review of *The Quiet American* which imputed to Greene the political sentiments of his narrator, Thomas Fowler, Greene replied: "A good deal of misunderstanding is due to the apparent ignorance nowadays of a novelist's technique. More people should read Henry James' Prefaces and realize the importance of a point of view. If one uses the first person the point of view has obviously got to be I, and one must put one's self in I's skin as intensely as possible. . . . I share certain of Fowler's views but not all of them." New York *Times Book Review,* August 26, 1956, p. 8.

[16] "Francois Mauriac," *The Lost Childhood,* pp. 70-71. Rayner Heppenstal discusses these two essays in a related context in *The Double Image* (London, 1947), pp. 58-60.

[17] "Man Made Angry," *The Lost Childhood,* p. 78.

[18] *The Responsibility of the Artist,* pp. 102-103.

[19] *The Picaresque Saint* (New York, 1959), p. 272.

[20] "Sheep in Wolves' Clothing," *Partisan Review,* XXIV (Spring 1957) 270-74.

[21] *The Double Image,* p. 76.

[22] Philip Rieff, *Freud: The Mind of the Moralist* (New York, 1959), p. 199.

THE SATANIST FALLACY OF *BRIGHTON ROCK*

[1] H. R. Haber, "The Two Worlds of Graham Greene," *Modern Fiction Studies,* III (Autumn 1957), 263.

[2] R.W.B. Lewis, "The 'Trilogy' of Graham Greene," *Modern Fiction Studies,* III (Autumn 1957), 195.

[3] Lewis, p. 199.

[4] Graham Greene, *Journey Without Maps* (London, 1936), p. 15.

[5] A. A. DeVitis, "Allegory in *Brighton Rock*," *Modern Fiction Studies,* III (Autumn 1957), 216-24.

[6] Lewis, p. 215.

7 Haber, pp. 256-68.

8 By 'historical perspective' and 'spatial extension' I refer to an esthetic concept similar to that set forth by Joseph Frank, "Spatial Form in Modern Literature," *Sewanee Review*, LIII (Spring, Summer, Autumn, 1945), 221-40, 433-56, 643-53, *q.v.* "Mr. Frank considers the cultural context of the modern tendency toward spatial form, which he sees as expressive of a 'timeless world of myth' transcending historical limits and encompassing all times," Walter Sutton, "The Literary Image and the Reader: A Consideration of the Theory of Spatial Form," *Journal of Aesthetics and Art Criticism*, XVI (Sept. 1957), 112-23.

9 Lewis, p. 200.

10 Arnold Kettle, *An Introduction to the English Novel* (London, 1953), II, 166. Kettle is not actually discussing *Brighton Rock*, but there is no reason to believe he would object to having his general strictures applied to all of Greene's works.

11 This reference to Sean O'Casey's *Rose and Crown* (New York, 1952), p. 272, is cited by A. A. DeVitis in his article (above) as an important part of the argument.

12 Lewis, p. 198.

13 Ezra Pound, "A Few Don'ts by an Imagiste," *Poetry*, I (March 1913), 200-201.

14 DeVitis, p. 219.

15 Lewis, p. 200.

16 Lewis, p. 202.

17 *Journey Without Maps*, p. 10.

18 Lewis, p. 203.

19 It is most interesting to note how Greene's major philosophical interests revolve around St. Augustine's three main doctrines: original sin, divine grace, and the mission of the church.

20 A. N. Whitehead, *Adventures of Ideas* (New York, 1933), p. 154.

21 John McCormick, *Catastrophe and Imagination* (London, 1957), p. 290.

22 The sexual and religious implications, and the minor way in which these disparate interests are here linked, should not of course be ignored.

23 H. Rider Haggard, *King Solomon's Mines* (New York, 1957), p. 56. It seems unnecessary to establish the fact that Greene knew this novel, a popular product of 1885; however, he mentions it obliquely in *Journey Without Maps* (p. 8): "There are a thousand names for it, King Solomon's Mines. . . ."

24 *Journey Without Maps*, p. 97.

25 Karl Patten, "The Structure of *The Power and the Glory*," *Modern Fiction Studies*, III (Autumn 1957), 229.

[26] Lewis, p. 201.

[27] Patten, p. 225.

[28] Edwin Muir, *The Structure of the Novel* (London, 1928), p. 64.

[29] Lewis, pp. 198-99.

[30] Sean O'Faolain, *The Vanishing Hero* (London, 1956), pp. 73-97 *q.v.* For an alternative position see my article, "Existentialism in Greene's *The Quiet American*," *Modern Fiction Studies*, III (Autumn 1957), 241-48.

THE HEART OF THE NOVEL

[1] Mr. Laitinen's essay is translated from the Finnish by Ants Oras.

MORAL SITUATION IN *THE QUIET AMERICAN*

[1] Robert O. Evans takes a different view in "Existentialism in Greene's *The Quiet American*," *Modern Fiction Studies*, III (Autumn 1957), 241-48.

[2] It is quite in keeping Greene's practice to play with the names of his characters in this way. See Philip Stratford, "Unlocking the Potting Shed," *Kenyon Review*, XXIV (Winter 1962), 134 and *passim*.

[3] For a fuller discussion of the theme of pity in Graham Greene's novels, see Kenneth Allott and Miriam Farris, "The Universe of Pity," *The Art of Graham Greene* (London, 1951; repr. New York, 1963).

[4] Passages from Albert Camus' *La Peste* are given throughout from the 1948 translation by Stuart Gilbert.

THE CURSE OF THE FILM

[1] This essay appeared in substantially the same form in John Atkins, *Graham Greene* (London, 1957), and is used with permission.

THE WITCH AT THE CORNER

[1] In this paper the more recent Bantam edition (New York, 1960) has been used.

[2] *The Explicator*, XV (December 1956), item 13.

[3] "Hell on Earth: Six Versions," *Hudson Review*, II (Summer 1949), 311-17.

[4] Young, p. 312.

[5] *The Vanishing Hero* (London, 1956), p. 73.

[6] "Innocence Revisited," *Renascence*, XII (Autumn 1959), 29-34.

[7] *The Lost Childhood and Other Essays* (New York, 1952), pp. 13-17.

[8] *Journey Without Maps* (London, 1936), p. 313.

[9] R. W. B. Lewis, in "The Fiction of Graham Greene: Between the Horror and the Glory," *Kenyon Review*, XIX (Winter 1957), 56-75, discusses the importance of the Liberian trip to Greene but does not make very explicit connections with the works themselves. He also overlooks the role of the devil and his character of Power. Joseph M. Duffy in "The Lost World of Graham Greene," *Thought*, XXXI (Spring-Winter 1958-1959), 229-47, discusses the world of a lost Eden in Greene's novels, which source he traces to the Liberian trip.

[10] *Journey Without Maps*, p. 213.

[11] *An Outline of Psychoanalysis*, trans. James Strachey (New York, 1949), pp. 49-50.

[12] *Journey Without Maps*, p. 311.

[13] *Ibid.*, p. 219.

[14] *Ibid.*, p. 278.

[15] *Ibid.* (italics mine).

[16] *Creative Intuition in Art and Poetry* ("Bollingen Series," Vol. XXXV, No. 1; New York, 1953), pp. 90-95.

[17] *Journey Without Maps*, p. 219 (italics mine). Greene has a rather limited view of James here, unlike his later appraisals in a series of essays where he suggests echoes of "supernatural evil" and "savage elementary beliefs." "Henry James: the Religious Aspect," *The Lost Childhood* . . ., p. 36.

[18] O'Faolain, p. 75.

[19] "Walter de la Mare's Short Stories," *The Lost Childhood* . . ., p. 79.

[20] "The Basement Room," p. 13.

[21] *The Lawless Roads* (London, 1939) might also serve as a source of myth.

[22] "The Basement Room," pp. 10-11.

[23] "The Basement Room," pp. 8-9.

[24] "The Basement Room," p. 19.

[25] *Journey Without Maps*, p. 104.

[26] "The Hint of an Explanation," p. 119.

[27] *Journey Without Maps*, p. 100.

[28] *Ibid.*, p. 104.

[29] *England Made Me* (London, 1935), p. 264.

[30] *Journey Without Maps*, p. 278.

[31] "I Spy," p. 44.

[32] *Journey Without Maps*, p. 220.

[33] "Proof Positive," p. 98.

[34] In his "Congo Journal," the diary Greene kept of his struggle to formulate the character of Querry, he asserts: "I had the forest outside Imbonga in mind when I described Querry's search for Deo

Gratias, mingled perhaps with memories of the deeper forests of Liberia." *In Search of A Character* (London, 1961), p. 63.

[35] *A Burnt-out Case* (New York, 1960), p. 89.

[36] *Ibid.*

[37] *Ibid.*, p. 189.

[38] *Ibid.*, p. 197.

[39] *Journey Without Maps*, p. 104.

[40] "Henry James: The Religious Aspect," *The Lost Childhood . . .*, p. 36.

[41] *Ibid.*

[42] "The Lost Childhood," *The Lost Childhood . . .*, p. 16.

223